A Shoulder to

Books by the same author

A Shoulder to Laugh On

BASIL BOOTHROYD

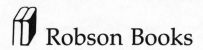 Robson Books

To
JUNE
and Oliver, Shirley, Jane, Chris, Peter, Barry, Andy, Carl,
Claire, Jeremy, James, Kirstie, Thomas and Sam

First published in Great Britain in 1987 by Robson Books Ltd.,
Bolsover House, 5–6 Clipstone Street, London W1P 7EB.

Copyright © 1987 Basil Boothroyd

British Library Cataloguing in Publication Data

Boothroyd, Basil
  A shoulder to laugh on.
  1. Boothroyd, Basil 2. Broadcasters—
  Great Britain—Biography
  I. Title
  791.44'092'4   PN1990.72.B/

ISBN 0-86051-393-9

Printed in Great Britain by
St Edmundsbury Press Ltd, Bury St Edmunds, Suffolk
Bound by Dorstel Press Ltd, Harlow Essex

Contents

Introduction

RESEARCHES DISCLOSE THAT I was born an Edwardian. It was a near thing. The era ran out after my first three months. But Elizabethans, already into their thirties and fancying the best years behind them, may be surprised, if no more so than I am.

All that time gone by, and not a lot to show. If Shakespeare had been my age he would have been dead for twenty-five years. Mozart for thirty-six. It's hard not to envy their snap and drive. They got down to things. None of the fidgety idling that consumes energy without applying it, like a mower left chugging on the lawn when the phone rings.

They were lucky. In a different way, and not to push the equation, so am I. My lawn, largely neglected, has blessed me with small, useful nuisances: molehills, to be made into mountains for a week, swept into print, and disposed of into readers' gardens. One day I shan't be able to do this any more, but just chug in the long grass, idling full time until the fuel runs out.

Still, I shall have been expecting this, week by week, more or less since the Edwardian era. That's a long time to have been lucky.

BASIL BOOTHROYD
Cuckfield, Sussex, 1987

One

TREBLE CLEF

IT WOULD BE pleasing to claim, just for the drama of it, that in November, 1919, I set fire to Burghersh Chantry, Lincoln's low old sprawling Choir School, tucked down an obscure lane off the cathedral precincts. I was nine, young for an incendiary, and in fact innocent, having slept through it all and missed it. What a swizz.

The first I knew was at breakfast in the morning. We were all bidden to kneel by our plates of salted porridge while our headmaster, towering, Scottish, and disapproving of sugared porridge, offered up thanks for our deliverance. We called him 'Gulliver', though he was officially Canon Elliott, and I've since wondered who among us Lilliputians had read Swift.

It emerged that last night's embers in the grate had ignited ancient beams, which started it. But it could have been me. I had somehow acquired, perhaps a week before, a box of fusees. These were, perhaps still are, a particularly exciting type of match, combustibly coated for most of their length, giving a fine effect when struck in bed after lights out. I hadn't long left home, where even boring single-flicker domestic matches had been kept where I couldn't reach them. Fusees signalled emancipation. But Gulliver, on his nightly round, had caught me enjoying these long, flaring radiances.

'You foolish child!' I may not have been clear about the gravity of the offence, but his wrath was as terrible as God's. We slept several to a room. And I can't now think what the others, older than me (everyone was older than me) could have been doing while I came near to burning them alive. Just sleeping, perhaps. Dreaming about tomorrow's matins or evensong. Would they scoop up successfully to the high B-flat of Stanford's *Magnificat*? How much would old Bennett grunt from the organ-loft, striving to hold us back from hurrying the psalms? Hurrying was a great crime, especially in the psalms. Organist and choirmaster G.J. Bennett, Mus. Doc., was a great grunter, though fighting the habit, with passable success, when he descended from the loft to conduct us unaccompanied for the Christmas Eve carol service. *A Virgin unspotted, See Amid The Winter Snow, Though Poor be the Manger*. We left the stalls for that, circled under the central, multi-flamed candelabra. Mr Moss, baritone, traditionally took the *Manger* solo with a throbbing vibrato which he claimed to achieve, when questioned on technique, by standing on one leg and shaking the other.

Old Bennett was a great cigarette smoker. I had my first taste of tobacco from his yellowed fingers. Open, open, open, boy! Knocking apart one's upper and lower teeth. This during twice-daily practice in what was called the Song School, above the cathedral's south transept. It contained a hand-pumped organ, whose stool he moved on to when performances had attained suitable shape. It was sizeable. A country church would have been glad of it: but a mere pipsqueak compared with the huge Willis organ down below, electrically powered, its bass pipes, the 64-footers, distanced along the clerestory above the nave so that the man in the loft had to be half a bar ahead of singers and orchestra on big oratorio occasions, allowing for the time-lag of sound. The man hired to pump in the Song School, elderly, wizened, music no part of him, found the louder passages of Stainer's *Crucifixion* exhausting beyond his rewards of sixpence an hour. Oh, that Strainer! he would complain.

The Doctor also smoked a hookah or hubble-bubble, though only in the privacy of his home, invaded on Sunday afternoons by boys with solos at forthcoming evensong, summoned for a final polish. He owned another oddity, an upright piano with a pedal keyboard, for his own polishing of organ works. I had never seen before, nor have since, either of these curious engines, but took them in the unquerying stride of youth, assuming long afterwards that hubble-bubbles, and pianos with a heel-toe substructure, were standard in all the best musical homes.

I don't often go back to the cathedral, and then seldom to a service. It is too hard on the tear-ducts, looking down from a high stall on the boys who used to be me, singing the music I used to sing. And I stay out of the vestry, which was sometimes invaded in my own day by ancients claiming to have been boys there themselves. As we shed cassock and surplice, eager to rush off, I suppose we gathered dimly what the old men were on about, though unable to relate it to anything much. That would take half a century or so.

We might have been rushing off, if less eagerly, to the class-room. Academic timetables were geared to musical commit-

ments. The mornings mostly went on the Song School and
matins, afternoons on the Song School and evensong. Somewhere between we had to wedge in a little Euclid, or the declen-
sion of hic-haec-hoc. As to the last, we could study and sing
simultaneously. By a lucky chance our Tallis's *Responses* books
were small, blue and floppy. So were our Latin Grammars. When
we turned to the east for the Creed, well placed worshippers
could be surprised to see, down both Cantoris and Decani sides
of the choirstalls, that we had been fluting, 'O Lord, make haste
to help us', from *First Steps in Latin*: its title, by accepted practice,
always amended to *First Steps in Eating*.

For returning ex-choristers of a sentimental turn, I would recommend a safer listening point just inside the great West Door.
There, with the long nave between them and St Hugh's Choir,
and the four-part harmonies of, 'O, Lord, open thou our lips,'
opening like a flower, an eye can be dabbed without drawing
attention.

If it's all too much, step outside and have a look at the West
front. The light on its broad expanse, notably when the sun is
going down, shivers into pastelly pinks and golds, bathing the
Norman arches, the seated ranks of carved bishops and kings,
their robes and crowns blurred with time. A sight to see, memo-
rably from the upper windows opposite of No. 19 Minster Yard,
at an early summer bedtime, a stone's throw away across the
lawns.

I saw it from there for about five years. The Choir School had
foundered and sunk, striking some financial reef. The boys, in
small groups, were thereafter lodged with vergers and their
wives or other good cathedral souls. Three of us, the two Biggin
brothers and myself, moved in with Mr and Mrs Newborn at No.
19, becoming predictably known, in jesting clerical circles, as the
Newborn Babes.

Ernest Newborn was the Head Verger. The Biggins particularly would have settled for nothing less. They had been
brought up to enjoy and expect the best in all things, and continually proclaimed the superiority of all things Biggin. Today,
when I need a mental grope before addressing intimates by name
with any confidence, I can name the Biggins in fully, sixty years
after. Alan, the elder, was Douglas Alan Elmhirst Biggin, probably pushing twelve when we first met, and unapproachably
impressive by weight of years alone. Geoff was Geoffrey Philip
Elmhirst Biggin, younger, but still my senior. Alan was inclined
to be aggressive and self-projecting. Geoffrey softer, but not
unaware of a select station in the world.

The Elmhirst – I was warned early and often about the correct spelling – had been a famous admiral, a lord of battles, his cocked hat and epaulettes lodged way back in the Biggin annals. His maritime triumphs were often recounted, and I have no doubt that he is a figure of fame and awe to naval historians, though I have never been able to find him anywhere myself. They were from Sheffield, or, rather, nearby Hathersage, both places much spoken of. Their father, Albert E. Biggin (I would have to guess what the 'E' stood for) was in steel, and seemed to have invented the stuff; if not that, some revolutionary stainless process. The village was the finest in Yorkshire, their house the finest in the village, which I gathered was in the heart of, or perhaps at the top of the Peak District, whose rare beauty and unusual topography rivalled the Rockies for awful grandeur.

Father Biggin came often to visit. By car. A Humber, I think. Like him, it had a lot of brass. He would take us to the races in it, buy enormous teas. He and Mrs Biggin stayed at The White Hart, Lincoln's four-star best. Hotels may not have had stars then, but only the best would have done. Once, when he was there, something happened that spoke to me more eloquently of wealth, the simple not having to worry about money, than anything of the kind that ever so impressed, or so ineradicably stayed with me. He walked abroad one day leaving his raincoat in the hotel. It rained. He went into a shop and bought a raincoat.

I would not have learnt this from him. Guess from whom. He was a quiet man. Told nothing of admirals or revolutionary inventions. Musical. His wife slight and pink, remembered in furs. He wrote a pretty song or two, for Alan to sing, in a voice a little breathy (old Bennett's word, not solely for the elder Biggin). I can still play one of them, a setting of Byron's 'Maid of Athens, ere we part, Give, Oh, give me back my heart. . .'

With the collapse of the Choir School (since reconstituted and flourishing) we not only lived but learned in fresh settings. The three Newborn babes were disruptingly whisked into Lincoln School as day boys: with us, no doubt, other outcasts from Burghersh Chantry, though we retained our respective lodgings, some with the Clerk of the Works, who was of interest for having a stiff leg, some with vergers, also of interest in their several ways: Mr Woolham was said to have only one lung, but this didn't seem to show; Mr Cotgrove was an obsessive pianola player, sweating ripely during performances and going through such ecstasies of execution as he drove the pedals and manipulated the thumb controls that Mr Newborn, always matter-of-fact over the arts, said as we walked home from one Cotgrove recital, 'You'd think he was bloody Paderooski.'

'Ernest!' said Mrs Newborn.

Mr Newborn had come through the First World War only a year or two before, in what capacity I never knew. If I thought of him as having been solid and heroic it was perhaps not just a romantic childish idea. He had the bearing and the quietness, and rebuked us once for laughing at a pitiable local figure known as Shellshock Sam, who marched round the cathedral at a military pace, shouldering his walking-stick and crying hoarse orders.

But the colourful language of that war was hard to erase: distressing for Mrs Newborn: interesting for us, and had its special moments when Ernest had let a few whizzbangs drop at 19 Minster Yard, and was next seen, bowed over his silver mace, escorting the Dean from stall to pulpit.

They must have been quite young, perhaps thirty-five and thirty, but that was centuries old to us. They were childless, and remained so. Parents wasted. Mrs Newborn was large, motherly, enveloping, yet determinedly unsentimental. We must have given them problems. At least annoyances. She once skinned my nose with a Boyce Book, when I got out of hand in some disagreement with the Biggins. It hurt her more than it did me, intended more as a feint than a blow. But the weapon was unwieldy. The Boyce Books were ancient and leatherbound, about the size of a bank ledger, containing miscellaneous scores, many by William Boyce, but there would be William Byrd, Orlando Gibbons. . .I forget. They were ordinarily kept in the cathedral's music library unless wanted in the choir stalls, but one had been brought home that evening for some private brushing-up. I believe the quarrel was actually to do with the book, possibly a split of opinions, rigidly held on both sides, over the key-signature of *God is Gone Up*, or whether or not there was a soprano lead in *Lift Up Your Heads*.

I think I was proved right, and the Biggins thereupon claimed the dispute to have been about something else, and I screamed protests and got hit. Or it could all have been the other way round. It seemed important at the time, whatever it was, and whichever way round.

With us, it would have been just the sort of trigger for high words. Our lay contemporaries might clash over the rival merits of their bicycling with no hands, superior systems of lacing football boots. Our contentions were ecclesiastical-musical. Would we, given appointment to the Precentorship, expel mem-

bers of the congregation for joining in the singing, waywardly
and an octave too low? Had Mr Hewitt, old Bennett's deputy, by
error or design stepped on the Full Organ pedal in a quieter
passage of the *Nunc Dimittis*? Did the great central tower, in a
gale, sway as much as a yard from true? Six feet? And if it fell
down, would its scattered masonry reach as far as Hathersage?

The Precentor of my time, responsible by his office for the
cathedral music and for our spiritual welfare through the
medium of the Sunday School sessions just round the corner at
the Precentory, was a gentle man with what would now be called
charisma; he was a vigorous preacher, his fully-fashioned surplice sleeves billowing in outflung gesture. He was nicknamed,
totally inexplicably, 'Snat'. But became more widely known, and
tragically, as Archdeacon Wakeford. It was brought to the notice
of the Dean and Chapter by some vigilant watcher for righteous-
ness, that he had spent the night with a woman at a Peterborough
hotel. She was never named, and never appeared, but the Con-
sistory Court unfrocked and banished poor Snat, and he faded,
with his loyal and forgiving wife, from the Precentory, from
Lincoln, and from the front pages of the national press, who were
not to have a feast of self-righteous fun on that scale until their
romp over the Vicar of Stiffkey.

How, I wonder, was the nine days' scandal received in Worksop, my home thirty long miles away? Lincoln had been my
devout Father's great success with me, where I should be
watched over by the godly and grow up in the Lord. He must
have been downcast and bewildered.

We didn't learn much about it. The Newborns had prudently
kept the papers from us, evading a hail of difficult questions.
What was so wrong in staying the night with a lady, as openly
practised by Albert E. Biggin at The White Hart? We were at an
age – and in an age – of innocence, the secrets of fleshly passion
less accessible than they are today. But the disappearance of poor
Snat was a matter for inevitable speculation, and some of our
questions got through. We were told, in the end, that he had
been caught forging five-pound notes. Such wickedness. It made
dramatic vestry-talk. After that, like the papers, we soon forgot
him.

At Lincoln School we were creatures apart. Eton suits and
collars, mortar-boards, the Choir School's retained uniform, contributed to this, inviting scorn, but also envy. We rose and left
classrooms at will, on an understanding with the staff, scarcely
drawing a nod from the dais as we trotted smugly off. We had to
go and sing. That was the priority.

We needed time not only for practice and service, but for walking. The Chantry had been a mere two minutes' scuttle from the cathedral. The School was a mile off down the Wragby Road. I daresay we abandoned long division or Pitt the Younger with ample time in hand, and not a lot of interest in what either was trying to prove. I still blame my yawning gaps of ignorance on all that lost instruction. But I may not always have been justified in dismissing examination posers with the useful formula, 'Not present when taught'. How did they go on about the marking?

Perhaps allowances were made. But were eroded by my answers on subjects taught when I had indeed been present but thinking of other things. Perhaps the coming top A in *The Wilderness*. Whether, at old Bennett's summer party, I should earn sixpence by catching one of the tennis balls he traditionally whammed over his chimneys from the far side of the house. Old Bennett, I since realise, could not have been so old after all. In any case, I was never a sponge for knowledge, and still credit the better crossword for what little I have. And the School was nothing. The cathedral everything.

But the voice went. From top A's to bottom B flats, with intervening yodelling. I became a boarder. Full classroom attendances, but too late to fill the gaps. Corn Laws and Factory Acts mingled inextricably with Home Rule and the Reformation: lowest common denominators with highest common factors: the East India Company with the South Sea Bubble. It was like trying to pick up a *Times* correspondence in its later stages. What was this all about?

At sixteen and a month or two I entered that limbo, if without infernal connotations, between school and real life. School had been all right. I had neither enjoyed nor disenjoyed it. On life and what to do with it I had no ideas. There was no thought of a university. Not only no thought but no mention. We were not of what was then the university-going class. In any event, Father hadn't the money, and I hadn't the brains. As for earning a living, school reports stayed gloomy to the last, the Headmaster's summaries suggesting a bemused, but eventually resigned, desperation. I passed no examinations, and still have not. I got 14 out of 400 for my last maths paper. I lacked any reasoning faculty or sense of any proper sequence of things, and still do. It meant then that an invitation to remove the brackets from an algebraical equation slammed down a mental shutter of absolute incomprehension. Now, that if I don't get the drift of a printed sentence the first time, I can read it a dozen times and still not see a glimmer. History is a jumble. Only Shakespeare can remind me, and that ephemerally, whether Lancaster or York wore the white rose.

My essays were more successful, and I would direct Father's attention to the master's favourable comments. These he disappointingly took for granted. Our house was full of books. If I had rejected *The Heart of Midlothian* and *The Cloister and the Hearth* in favour of Jeffery Farnol and *Sexton Blake*, words must at least have got into me, and would naturally come out again.

From general lack of adventurousness and an instinct to keep out of trouble I was a law-abiding boy. Let others climb the roofs by night and carve their monograms on the school clock. But I did take risks over the essays, finding a way to get into the locked common room by the window and sneak a look at my marked exercise book. To go to these lengths might have suggested, if only to me, that to write for a living might be the answer. It didn't. Nor to anyone else. Even the master, who had once marked an essay 20 out of 20 – perfection, surely – told me that I ought to be an actor. I think he meant it. There were no careers masters at that time. Had there been, how many would have ventured such a recommendation?

Luckily for him, he made the suggestion at the end of my last term. When I told Father, hoping to cheer him with a hint that I might after all be good at something, he went into shock. To put such ideas into the head of an innocent boy! The man was out of his mind. And should be out of the profession. Had I been going back, Father might well have gone with me, to demand of the headmaster, the Rev. Moggy Moxon, DD, a remote man of pasty aspect, that he pluck this viper from his bosom.

It was thirty years before I went back, and a surprise to be invited, nothing of the kind having been prefigured in my pupil days. I gave away the prizes, one of those anonymous old buffers I remembered on the same platform assuring me that the race was not always to the swift. At least I kept that out of my speech. It is a maxim I have never made sense of, myself. If life has taught me anything, it is that the swift are the ones the race is invariably to.

My English master was still there. Another surprise. I had expected him to be either a hundred or dead. As he was far from either I realised that he must have been about twenty-three when he outraged my father by trying to put me on the stage. I was surprised, too, to rediscover modest grandeurs. Cloisters, fives court, pool, all forgotten. Though I was reminded, handing over the prizes, that I had once myself been handed one. For English.

Lockhart's *Life of Napoleon*. And that I ought really to read it one of these days.

That, and a paper-knife with a rabbit's head handle as a gift for Father, evidence of my achievements at woodwork, though the design had developed more or less by chance, were about all I brought away.

But of the cathedral all remains haunting and clear, the sounds, the echoes, the solemnities, the smell of the stone. Returning there, all too seldom, and approaching the small south-west door, I know just what the feel of its brass handle is going to be in my hand.

Two

AS THINGS WERE

'WELL,' SAID MY mother after a pause, speaking from the ditch, 'We may as well eat the sandwiches.'

She was fair and still pretty. The Edwardian child was not encouraged to know the age of his parents, but for some official reasons connected with school I had recently had to ask their respective ages. Mother first. 'You'd better ask your father.' He wore a disapproving face and went back to reading his Walter Scott, but later supplied the information by long distance, calling up the stairs. I could tell them that my mother was fifty-five. . .I waited. And that he was. . .five years older. I wasn't hot on maths but I could work that one out.

They had married late. I never knew any of my grandparents, except for a bedridden old lady in a lace cap, who was probably one of them. If I stood on tip-toe, she could just reach down to put a piece of buttered toast in my mouth. I don't think it happened often. Perhaps only once, becoming memorable. I'm not sure about the lace cap. I could be confusing her with Whistler's Mother.

Is it only in retrospect that I feel admiration for my mother's calm as she spoke from the ditch that day, mud-streaked and with her hat drooping sideways from its pin? Certainly it is only now, at this moment, that I see a genetic pattern: her patience, unselfishness and practicality crossing down to my sister, though sparing some of her humour for me, while my father's ready irritability, love of words, and highly personal antipathies came my way. But not his clever hands. Among his standing hates were glass-fronted bookcases, long-handled bags, and bank clerks who kept pens behind their ears. My own are different, but of equal irrationality, and much multiplied, from dogs, athletes and shopping, to board games and operatic sopranos.

His love of words was such that, in reading aloud, he would often be overcome by tears, not at the sentimental content, but just affected by the way a phrase was turned. I have something of this from him. The hands, no. He could make anything, mend anything. The mechanical toy, no matter how sickening and seemingly final its death rattle, would be restored to life, with infinite patience for a man on the whole impatient. I took this for granted, as my own son took it for granted that any failed mechanism presented for inspection, rather than any hoped-for resurrection, was only calling at a staging-post on the way to the dustbin.

On my father and mother's first – I think only – visit after our marriage, he brought with him an unsolicited grandfather clock in a number of variously shaped boxes. These, it turned out, as he insisted on demonstrating before so much as taking his hat off, had been purpose-fashioned to contain the clock's internal organs: a pendulum-shaped box, a weight-shaped box (well, two), a works-shaped box, perhaps even a winding-handle-shaped box. He had come by train, must have been in his late seventies by then. I thought of all the planning and care and skill. We got his hat and coat away from him eventually, but he would neither eat nor sleep until the thing was assembled, sited, ticking, and showing the right time.

I shouldn't have said that. He hated people who talked about, or more particularly asked him for, the 'right' time. Clocks and watches might be wrong, though his never were. Time was always right.

Inside the door of the clock he had pinned a typewritten verse.

> Master, behold me, here I stand
> To tell ye time at thy command;
> To do thy will is my delight,
> To tell ye hour by day or night.
> Master, be wise, and learn of me
> To serve thy GOD as I serve thee.

It is still there. On winding days I am sometimes conscious of falling short of its solemn bidding, and of envying the rocklike faith of both parents, unquestioning of God, of His ways, of the assured Hereafter. Father died first. When Mother was dying she was firm with the doctors. 'Don't you do anything to keep me here.' My sister's last words to me, devout though she was and confident that Heaven was her destination, were less devotional, but characteristic. She was in pain, and stuck all over with drips and feeds. 'Don't make me laugh.' But managing a smile. By then I was in the laughter business professionally, in so far as I have ever been professional about anything, and she was marking her pride in that.

She was not a member of the accident. Six years my senior, she would have been briefly out into the great world by them, in the office of a St Alban's solicitor. I have an idea that he was a sort of cousin of Mother's, at some remove. My mother had been one of eleven children. Or was it twelve? Cousins abounded. Many seemed to have removed across the Atlantic, I suppose before the First World War, and were always for me shadowy if adventurous figures, uncles in Toronto, aunts in New York, from whose descendants I hear at long intervals, but in very long letters, always warm, often funny, but packed with gossip and unidentifiable Toms and Georges and Emilys.

Even of my parents' parents I know little. Mother herself was a schoolteacher in Derby, I know that. I have wondered how Father ranged so far from his native Worksop and mine, a good forty miles. How did they meet? The bicycle was fast coming in. Perhaps a group of young Worksop blades, on cross-barred and back-stepped male machines, pedalled into encounter with a group of Derby girls with basketed handlebars and dress-guards. I remember photographs at home of my father and stiffly posed bicycling cronies. Small round caps and knickerbockers. Cascading dark moustaches. No girls, though. Nor could he have been so young a blade. Or, if so, the courtship was long. I heard, I suppose from my sister, that his mother was clingingly possessive. They could not have married until he was forty. There would have been terrible scenes, tears, protests, charges of brutal unfiliality. I don't know. How little one knows. Did his mother survive to become the buttered-toast dispenser?

My father's father stuck in my mind as a woodcutter. It sounded honest, humble. I don't know where I got that from. But I found vague references in my father's papers suggesting something a little superior, some sort of expert on timber, inspecting and pronouncing on trees. Sherwood Forest was near to us. And the Dukeries (of Portland, of Newcastle). According to whim, and perhaps company, I would locate Worksop, for the ignorant, as being in the grimy heart of the Nottinghamshire coalfields or on the edge of Sherwood Forest. This grandfather perhaps advised the dukes? My father had associations with the dukes. Not close. He would wind their clocks at one time. This I know, because as a very small child I sometimes went with him to attend the winding. No impression was made on me by the ducal glories of these grand estates, though I was told I once picked up one of His Grace's golf balls and threw it to him, hitting him on the calf.

Neither the throwing nor the hitting would have pleased him much. I don't know what we were doing on his golf course in any case. Making our way to outlying clocks perhaps. About to descend to the underground ballroom, which one of the estates had, if not both.

It must have been during one of these subterranean journeys that a couple of dramatic incidents occurred. We were certainly in a dark tunnel. The first was that I had hiccups. That was less the dramatic incident than the extraordinary behaviour of my father. He was a quiet man, but suddenly bawled deafeningly in my ear, 'ROW-ROW-ROW-ROW-ROW!'

To shock, though I didn't know it at the time, and was very frightened, was then, perhaps still is, a recognised cure for the hiccups. It didn't cure mine, as I remember. This was effected by the second incident, in which a box of matches suddenly exploded in my father's pocket. What caused this I didn't know, and still have no theories. I have a feeling that he blamed me for it. He was a gentle man, as well as quiet (hiccup remedies apart), but by temperament would lay blame for life's small miscarriages on anything, anyone, but himself.

I know the impulse well.

At other times my outings would be to the colliery village of Shireoaks. He collected rents there, loathsome occupation for a compassionate soul. The little houses, identical by the score, front steps bravely bathbricked, were not readily thrown open to us. Money and rent book passed round the door by resigned ladies of the house, our progress down the street already monitored through decent net curtains. No resentment, or none that came over to a four-year-old. This could have been from dulled susceptibilities on the tenant's part, or from the collector's hesitant approach, diminishing his role as an agent of oppression. I don't know who got the money, after Father's no doubt modest cut. Probably the dukes.

There were miners' houses in the less 'residential' areas of Worksop itself. Off duty the colliers – we always called them colliers – would take their leisure squatting, never sitting, on the front step, knees spread, a cigarette dangled between them, turned into the palm. No collar still, but usually a stud, denoting a move towards formal wear for when the pubs opened, this being marked by black caps and white artificial-silk scarves, almost a uniform. I did not associate the colliers with the horse-drawn carts lumbering down our street to cries of 'Coal, coal!'

I was vaguely afraid of them. At least vaguely apprehensive. This was from my mother, who felt the same, perhaps just as groundlessly. When the pubs shut, having been open, and we were out together in the afternoon, they walked unsteadily, and we would cross the road. They had had, she would explain, 'a drop too much'. In open fields we would sometimes see a group of them, looking first in the air, then on the ground. My mother shielded my eyes, if only metaphorically. This was their other form of depraved recreation. Gambling. Pitch and Toss. Coppers thrown up to fall heads or tails. My mother sorrowed, not condemned, but would take the opportunity for a little talk on the evil of games of chance.

I see too late that I fell short as a son. I don't mean that I was made to feel this at the time, not in general, though in a series of particulars I was aware of being a disappointment. It didn't worry me. That was probably even more disappointing. I was loved and cherished beyond my deserts. A demonstration of this, on Father's part, I look back on even now with shock and disbelief, though I must have been quite small when it happened. The cat scratched me, very probably provoked. He took it out at once and drowned it in the water-butt. What was this, in him? Something more than an eye for an eye, a precept which in life he would surely forbear to practise.

I couldn't drown a cat myself for its weight in gold, however fond and just the cause.

When I said on 'Desert Island Discs' that I wasn't sure what Father had done for a living, my sister was upset. Rightly so. But it was true, over my recollection of his whole employment span. The rent-collecting. The clock-winding. Though the last, I suppose, was a spin-off from his ownership, at one time, of a jeweller's shop. This embraced eye-testing and the provision of glasses. Had he any qualifications? I don't know. He seemed to me to know all about the constituency of optical glass, and would revolve a lens against the light, making small brisk notes, as I have seen the professional opticians do. But my sister had herself told me that as a watchmaker and jeweller he preferred to spend his working day in the room behind the shop, playing chess with a crony, and was exasperated when the bell rang, threatening customers.

Then for a period, which could have been long or short, he must have been on the fringes of insurance. His office was in the house. I was old enough to read, because I remember the scatterings of forms and leaflets, Royal, Northern, Commercial Union, the quaint and sad Scottish Widows. Perhaps other occupations I never heard about. He had fluent shorthand. Was this ever applied for gain?

After some twenty or twenty-five of his later years he retired from the secretaryship of the Victoria Hospital, with an illuminated address and a fulsome note in the *Worksop Guardian*. And saw that, I suppose, as his career. But he would be a late-developer, taking to it, and I would have been getting on towards leaving school.

Had he enjoyed being a hospital secretary? Meetings, letters, minutes, accounts? An improvement on collecting rents. But it seemed a barren landfall for a man who read so much, knew so much, could do so much, from mending a watch to building a summerhouse – this still up after half a century, flagpole with ratchet lowering-device at the foot of its steps, outside the house that Auntie Annie built.

Perhaps he never framed. 'Frame!' he would tell me. An injunction to show some flicker of purpose or direction. It has that secondary definition in the dictionaries. Other items in his vocabulary of exasperation, no. 'Don't orm about.' Perhaps 'awm'. The nearest the dictionary gets is a series of referrals from 'Awm' to 'Aum' to 'Aam', a Dutch and German liquid measure. I saw what he was trying to say (as John Betjeman once commented when I showed him a poem by Mortimer Wheeler). Orming about was idle sitting, failing to fill the unforgiving minute. It was a speciality of mine, which to some degree has weathered the passing years.

My sister never ormed about. She was studying, passing examinations, painting in sepia, doing intent and beautiful needlework. Even she, however, was just occasionally 'mardy'. The lexicographers equally fail me on that. No mention. I can tell them that it signifies an elusive discontent with one's lot, both annoying and inexplicable to parents. In my case it was compounded by orming about.

From time to time my father would screw up his shoulders and complain of feeling 'nesh'. A good word, and known to dictionaries: a vague rawness, a sensation of nerve-ends exposed, the hope that nothing difficult will come along today. I often feel nesh. How often my father felt it on account of my mardy orming is something I can only guess.

I guess pretty often.

A fear that he himself had never really framed may have been at the back of his eagerness for a little framing on my own part, and his fits of despondency at seeing no signs of it.

'Bally' was the nearest he ever came to foul language. He had private swears. 'Dished' was for mild annoyance. The dished fire wouldn't light. His dished pipe wouldn't draw. 'Bosted' was reserved, or, more accurately, impelled out of him for occasions of rage.

The afternoon of the accident was one of these. As my mother emerged from the ditch, placidly proposing to hold the picnic, he was struggling up from the grassy bank, momentarily lost for words. Then, 'Bosted boy! I should never have let you have a licence!'

The motor-cycle combination, its oval front wheel into a tree, had shed its whole load. Him from the pillion, Mother from the sidecar, me from the saddle. Of all vehicles, particularly on a left-hand bend taken too fast, the motor-cycle combination is the trickiest. The sidecar comes up, control goes, crash, silence.

I scrambled undamaged from the hedge-bottom. Mother turned an ankle but didn't mention it until later. Father was hurt, and said so. My sister told me years afterwards that the back trouble stayed with him, if in modified form, for the rest of his life. He didn't go on about it. Swift to anger, but not nursing it. He may have let the sun – still heartlessly shining – go down on his wrath that day, but not the next. He did tell me later, conversationally disguised but with cautionary undertones, what the repairs had cost. The exact figure has gone from me, but I know it was a colossal sum. More than ten pounds, I think.

It couldn't have been easy to come by. I don't know how he came by the combination in the first place. Financial margins were always narrow. It's possible that his sister, my Auntie Annie Hodges, considerably older, and rich, supplied a grant-in-aid. Eventually, when her husband, Uncle Harry Hodges, died – it was thought sensible and practical, by everyone but me, that I should attend the funeral wearing his bowler hat, though a little large – she built a new house for all of us, including her. It was handsome, spacious, no expense spared in the way of fine doors and mahogany banisters, and cost a thousand pounds to the penny. That would be in about 1927. I know the cost. The phrase went about, between my mother, my father and my Auntie Annie Hodges. 'A thousand pounds to the penny.' Whether this had been aimed at, was a cosy numerological freak, or just lent the solid, unassailable feeling of a round figure, doesn't matter much one way or the other. It was a lot of money. But she could afford it. This is not to say that her liberality was at all taken for granted. Simply that a grocer's widow, having sold the shop, the business, the goodwill and the house adjoining, prime corner site, for £6,000, and probably a few hundred tucked away already, was in a bracket difficult to compass.

We thought in smaller change. When, after Mother had fol-

lowed Father to their assured reunion, I went through the house
for the dismal sortings-out, I found at the back of various drawers
in desks and chests a number of envelopes containing coins.
They were marked in Father's even hand, 'Sixpence a day saved',
'Shilling a week saved'. Against what contingency was
unguessable. Perhaps none. Thrift was good in itself.

He had his prodigal moments, all the same. I remember, with
the clarity that shines a fierce, unselective light on trivial recollections, the day he walked into the kitchen carrying a glossy new
horn-gramophone. It was cumbersome, but his irritation at the
difficulty of manoeuvring it through the door was subordinated
to emanations of triumph and expectation. Pride of acquisition,
Mother's looked-for delight. In the second he was disappointed.

'Oh, *Jim*!' Her voice always had a falling, die-away cadence. On
this, it was a sigh, underscored with exasperation and resigna-
tion. Quick to scent a failure, Father dumped the instrument on
the table, lopsided amid the cooking, and stamped off, wishing
he'd never bought the bosted thing. It had a record with it, and he
dumped that too. 'Hark, the Herald Angels Sing.' On the flip-
side, 'Take a Pair of Sparkling Eyes'.

It would have been wartime. Just as clearly, I remember
another 'Oh, Jim,' with a deeper drama and an awful dying fall.
'Oh, Jim, I hope you don't have to go.' Higher and higher age
groups were being called to the slaughter. 1916, 1917? This time
the emotional interchange was so highly charged that I was
physically aware of it, and still see their faces, as in a frozen film-
frame: perhaps my outstanding memory of the Kaiser's War,
unless you could count the wounded soldiers who seemed to be
everywhere, in their red ties and heroes' thick blue shapeless
suits. I fancied myself as a wounded soldier, running about the
house with an arm in a sling, announcing my adopted status:
until Mother said, 'Oh, don't, don't;' and because of her voice I
didn't. Her favourite brother had gone to France early, and was
back in three days with an arm and a leg blown off. My Uncle
Lawrie. He was quiet and uncomplaining. When he had mastered his artificial limbs, clumsy contrivances then, all straps and
buckles, we would take the train to Derby and visit him: visit,
rather, my mother's sister Elsie and printer Uncle Harry Harpur,
her husband (as distinct from Uncle Harry Hodges). He supplied
a roof, and some sort of job at the printing-works, for that gentle,
ruined man.

My father didn't have to go. Too old, even for the extended
trawl. He must have busied himself with civil defence, and once,
when I was grown to an age when we could be man to man,

stepped alarmingly out of character with a remembered line from a fellow special constable as they patrolled for infringements of the blackout. 'Put that light out,' shouted this wag, spotting a chink from a small upper window – 'You'll have to shit in the dark.' Father slightly blurred the operative word, unaccustomed to form it. I didn't recover for some time, and my looked-for laugh must have had a hollow ring. I never heard anything of the sort from him again. Perhaps it was just the phrasing, as with Scott or Dickens, that had taken his fancy. Perhaps there was an impulse to test his footing in my younger and wider world.

There was a speedy reconciliation over the gramophone. The Herald Angels sang the same evening, and often afterwards, becoming for some time a standard item before church on Sundays. Or it may have been chapel. My early worshipping was certainly at chapel. I don't know of what nonconformist denomination, but my Uncle Harry Hodges played the organ there, and with some skill.

He had a pipe organ in the drawing-room over the grocery, and by request would sing at it. By my request, mostly, since his songs were not sacred but comic. I suppose he really was a funny man. He sang 'When Father Laid the Carpet on the Stairs', and 'When Father Papered the Parlour'. Did my laughter at all spring from identifying the father in the songs with the Father who would have laid a carpet or papered a parlour with final success, but only after outbursts of rage over the intransigence of the bosted equipment?

At some point, Father and Mother, or Father with Mother's loyal acquiescence, 'went over' from chapel to church. It must have been a huge decision. A new way of religious life, infinitely more of a plunge than any change of political allegiance which, in other households, would attract comparable heart-searchings, breed rifts and acrimony. We had no truck with politics. The ways of God took precedence over the follies and fancies of governments.

Chapel against church was the stuff of reality. Asquith against Lloyd George was just names in the papers. For Father and Mother there was a week's talking point in a new design of hassocks, or a decision to take up the collection in bags instead of plates. A change of vicar meant longer discussions. But there was never more, or more highly charged debate than when Uncle Bobby 'went over'. This was not a matter of chapel to church, but England to Rome.

I felt the shock waves. Relations with that branch of the family were seriously imperilled, even severed for a time. I learnt later that the lapse had been temporary, that the lost sheep returned to the fold.

Uncle Bobby I recall as short, brisk and ruddy, with a stick and rather smart knickerbockers, crunching the Worthing shingle with my cousins, three girls and a boy, scampering alongside; all in the buoyant spirits befitting a family living in fairyland. That is to say, at the seaside. The sea was not readily accessible from Worksop. Visits were short and rare. To be able to walk into it, more or less from your front gate, was hard on the imagination. As it was hard, looking back, to imagine that carefree man, inside his confident Norfolk jacket, racked in a soul's dilemma between Protestantism and the Pope.

The church we joined was as low as you could get. No bobbing in the aisle before taking a seat. Black cassocks in the choirstalls, and none of your frilled collars. We did not cross ourselves at the name of Jesus, though we may have bowed the head, self-consciously for my part, but glad not to have missed the place for it. Anyway, nothing showy.

I don't know what I thought of it all. I concentrated hard on my prayers, trying to send them up. In the Confession I confessed the little lies, the little thefts from the larder, the smoking of blotting-paper cigarettes up the bedroom chimney. And wondered what could be the murmured disburdenings of Mother and Father beside me, so good, so kind, so innocent, so loving of God, as they pleaded with tight-clenched eyes, 'O Lord, have mercy on us, miserable offenders.'

Father's mistrust of showy worship served me well on a Cornish holiday once. Just the two of us. All men together. This would have been earlier than the days of the big BSA and sidecar. The days, indeed, of the two-stroke Sparkbrook, Father in First World War flying helmet, goggles, and belted leather jerkin, against the rush of the twenty-mile-an-hour slipstream. I was on the back, and sometimes slipped off on abrupt engagement of the clutch. This made him very cross.

I could not have been a very satisfactory travelling companion, and once failed him badly on some expedition or other when, stopping to get petrol, he espied a particularly appealing cheese in the shop-window opposite and sent me in to buy some while he completed the business at the pump. We chugged on, out into the countryside again, and chose with care a suitable spot to enjoy the cheese. On unwrapping, it proved not to be the particularly appealing one, but something that didn't appeal at all. Bosted boy.

We enjoyed ourselves on these adventures, but I never quite

got my enjoyment up to his. He was an antiquarian. Ruined abbeys, historic sites, interesting tombs were his delight. I understand now that he wanted them to delight me just as much. I wasn't ready for them. No emanations reached me. What would I have been then, twelve, thirteen? Despite his explanations and commentaries, always a little diffident and understated, not wanting, I suppose, to damp any interest by being oppressively informative, I could never share his excitement at standing on Hetty Pegler's Tump – I believe there is such a thing, but could not now say what or where – or clambering the crumbled fortifications of Kenilworth trying to see, as he did, the shades of dead nobles and their ladies.

On Sundays, even on holiday, we went to church. That was a matter of course. Except for the little church on the Cornish cliff that time. I forget where it was, but we had been to the ruined castle of Tintagel on the Saturday, so it couldn't have been far. We made an early reconnaissance, well before service time, in quest, perhaps, of quaint misericords or balustered Saxon windows. We got no further than the inside of the porch. Father checked like a bird flown into glass, snuffing the tainted air. Incense. We spent a secular morning lying in the grass, his pipe going well. 'I could have smoked this in the church,' he said, 'for all anyone would have cared in that stench.'

My sister Winifred was more satisfactory than I. She framed, and not in *passe-partout* only. We had to call her 'our' Winifred. Mother's youngest sister, not among those to disappear across the Atlantic, was also Winifred. This was Uncle Bobby's wife. Uncle Bobby was also called Uncle Will. He could be both, in a single conversation – except during his spell of apostasy, when he dropped out of all conversations. Their eldest daughter was another Winifred. The family likeness was marked on the female side. My mother and her sister, only a year or two between them, might have been twins.

In my cousin Winifred, at seventeen sparkling and beautiful, I saw my mother when young. This didn't stop me, at about the same age, from falling in love with her, and she with me. We hadn't seen each other since we were children. She had just been one of the carefree Worthing laughers and skippers. I almost think that we were re-introduced. 'You remember Cousin Winifred?' Oh! what a change was there. In me too, I don't doubt. There was an immediate interplay of magnetisms as she came into the room. This would be at home, I think. Agonising elation set in. Necessarily, the affair was mainly conducted by correspondence. We met once at the Derby house, some kind of family get-together, suffering keenly from unguessing intruders. Only Uncle Lawrie, that sensitive, deprived creature, read our secret signals, and somehow fixed it that we were left alone for a few minutes. I forget how, but I imagine that if Lawrie, gathering his awful trappings together, proposed a walk in the garden, or whatever the pretext was, the rest would humour him and go.

The thing came out in the open in the end, with serious talk of an engagement. But, well. Cousins. It was deemed better shelved. Think it over. We probably never believed anything would come of it. In the event nothing did. But it was a fierce baptism of love. Afterwards she wrote to say she had found her true mate. He proved as false as they come, and stayed just long enough to father a child and walk out. Fifty years later I went to see her. It was a shock when she opened the door. I thought it was my mother.

I had no idea what I wanted to do for a living. The Church was my father's cherished hope. Mother's, too, perhaps even more. Arthur, her youngest and most serious brother, had been a clergyman, the word we used always, and was the quiet joy of them both. I never knew him. He died in his time of curacy. It was a monstrous grief, as Mother's rare references made unmistakeable. But God's will. The infinite wisdom accepted. No questions.

I continued to orm about. There were predictable changes. The view from the sidecar, low on the road, became more interesting as we overtook girls on bicycles. The view from the saddle was yet to come, and it may have been about this time that Father's desire for me to frame, if only towards the internal combustion engine, prompted the driving-licence and its most notable consequence. I combed my hair a good deal, then blond and plentiful; took pains with my tie-knot; intermittently shaved; drew pictures of naked woman, biologically inexact, as I learnt later, though not from any parental information on the Facts of Life. They could never have brought themselves to that.

The pictures I hadn't even the gumption to keep in a secure hiding place. A painful confrontation followed their discovery. I maintained, feebly enough, that they were art. It was plain that my future in that direction was unpromising. Father, crumpled with distaste, looking nesh, readily quoted Isaac Watts, the grand old hymnster. Satan would find mischief yet for idle hands to do.

The debate continued. He now saw me ending, or at any rate starting, as a shop's delivery boy. 'Errand-lad', he called this. It was the lowest he could think of.

A.A. Milne's father, in a similar though socially up-market plight over his son's future, had told him that his only hope would be to go into a bank. The lowest he could think of.

Father's suggestion was sardonic. But Winifred, quietly threading coloured silks in her corner and keeping a sober face, said, 'Perhaps Auntie Annie would have him.' She had a flat tone in jest. Mother, taken in for a minute, said that at least it would be near home. The Hodges grocery was at the bottom of the street.

Father left the room.

Three

MUSICAL BANKS

AUNTIE ANNIE DIDN'T take me. Lloyds Bank did, to Father's comfort and joy. Respectability, security, white collar, pension at sixty. I was set up for life in The Bank. It was thought of at home, and almost enunciated, with the capital T and B.

Initiation took place at Bourne, one of many small Lincolnshire branches I was shuffled round during the next few years, successive managers speeding me on my way without regret. I was eventually shuffled up to London, Head Office, and the Editorial Department, where I could do no harm.

Wodehouse once wrote to me, 'I have often thought it curious that you and I should both have started in banks. I have a feeling that you were really rather hot banking stuff, but I never got the first notion of what it was all about.'

He was wrong about me. And perhaps not quite truthful, since no humorist is ever quite truthful, about himself. He told me the only time we met – did he tell me, or write it somewhere? – of his shrewd handling of a literary agent's bounced cheque. This was during his first spell in America, when he was as hard up as the agent. Noting the official grounds for bouncing as 'Insufficient Funds', and having an acquaintance in the bank, he persuaded him over a drink to a breach of confidentiality in which the amount of the deficiency was disclosed. It was small. Perhaps a mere ten dollars short of the required two hundred and fifty. Crediting the defaulter's account with a ten-dollar bill of his own, he re-presented the cheque, which was then honoured, if by a hair. So something of banking procedures must have rubbed off on him.

It pleases me to name T.S. Eliot as a fellow Lloyds alumnus. We literary men. He only put in eight years, though in some more rarefied capacity at Head Office. As *The Confidential Clerk*? Head Office, for me, hopping the Lincolnshire archipelago, had been merely a distant, shimmering mirage: if real at all, just the address to which the sacred daily Letter had to be despatched. A task sometimes entrusted to me, as junior, though I occasionally lost it, and once left it on a bus. Had I ever met Eliot, with ensuing banking reminiscences, common ground would have been scarce, as between his advising on the movement of millions – I speculate – and my concern with remembering to fill the counter inkwells, stoke the anthracite stove, and wind the wall-clock on Monday mornings.

The anthracite stove I wouldn't swear to. I think it is true. There was certainly, at Bourne, that first branch, some bulbous device at the back of the office, in a stone surround, which I was responsible for feeding, and often failed in that, to the on the whole tolerant abuse of the staff, as a chill came on towards the end of the day. 'Boothy! Stove!' Offices did not then bandy Christian names, either with the later false intimacy of the broad-casting studio or, as at *Punch*, because we liked each other. At seventeen, I was 'Mr Boothroyd' to Mr Reade the manager. They were syllables I dreaded to hear fall from his lips, often on a wave of whisky and wrath: the wrath justifiable, whether because an enraged customer had complained of my erratic hand-delivery of passbooks, since the fun of reading another customer's secrets meant he was getting the same enjoyment out of yours: or because, a more regular offence, Mr Boothroyd had once again soaked, blotched, ripped and ruined the managerial correspon-dence.

This was written in a flourishing hand, and required to be copied in a primitive press topped by an immense twirling han-dle. Quantities of water were involved, applied with a broad paint-brush. It called for fine judgement. Every letter was a gamble. It could turn out a perfect reproduction or a drenched, illegible mess. In that event, the original was also exterminated.

No nervous and defenceless boy should have had to present these handfuls of mush to the man in charge of his destiny, who had no alternative but to do again.

Not only was Reade's handwriting flourishy. He was a flour-ishy mover, and affected loose flourishy suits, the jacket always unbuttoned and heightening the general air of sweep and dash and affairs of great moment.

He mostly swept and dashed in and out of the Angel next door. Legitimate enough, this, in terms of banking practice: consorting affably with one's own customers, and not past poaching a couple from Barclays or the Midland, a technique, I believe, more often exercised on the golf course in modern times. Market days were his busiest, since under some local dispensation the pubs then kept open longer than the banks. He was therefore apt to return, hugely genial, when the rest of us were impatient to leave but couldn't until he had signed the letters. Should these be handfuls of mush the geniality faded fast.

He was an energetic lay-preacher. Father would have liked that, if finding it hard to reconcile with the whisky fumes. Once, whether from curiosity, a hope to ingratiate, or a conscientious endeavour to keep up with God, I went to hear him preach. Once was enough. It is always interesting to see people in an alien element, but assumptions of holiness did not sit well on him. For all I know he may have been as holy as the next man, but his office persona got between me and the Word.

The stove at Bourne, together with other features of banking life in small country branches, went into my first appearance in print (not counting the statutory school poem in *The Lincolnian*, containing the words 'fissiparous' and 'ineluctable') in the bank's house magazine, *The Dark Horse*. It took its name from the Lloyds emblem, a black horse on a green ground, now familiar in the commercials. It used to have a date under it, 1677, suggesting the bank's impressively long record of service. Honesty has since broken in, and it has been dropped. It was the date on which a goldsmith had occupied the Lombard Street site acquired considerably later for the bank's head office.

Eventually there were more articles, ultimately collected into a small green book, *The Adventures of Mr. Pitkin*. For private circulation, as the catalogues say. And would now say – had it ever appeared in them – 'Rare'. Copies have been shown to me in unlikely places. Twenty years on, at Lloyds in Monte Carlo. Forty, when cashing a traveller's cheque at Wells Fargo in Pasadena. In cold, flat Lincolnshire, Monte Carlo had itself been a dream, and the notion that fellow minions of Lombard Street should actually be stationed there a dream inside a dream. I came within gasping distance of such fantasies when, after my first branch or two, I was transported to Skegness, the Monte Carlo of the east coast and fabled haunt of unbridled joy.

Perhaps the real Monte Carlo, for those locked on the wrong side of the bank counter, also fell short of romantic expectations. Skegness, loud with bands and funfairs, and inducing holiday girls, home proprieties abandoned, to walk the streets in permissive garments known as beach-pyjamas, never really opened its glamorous doors to me. While visitors dallied on the dunes, I was immured behind my barred window. In the evenings revelry was denied me, from a combination of having no money and being loosely preoccupied with Part 1 of the Institute of Bankers examinations. It was my driving ambition to pass Part 1, at least. The bank, of its bounty, rewarded successful candidates with a bonus of £15, a sum remote to the imagination, but good for a second-hand motor-bike should it ever be achieved. It never was, with me.

I have few recollections of that notoriously bracing resort. I know I was impressed by my landlady's assertion that since her husband had taken to drinking three or four pints of beer a night his constipation problem had been solved. It seemed to me, free of such mature anxieties, a staggering expenditure in so small a cause. A sharper memory is of a girl. It was not personal. I was idly lusting after her as she approached outside my window, dressed for bed or beach, when she paused, with her laughing escort, and tossed a handful of monkey nuts through the open few inches of the top sash. Feed the animals.

Landlords and landladies were then a salient feature of the young banker's life. He was moved quickly from branch to branch; in theory, no doubt, to get a variety of experience, though most of my branches might well have been interchangeable in terms of customers, who were chiefly agricultural, and of staff numbers, usually six or seven, mostly with no marked vocation for the profession.

But it was better for customer-relations not to keep us long in the same small community. We knew too much. Customers repeatedly meeting us at vicarage garden-parties in charge of the hoop-la, and also in charge of their secrets, felt uncomfortable.

Money is a secret and sacred thing. People will confide their sex life, bowel movements and whether they have their own teeth; but never the bank statement's holy writ. I was slow to grasp this, and once at Horncastle branch got into bad trouble over a customer called Birdman, an elderly manufacturer of sausage skins. His business did not prosper, and he was regularly at the counter asking the state of play. The 'position', as it was always called. What was the position? The words would be almost noiselessly confidential.

On this market day, the office crowded with farmers and loud with gossip of ewes and tups, beets and swedes, I happened to have Mr Birdman's position before me on the ledger desk when the cashier passed back his enquiry. For once it was good news, and I was glad to be its bearer. 'You're all right, Mr Birdman' – a good carrying voice, topping the tumult – 'Nineteen pounds to go!'

Unluckily for me, the voice carried to manager Ginger Willie, who soon had me in his room to hear the correct procedure in these matters. The position is whispered to the cashier, who writes it on paper, folds it discreetly and palms it to the customer, who reads it in the darkest corner of the public space, commits it to memory and in extremely delicate cases eats it.

Unluckily for Birdman he was in no position to take his account elsewhere. Lost accounts drew Olympian thunderbolts from head office – a nightmare for managers, especially of Ginger Willie's forcible-feeble kind.

The staff, however, had no secrets from each other. The staff ledger was an open book. Our accounts, if narrowly by the month's end, showed an obligatory credit balance: or in my own case often a bleak NIL, and didn't have to wait for the month's end for that. I would already have borrowed recklessly from better-placed colleagues. There was no escape for them in pleas of personal poverty. I could check their 'position'. They were on the whole forthcoming, and knew my own position. On £6 a month, and a weekly thirty shillings going out for landladies alone, they could see I needed help.

What has become of landladies? Junior bankers now seem to live at home, parental or matrimonial. (The bank's Rule Book, in my time, ruled out matrimony below a stipulated salary scale.) The policy of rocketing them from branch to branch has apparently been abandoned. Perhaps just resisted. Enlightened conditions of labour. Whatever the cause, they don't see the world as I did, forever pulling up my shallow roots in Bourne or Brigg to put them down afresh in Horncastle, Sleaford, Spilsby. And off again to wider-flung adventure spots in Norfolk or Cambridgeshire: Watton, Diss, Ely, Cambridge itself.

A cosmopolitan in miniature, I soon learned at each new, indistinguishable destination, that the street from the railway, at first mysterious and strange, would after a week be familiar; the shuttle from bank to post office to pub to lodgings settling into a trodden way. I acquired skilled appraisement of landladies. Cooking is not to be read in a face. But their mien, even as they opened the door to their new young gentleman from the bank, was a pointer to the chances of sock-darning beyond the call of duty, or tolerance over rent arrears. Were they in it for the money, or the mothering?

Mostly the last. Whom do they mother now, that vanished breed? Is there today, if without her beautiful name, a Mrs Waterloo (Brigg), who beside her black-leaded grate comforted me with cocoa and sympathy in my days of star-crossed love? I had left my heart in Cambridge, its strings still anchored there and twanging at a touch. Mrs Waterloo asked no questions but read my pain. She was tiny, smiling, grey, an eager darner, and must have had pangs of her own in her time, whether over Mr Waterloo, long gone, or some old star-crossing gone even longer.

Where are today's Mrs Lingards (Cambridge)? Mrs Lingard was pale and patient, with a pale, patient voice, her husband believed to be worse than dead, in either prison or permanent psychiatric care. No doubt I did nothing to disguise my money troubles, chiefly represented by a selection of library books from W.H. Smith, long past their due date of return and with mounting, unaffordable penalties. They glowered daily from the top of my piano, blackening breakfast: until one morning, darting the routine, despairing look, I saw that they had gone.

'Well, they were a nuisance with the dusting,' she explained, on her dying fall. It must have cost her a good ten shillings. The house was well out along the Chesterton Road. There would have been the busfare to the station and back.

My piano should strictly be 'my' piano. Hired, and the hire not paid. I also had 'my' saxophone. Hire purchases, and the instalments in arrears: was later to have a snare-drum and high-hat cymbal. These were on approval, but enabled me to order a hundred professional cards from Messrs Johnson & Nephew, inscribed with my name and 'Pianist, Percussionist and Saxophonist'. No address. I kept moving.

Mrs Lingard, whose heart was in the right place but her nervous system frail, had grounds for complaint after bearing the early brunt of the saxophone. 'I'm afraid you'll have to go,' she said. 'If it makes a noise like that now, what's it going to be like when you can play it?' She sounded sad, but she always did, and saw me off at the front door as she always had, echoing my last 'Cheer-ho'.

We Cambridge men were saying 'Cheer-ho' at that time. Our adjectives of approval were 'wizard' and 'masterly'. I took to the vocabulary with ease, also to the undergraduate life – as a mere Cambridge bank-clerk having no claim to either. This happened through music, if the word doesn't overstate. I was 'up' at the same time as the vicar's son from Bourne. I think an invitation to tea, perhaps to breakfast, even more dashing, led to wider university ('varsity) contacts. These were the music-makers, centred on a tubby, rich Dutchman, who owned the full range of instruments for an eight-piece orchestra and couldn't play any of them. Bakker's collection included the whole glittering family of saxophones, from two sopranos, one curved and one straight, descending through even a C-Melody (rare) to a B-flat bass as tall as he was. Advertised in *Rhythm* or *The Melodymaker* (required reading), all would have carried the coding s.p., g.b. Silver-plated, gold bell.

They put my leaky E-flat alto (nickel all over) in the shade.

Musicians are drawn together. With the indulgent Bakker as non-playing captain, we students of Ellington, Armstrong, Waller, Tatum, Teagarden, – Jack Hylton nearer home – formed the magnificently equipped Syncopeppers. I don't know who devised the name. Bakker devised the tie, a limited edition, crimson crotchets on a silver ground. I treasured mine until no knottable area survived unfrayed. Banners hung from our music-stands, gleaming in purple and gold. We wore grey flannel suits and took jazz to the people. Or to those of them who would have it, at no charge, in the outlying village halls of Rupert Brooke country: Ditton, Coton, Trumpington, Madingley: we came down on them like wolves on the fold, and our howlings curdled their blood. Return dates never requested, we ran through available victims quickly. Those who heard us once, and lived, must have long remembered our 'Varsity Drag' and 'Tiger Rag', though not easy to tell apart.

We jointly owned a punt. Its name was *M'Gwenya*. I can still see the faded lettering on the stern. Selected instrumentalists, reduced from the full complement by limited deck space, would pole out to Grantchester on those warm summer evenings, the air heavy with Brooke's river smell, 'thrilling-sweet and rotten, Unforgettable, unforgotten'. The lines retain their evocations. Today, walking by local streams, I get a whiff and the picture comes back.

It has been said that the Thames, as a resort for peace and pleasure, was ruined by the portable gramophone. The Syncopeppers did the same for the Cam. I had made strides with the saxophone, now within reach of Mrs Lingard's dreaded moment when I could actually play it. Drums being unmanageable, let alone tubular bells, our percussionist, the eternally laughing and amiable Spiller (Eton, I think, and King's), did the poling and vocals. He affected an eyeglass and wore expensively bespoke white trousers, occasionally stepping deliberately off the poop into the water, coming up smiling and the eyeglass still in place. Rolf Holdsworth, owner-player of the banjo and ukelele (fingering conveniently identical) was the rhythm section. Bakker went through the flatulent motions of a trombonist. General thirst ensued, and we trailed bottles of hock on strings below the surface. It must have been the finest and hottest summer since records were kept, though one has doubts in retrospect. They

were already creeping in, I see, a quarter of a century back, when
I wrote, with a bow to nostalgia and Ogden Nash:

> *I so clearly remember*
> *September*
> *1927.*
> *It was under its blue heaven*
> *That I fell*
> *Under first love's spell.*
>
> *Forget how it started,*
> *Even how we parted,*
> *Can't place*
> *Her face,*
> *All*
> *I recall*
> *Of those thirty days*
> *Is the solar rays*
> *That burned on and on,*
> *Shone*
> *From pearly dawns*
> *To dancing on lawns*
> *Until the sun,*
> *Like a ginger bun,*
> *Sank*
> *Into the cloudless blank,*
> *And the night*
> *Turned moon-bright.*
> *That was the sort of weather*
> *We had together.*
>
> *Which is why*
> *I*
> *Was quite surprised the other day*
> *To hear a meteorologist say*
> *That the September*
> *I so clearly remember*
> *Because of my first dates*
> *Was actually in the records as the wettest until 1958's.*

Those recollections of a cloudless 1927 September were falsi-
fied at several points. It was more probably August. And the year
might have been 1930, again short of a suitably romantic rhyme. I
have never danced on lawns. I could be open to challenge by

met-men on their 1958 rainfall figures. But there is truth, if commonplace enough, in the remembered radiance of summers long past. Their unremitting sun. And though Dorice Bentley-Gunn was not my first love, it was on the Cam that we met that summer, whichever summer it was, and she lasted the longest: not in terms of active relationship, which barely lasted a couple of months. But in the sense that the ache, only acute for a year or so, grumbled on for decades. I suppose we all get one of those in a lifetime, and one is plenty.

The circumstances of our meeting were idyllic to the point of absurdity. A dreamy afternoon. Punts. She was trying to paddle hers out of the reeds in a sheltered reach as I came poling along in my expensively indebted trousers with rhythmic ease. I thought she was beautiful, and still think I was right. After the rescue I found she had her hair short like a man's, but only when she took her hat off, which was yellow, with a scooped-out arc at the back and curls pinned inside at the front. She never took anything else off much, though I would have relished it deeply.

What was I doing, alone in *M'Gwenya* on a dreamy afternoon, rounding a bend to such an adventure? Admittedly I was an adoptive undergraduate. But I must have looked in at the bank sometimes. Where were the rest of the Syncopeppers? Again, they must have looked in on their lectures sometimes. It doesn't do to dig too deep. But in any case they would be in the middle of the long vac. (as I called it) at the time.

If so, she didn't know. She was a hairdresser, newly from Bingley, with a touch of Yorkshire accent I found ravishing. She knew enough to ask my college. When I said 'Lloyds' it passed without comment.

She loved my piano. 'What'll I do?' I played, yearning with flattened sixths; 'Glad-Rag Doll'; 'I've got a woman', the last based loosely on the Ted Lewis arrangement, which was also ruining the Cam that summer via portable gramophone. Not all punt crews could make their own music.

She was an honest girl, and would never say she loved me, though my demands for that assurance must have been tiresomely monotonous. She was nineteen, with adventurous incidents behind her. A trophy for acrobatic high-diving at Blackpool. Imagine. But she had the photographs to prove it. Also of an excursion in the support boat accompanying Gertrude Ederle on her Channel swim. Dorice would swim in the sluggish river currents to Grantchester, myself accompanying her in the support punt, custodian of her towels and clothes: averting my glance, by request, when these came into play in some discreet, ultimate glade, until the permissible time to hand over her yellow hat with the curls inside.

Hairdressing was itself a glamour profession then, air-hostessing and modelling yet to displace it in that regard. She was on big money – three pounds a week. Reluctantly, but with no choice, I let her pay for us both to go to the pictures, just beginning to talk, play and sing, their American accents and idioms surprising to British ears. Taking our seats for *Broadway Melody*, we were handed helpful leaflets, explaining difficult words such as 'boloney', or distinguishing between US and UK usage of 'closet'. Despite television's scrapings of Hollywood's grainy old barrel I have never seen the film since, but such are the raw sensibilities of love that I still remember the cast (Anita Page and Bessie Love with top billing), most of the scenes and some of the dialogue. 'He's going to give me a ring,' says Bessie, tearful and applying make-up remover at her dressing-room mirror. 'Oh, yeah, sure,' says the hero in full evening dress – 'on the telephone, but not here' (tapping a third left-hand finger).

Ah, ah.

The rest of the Syncopeppers then being 'down', I can only assume, I somehow secured nightly employment at the piano of the Rendezvous dance-hall – still going when last I heard - and trilled personal flourishes at her as she danced with the young men of the town. Later of the gown. One of these she presently married, an economics student of faintly Oriental features who sailed her away with him to California. Either he or she must have done all right. Just before the war she gave me lunch in her small suite at the Dorchester. So I still wasn't paying. It was fairly formal, but with reminiscences. She showed me, with love and pride, photographs of two teenage sons, very Japanese. No piano in the suite. I would have played her one of the Rendezvous numbers. 'The Song is Ended', perhaps ('but the Melody lingers on'). We never met again. Where are you now, Dorice Bentley-Gunn, lately of Bingley and Cambridge? At the time of this writing you would be about seventy-seven.

Sometime, that year of *M'Gwenya*, I had a week's leave from the bank. Looking back, I seem to have been on leave from the bank all year, which can hardly have been so. I went home to Worksop, where I assured them that I was happy and industrious in my work, thought well of by my superiors, studying for Part I, avoiding bad company and getting early to bed. Unfortunately it was Father who opened the telegram from the Rendezvous management saying 'Permanent Job Yours If Return Thursday'.

This took some explaining. It wasn't difficult to explain that my piano job had been temporary, the regular man having shut his hand in a door; or even to offer speculation that his return to try out the restored fingers in my absence had shown them restored insufficiently, so that he was now out again and I in. These were not the details Father was looking for; he wanted the broader picture. I don't remember how successfully I painted it. I know I assured him I was still in The Bank.

I returned Thursday all the same, to suffer one of those cruel blows making show business such a bad business to be in. Some dark horse not even in the running had mysteriously beaten me to the post. My services were no longer required. It was a bitterness different from that already eating me over the now fast-fading Dorice, but the two together were terrible. I may not have seriously contemplated suicide, but I stood more than once on the Bridge of Sighs, looking down at the water. Life was clearly over. A hard thing at eighteen, when at seventeen and a half it had promised so much.

A hero of the Cambridge days was, and remains, a fellow-junior named Cobber, sacked during my time there for committing several months' voucher-sorting arrears to the basement boiler. Sorting paid cheques and other paper into alphabetical drawers of knife-edged cards was a chore of great tedium, and played hell with the cuticles. Cobber preferred the furnace. His gesture was in itself a many-splendoured thing, but the true glory was to come. He presently began to appear on the public side of the counter to conduct his new masters' business, grandly uniformed in commissionaire's braided chocolate, with 'Central Cinema' in gold on his hat.

Bills pursued me at Lloyds Bank, Brigg, my fresh official posting: for the tie, the grey flannel suit, the punting-trousers; for saxophone instalments, piano-hire, wire brushes, cymbals, bird-call effects. They were beyond all hope of settlement. The burst of Rendezvous earnings, probably aggregating as much as ten pounds or a small fortune, had gone on my last landlady, who was no motherer, and a disgrace to her kind. A Christian Science widow, Mrs Godolphin must have had her softer side. She kept a love-token in the umbrella-stand, the late Mr Godolphin's artificial leg.

Lily, her big, plain daughter, who threw herself about showing the lisle tops of her stockings, was an anxiety to her. I felt myself watched. Without need. The hole in my heart from Dorice could not have been filled by Norma Shearer.

That was my last Cambridge address. I had notified it by

postcard to the heavily owed piano shop, with directions to transfer the instrument. A call in person was not advisable, as even I could see. Indeed, for some weeks I had given the place a wide berth, with those of rival creditors. It meant walking to the office by ever more circuitous routes, bus travel being out of the question, except for luxurious plunges around pay-day. The fear of being pounced on from doorways may have been exaggerated. In a university town of 1930 unpaid bills were a tradesman's way of life. In the last resort a rich father would always come across. Fathers of poor bank clerks were less to be relied on.

The piano never turned up. In the arrogance of youth I was annoyed. Mrs Godolphin was also annoyed. I had announced on arrival that the instrument was on its way and I should require her sideboard to be moved out to make room. She and Lily helped me, with bad grace, and after a period of unfaded side-board-shaped paper helped me to move it back.

Relations remained scratchy throughout our short association, which wouldn't have lasted long, I fancy, even without a bank directive to repack my Gladstone bag for Brigg, Lincs. It was disappointing. I had winsome ways, and knew it. I rate Mrs Godolphin as one of those, recurring at intervals along life's path, who saw clean through them. Certainly not a woman to be charmed, on parting, into writing off bad debts.

She got the Rendezvous money. Neither she nor Lily came to the front door to see me off. At the bank, on my last day, there was a farewell ceremonial. A grand tearing up of my notes of hand, by a party of creditor colleagues. Not in large amounts individually, ten shillings here, five there, but in total not an obligation I could have wished added to other long-running liabilities.

To meet immediate needs I sold Rolf Holdsworth's bicycle and banjo, which he had entrusted to my care during the long vaca-tion. No moral twinges assailed me at the time. I had my lifestyle to keep up, which included Turkish cigarettes. Abdulla No. 11? They were creased down the side, in the fashion – as Richard Mallett once pointed out, of Edward VII's trousers (Mallett was *Punch* film critic, parodist, intricate light versifier, surrealist funny writer). But remorse later caused me to spill my conscience into print, naming the betrayed Holdsworth and offering restitu-tion, wherever he might be some forty years on. This turned out to be South Australia. He presently wrote saying that he was now a grandfather, had become reconciled to the loss of both articles, and I could keep the money.

It must have been about the same time, on a radio programme, that I invited trumpeter Billy Clark to get in touch, when I should be glad to let him have back the pound that I had owed him since roughly the time of the Reichstag fire. One listener did respond, admitting that his name wasn't Clark and he was no trumpeter, but agreeing to take the pound if it would ease my mind. Nothing from Billy.

He wasn't a trumpeter either, in any effective sense. By trade a house-painter, he shared with me Mrs Waterloo's kindly roof in Brigg. I learnt from him the expression 'daft as a brush', and long thought it either his own invention or understandably endemic to the house-painting profession. I have since heard it in circles unconnected. However, Billy had a trumpet, and all the feeling for it. I had my saxophone. Gathering others around us, notably a Mr and Mrs Trott, who played the violin and swinging 'cello and were both something at the waterworks, we soon had a band.

Billy was small, neat, in his early twenties, a great laughter, immemorially an orphan, idolatrous of Louis Armstrong and, nearer home, Nat Gonella. He had all the flourish. Legs spread, foot pounding, he tore into a shipwreck chorus* like a typhoon. Village hall bunting tugged at its moorings, passing dancers fell sideways. Real wild.

But after four bars his lip gave out. Or possibly his teeth, which had mostly been supplied locally. He would meet my reproving look, as I tried to salvage a few crotchets, by externalising his bottom set in a contrite death's-head grin. He sometimes held on longer in waltzes. *'Parlez-moi d'Amour'*, with slower notes, was almost a showpiece. He called it *Pa and Ma in Armour*.

We could scarcely have been as bad as this sounds. We got engagements. Were even paid. Not a lot. Fifteen shillings apiece for a big night, 8 p.m. to 2 a.m. From 8 to 12 only ten bob. But it was money. Waking to the glint of silver on my bedside table started the day right. There were inevitable disbursements, eventually on actual band-parts. Unwrapping those heavy bundles was a thrill as uncapturable as a child's Christmas morning. Talking of this recently to Benny Green, a real, that is, professional, musician in his time, I found that he had felt the same sizzle of expectancy. In his case, of course, the bundles would go into full use. With us, it was largely waste paper. We lacked trombonists. Second-clarinet parts were surplus to requirements.

Failing engagements of our own, I would often guest, as they now say, with a pub band in Scunthorpe. Frank Martin, pianist and brick-red furnace worker, used to get me home at three in the

*'Every man for himself'. We spoke the language.

morning on the back of his Norton, saxophone and accessories clutched to a starched but buckling evening shirt.

And so to bed, and shortly to the bank, gummy-eyed and still vibrating.

Brigg was a four-man branch under manager Harry Sellars. There had been over a hundred of us at Cambridge, so it was a come-down all round, and little chance of absenting myself, unmissed, on boating or musical duties. I have since wondered about the saintly Harry Sellars. How did he reconcile the stern, necessary duties of bouncing cheques with his guiding principles of Christian goodwill? Contesting loyalties. The Good Book and the Rule Book.

Like John Reade, he too was a lay-preacher, though with theory and practice kept less far apart. Not for him the enlistment of customers in the saloon bar or at the nineteenth hole. He sought conversions, if at all, among suggestible chapel-goers, to whom he preached either from the headquarters pulpit in the town or the tin-roofed sub-branch remote on the road to Skeg-ness. It made capital for me, in my letters home, to tell Father of the righteous inclinations of both Reade and Sellars, comforting him on the score of my secure guidance under God, despite intimations, as in the Rendezvous telegram, of the more secular life.

I never hear Sellars in the pulpit. He must have been torn over texts. Between Matthew 19:28, say ('And took him by the throat, saying, "Pay me that thou owest"') and Luke 12:54 ('Where your treasure is, there will your heart be also'). These conflicts have to be left to the theologians. Giving everything to the poor would offend banking practice.

But Harry gave to me, and I was certainly the poor.

After a few months under him I noticed a falling-off, then the cessation, of the bills from Cambridge, which at first had featured considerably in the bank's incoming post. Always optimistic, I readily accepted that the tailors and music-shops had given up (where money is concerned I have continued to read such things by a rose-coloured light) – but no. Harry had taken to siphoning off the bills into the top right-hand drawer of his desk, and produced them on summoning me one day to his mercy-seat.

'Basil, how much do you owe?'

I fumbled out a stupendous estimate.

Said Harry, getting a pad of debit-slips from his left-hand drawer and handing me the bills, 'Don't let me see any more of those': and wrote a slip for twenty pounds on his account. No strings. No repayments. A little uplifting homily. A bargain at the price. He had a noble soul, and if it has now gone where I think it has his fellow saints are looking shifty and self-seeking by comparison. It was perhaps as a quid pro quo that I got him a new customer, never to be despised at a small branch, in the name of William Clark, c/o Mrs Waterloo, 28 Scawby Road, Brigg. I don't think Billy did a lot to improve the branch figures, but at least his account was where I could keep an eye on it. It was thus, on being again uprooted and transplanted to Horncastle, that I knew he was good for a small loan towards my leaving expenses. Mrs. Waterloo wept a little when we parted. At least I don't think I owed her anything. Beyond nearly a long year's mothering.

Four

CHARACTER REFERENCES

AT HORNCASTLE, RESIDENTIALLY speaking, I was less mothered than fathered. Not in the sense that Father would have approved. Mr Ashton, whose oppressed but uncomplaining wife played little social or administrative part other than to appear, bedraggled and muttering, with the meals, was a fount of lecherous anecdote. He may have found an obscure satisfaction in my awed and often uncomprehending reception. There were less improper variants, colourful reminiscences of a long, globe-trotting life. The circumstantial detail was so rich that even his wildest improbabilities defied disbelief.

He must have been a handsome creature in his prime, perhaps some thirty years before, and was still – this would have been 1934 or 1935 – very much the country squire, in solid tweeds and good breeches. He had a large eagle nose and, as Conan Doyle described Lord Robert St Simon, 'the steady, well-opened eye of a man whose pleasant lot it had ever been to command and be obeyed'. Impressive. But a fake. He had picked up his style as landlord of many hotels: all over the world, to hear him talk, as he did for most of his waking hours. Local information was that he had never been out of Lincolnshire.

Thinking back to his wife, I now see what she reminded me of: Tenniel's White Queen in *Alice*. She may never have got her hairbrush tangled in her hair and left there: it just looked like that. She may not in fact have owned a hairbrush, and looked like that, too. She also had the royal chesswoman's face, pasty, button nose, chins in abundance, lips naturally pursed. To put it politely, she was plain. Old Ashton didn't put it politely, and early confided to me, in her presence, the circumstances of their union.

'In South Africa,' he said, scooping an enormous helping of stew, 'I married my first wife – come back, girl, let's have another dumpling – the most beautiful woman in Johannesburg. Did she lead me a dance.' He brushed up his cascading moustache, clearing it for action. Once doubtless bold and glossy, it now drooped, tobacco-yellow. 'I promised myself my next one would be the ugliest I could find. Kept the promise. See for yourself.'

His wife gave him a push of rebuke on his good tweed shoulder.

'I've shot her three times,' he said, tucking a yard-square damask napkin in his collar and reaching for the huge Victorian cruet. He drew in some gravy through long rabbit teeth. 'Still got one of the bullets in her.'

'Twice,' said Mrs Ashton. It was about the only time I ever heard her put him right on anything.

He was certainly handy with firearms, as I learnt suddenly after my first night's sleep there. On my arrival the previous evening I hadn't met him. He was in his own quarters, incommunicado, playing his gramophone record. He only had one, but enough surface remained to reproduce the Street Singer, a popular high-pitched tenor of the time, who continually bleated, 'Marta. . .rambling ro-o-ose of the wildwood'. Ashton never tired of this. A beautiful song and beautifully sung, was his regular comment as the needle rasped to rest.

My awakening resulted from a loud explosion under the bedroom window. A rushing noise down the chimney. Ashton presently walked in with a shot-gun under his arm, crossed to the grate and retrieved the rook in a small cloud of soot, leaving with a formal 'Good morning'.

After a week or so, when I was deemed a satisfactory audience, he would bid me to his retreat of an evening. A gloomy room, solidly furnished, it had a lot of pictures, mostly photographs. One of the coloured heavyweight, Jack Jones, was autographed, though not to anyone in particular. 'Good old Jack. I went three rounds with him in Melbourne.' Ashton's eyes glazed reminiscently. 'Knocked me down and I was out for two hours.' Some would have claimed the contest had gone the other way. Ashton never pushed a story. Indicating the fading photograph of W.G. Grace, he underplayed.

'Good old W.G. Know what he said to me? "Young feller,"he said, "you'll get me out if you go on bowling long enough." But I didn't go on long enough.' To claim that he had bowled Grace would have spoilt things: at his frank admission that he hadn't, one had to doubt one's doubts.

Mrs Ashton, if present during these recitals, would make little choking noises, either sceptical or confirmative, jerking her chins up and scratching her stomach, where her husband's bullets may have been lodged.

Two pictures in the Ashton collection had royal associations.

The print of Queen Victoria was less interesting for itself than for a comment on it by the Prince of Wales, Edward VII to be. 'We were keeping the hotel in Calcutta at the time,' said Ashton. It seemed that the Prince, dropping in for a drink, as a relief from the formal rigours of an Indian state visit, had jerked an approving thumb at the Queen Empress, and remarked, 'Good 'un of the old girl.'

Ashton would stand back at this point, eyes critically narrowed. 'Always thought it a poor likeness, myself. Still do. Wasn't my place to say so, of course.'

His other treasure was a vast, blackened oil-painting, the detail obscure, but there seemed to be trees and water, a blob in the middle distance acceptable as a boat. 'That's the mad king, you know. Bavaria. Insured for ten thousand. Rowed out on the palace lake, pulled the plug, drowned himself.'

A long story followed, concerning Ashton's acquisition of the painting. My memory isn't clear. Balkan intrigues. I know the adventure ended with his smuggling the thing out of Munich in a hollow walking stick. More, he produced documentary evidence: yellowed newspaper accounts of the exploit. These were from either the *Lincolnshire Echo*, or the even more local *Horncastle News*, studded here and there with, 'As Mr Ashton told our reporter. . .'

I was young. I think I believed quite a lot. But the material palled with repetition, and I soon did my best to escape to the pub when I sensed the memoirs coming on. Or one of the pubs. One of Horncastle's many. Ashton never sampled them. He drank at home, from an inexhaustible cellar of thin white wine, often further thinned by some sharp mineral water. For a time he sought to bribe my tiring ear by pressing this refreshment on me at no charge, which gave me acute stomach pains until I traced the source.

When a little drunk, as not infrequently, he shed the country gentleman veneer. Lascivious personal experiences in horrific detail, rich in lewd idiom, took over from the tales of glittering associations and sporting triumphs. Mrs Ashton maintained her standard responses. Wordless gutturals. Noncommittal spasms of the chins.

Then, for Ashton, tragedy struck. Not only was I phasing out as an audience, but his wife, who must have had a firmer hand on things than her demeanour suggested, took a second lodger, a towering, eighteen-stone dentist from the Orkneys. His name was Trouncer. He certainly trounced poor old Ashton. He had a wider and deeper fund of reminiscence, and a steam-roller tech-

Mother

Father

New boy

Lincoln. My view for five years

Mother with me

With my sister Winifred

With Father, Mother and 'rich' Auntie
Annie Hodges. Sherwood Forest

Phil with Toby

With Toby, outside 'Peelers'

With Kaaren (daughter-in-law)
and Angie (granddaughter)

At 'Peelers'. Five step-grandsons and one of my own (Peter Boothroyd, second from left)

Smug sergeant (front centre). RAF Police School

With unknown blonde and others in Cairo. (My Air Commodore drinking coffee)

nique that silenced even him. When Ashton, outmanned, withdrew to seek escape and solace with Marta, rambling rose of the wildwood, Trouncer would pursue him into his room. 'Did ye hear tell how I drew thirrrty-two teeth out of the wrong body, that time in Kirrrkwall. . .?'

Trouncer declined all drink. It would have meant a pause in the torrent of anecdote, or that was my theory. Occasionally, less from compassion for the suffering Ashton, than because of Trouncer's inconvenient habit of going to bed early with my library book, I tried to get him out to a pub. He was always adamant, almost fierce, in his refusal. One evening, to my surprise, he gave in. I had no idea why. It was a sudden decision, with an odd flash of the eye. We went to the Bull. Well, we started at the Bull. Then the White Hart adjoining. Over the road was the King's Head. I was spent out early, and ready to call it a night. 'Whisht,' said Trouncer, perhaps the only time I have encountered the word off the printed page. He was paying. He put away, I suppose, a bottle of malt, before I could get him home and up the steps.

In my innocence I had done a dreadful thing. I found later that under orders from Mrs Trouncer, whose existence had at no time been hinted at, he had come south to kick a drinking problem. He had shown much character, holding out for weeks against my temptations: in the end had lapsed terribly. I never discovered, though suspicion was strong, if it was in fact Ashton who spilt the beans to Mrs Trouncer. He had that much vengeance in him, I think.

She arrived two days later. Ashton, breaking the news to me that she was on the premises and packing her husband's bag, was darkly gleeful, his rabbit teeth seeming an inch long. 'Wouldn't you expect a small woman? Trouncer being so big and fat? Wait till she comes down. She's bigger than he is!' It was so. She was the size of a battleship, and as formidable. As she overspilt her armchair, waiting for the delinquent to get his coat on, I marvelled at the feats of corsetry that confined her. Ashton, with unexpected warmth, had begged her to stay the night. 'That I wull not!' was all she said.

How they would travel I couldn't guess. It was a long journey north. But I guessed she would find a way. 'Pity she wouldn't stay,' Ashton said at supper. He shook with laughter. Exulting in his victory? No. A thought had struck him.

'What I would have liked to see,' he said, tucking in his napkin, 'was the pair of them sitting up in bed of a morning, stark naked.'

'Eat your meal,' said Mrs Ashton.

'And Trouncer,' said Ashton, seeing the picture more clearly, 'with a silk hat on.'

It was at Horncastle that I received a telegram from Father. It said, 'Are you all right. Dad.' He could have saved a penny by sending 'alright', but to avoid the abhorrent usage was worth the money.

What could he mean? I couldn't have been righter. I was having fun. Playing in dance bands. Making my first appearance on any stage in the chorus of *Our Miss Gibbs*. Bedtime as late as I liked. No church. And the pubs.

And why the 'Dad'? I had never called him Dad in my life. What had got into him?

Though I sensed that only some powerful agitation could have prompted this strange signal, I deduced, after much puzzling, that it had some reference to my shortcomings as a correspondent. Where was the time to write letters, the crowded life I was leading? It was only after many years, when my own son was subject to long vanishings into pits of silence, but was, 'Fine, fine, OK, why?' when traced to a telephone, that I understood the rackings of a parental breast. Days going by, growing to weeks, still no letter on the mat: in Father's case, in the box: inexplicably, for a man so open and guileless, he had installed a box inside the front door. There was a ceremonial air about its unlocking and locking. No doubt he had made it himself, and got recurring pleasure from its silky hingeing and sturdy mechanisms. Or, it is not beyond possibility, he may have hated a letter-box being called a letter-box when it was only a flapped hole: and set himself to rectify that.

My mother, if my own son's was anything to go by, would have been the prime mover in the affair of the telegram. Discussions of mounting urgency. Those late-night voices I had once heard from my bedroom, the deeper rumble, the lighter response on the die-away note: even then worrying about my mild fecklessnesses, a gift for idle sitting, the repeatedly lost property (bicycle-pumps and fountain-pens left me like lemmings), the unvarying school report, 'Must try harder': an instinct for buying the wrong cheese.

In the end, increasingly alarming tremors erupting into the telegram. Mother's insistence, Father's reluctance. Drafts, re-drafts. The form of signature the final problem, not solved to the full satisfaction of any of the parties.

Through amateur dramatics at Horncastle I moved nervously into the neighbourhood change-for-dinner set. Well-breeched and well-spoken, they took their theatre seriously, to the point of hiring a professional actor from London, no less, to produce. His name was Frank Freeman, a figure of great glamour to me, though like thousands of his gifted but unlucky kind of small popular reputation. He was the first actor I ever met, though I have met many, and liked them, since. I sensed the ease and grace and mental aliveness of the breed, though not at that time the gallantly masked vulnerability: outwardly, masters of the earth; inside, frightened girls. All I ever learnt of Freeman on stage was a line, the last, in the 'original cast' list prefacing Galsworthy's play, *Escape*.

Policeman, it said: Frank Freeman. It still spoke glory.

I envied his ease and grace during rehearsals and productions (nothing oppressively intellectual, *Rookery Nook*, *Hay Fever*, but no expense spared in wigs, costumes and sets). He would be a guest, for this period, under one of the performer's spreading and handsomely-chimneyed roofs, relaxed among his peers. A fine performance.

During one of those rural assignments, a week or two's well-fed vacation, he confided to me his amusement at the vapours, the 'temperaments', the sheer creative toll taken of his high-toned actresses, who had to rest all day in preparation for the ordeal of curtain rise. He was drawing a comparison not with professionals but with amateurs in his London productions, the leg-weary shop girls of Selfridges or Harrods with nothing but a sandwich between the day's work and *Rose Marie* or *The Desert Song*.

It must have been in *The Ghost Train*, Arnold Ridley's inexhaustible recourse for amateurs, that I had a line doing its worst for my Worksop accent. 'That man's mad,' I had to say, and it probably came out nearer to 'Thut mun's mud.' The rest of the company, though based in Lincolnshire, made the sounds of the south. I envied that, would have liked to emulate it. As a schoolboy, southbound with my father on the back of the Sparkbrook, I had noted the progressive softening of accents. Even at the petrol pumps, it seemed to me that gentler voices prevailed, lacking the raucousness hitherto accepted as everybody's spoken word.

Phonetics fail of the finer shades, but I suppose what Freeman and anxious fellow-players wanted from me, roughly, was: 'Thairt mairn's maird', and I don't know whether I ever came anywhere near it. There would in any case have been other lines, with terrible pitfalls of vowels and stresses. My 'glass' rhymed with 'crass', my 'sugar' with 'lugger'. I worried about it, got into an ex-cited con-dition. Petty and absurd. I worry still, which is more than petty and worse than absurd today, when BBC (once 'received') pronunciation is regional trade-unionist and plate-glass educational, and Eton, they say, is advising its departing sons to concede to the common tongue.

That was bound to come. A part of the general levelling out. Peter Dickinson, my only old Etonian friend, confessed to unease when his mother, beside him in church, launched out boldly with 'When I survey the wondrous crawss'.

It was at Horncastle that Ginger Willie held sway. Short, a relisher of power, he moved with a bounce, rising on his toes, and was dominated by a tall, gaunt wife.

They had a flat over the office, always undesirable for bank staff, subject to awkward entrances through the communicating door. The preference is for managers to live at a distance, and leave in good time to get there. Also to be happily married: otherwise, as with Willie, they appear absurdly early in the morning, cut their lunch hour to nothing, and hang about long after the day's work is done, poring over ledgers and extrapolating the customers' lifestyle, noting cheques in favour of bookies and off-licences, displaying sudden interest in old, dead vouchers requiring to be exhumed from the book-safe. As with royalty proper, no one could go before Willie. This irked us all, but particularly me. Urgent engagements called from outside. For me the bank was an interference with living, for Willie a refuge from Mrs Willie.

On all too rare occasions Willie took an afternoon off, hiring a chauffeur-driven car and taking his wife for a run in the country. She had bladder trouble, according to ledger-clerk Bertie Clover. He envisioned the difficulties imposed on these excursions. An urgent tap on the dividing glass, and Willie's imperious, 'First cottage, driver!' Bertie would expand with closer detail. Willie's false jauntiness. The wait at the cottage door. The occupier absent or uncooperative. Mrs Willie under keen pressure. 'First bush, driver!' from the returning Willie. Willie himself in need of relief.

Clover's face, an assortment of bumps and wens, snaggle-toothed, wire spectacles askew over a malicious glitter, would glow at the vision. The mighty fallen was one of his special joys. To this purpose, indeed, he probably invented Mrs Willie's infirmity. He held humanity in zestful scorn, and rejoiced in the waywardness of God. Would recount how, on solitary excursions of his own, which were many and always solitary, he had noted that a bicycle careering into a devout pair of chapel-leavers left a passing drunk unscathed. 'That's a mystery, isn't that,

Barley-boy?' His 'it' was often a 'that'. East Anglian origins. His 'road' was 'rood', his 'boots' 'boats'. His form of addressing me was based on the city of Basle, as near as he cared to get to Basil.

As ledger-clerk and reserve cashier he was a notch or two above me, but probably older than the rest of the staff, barring Ginger Willie. He had been there before Willie arrived, and would be there after he had gone, still a ledger-clerk and reserve cashier. His outward geniality at the counter won all hearts. The bank was thought of by many, and indeed spoken of, as 'Mr Clover's bank'. It was the key to his survival there. A succession of managers must have wished him elsewhere, his ledgers at last restored to legible writing and cleansed of the bits of stamp-edging which he used, in carefree defiance of the Rule Book, to gum over a multitude of clerical errors. The page-headings, in his ludicrous attempts at copperplate, would be faintly annotated in pencil. 'Venerable Bead' under the name of the Vicar, whose permanent cold embarrassed with its nasal blob. His curate, Mr Elmett, was sub-titled with a parenthetical 'Crash'. No one could have been less crashing than that pale young man. Or less eques-trian than Major Scaynes-Tile, who insisted on his rank, which had a pencilled 'galloping' inserted before it.

The customers loved Bertie, at the counter a model of solicitude for their health, their holiday plans their children and dogs. He despised the lot of them. One day about Christmas time I went back to the office for something forgotten and found him there, engaged in solitary rites. It was the season when Ginger Willie received gifts of flesh and wine. Bertie had collected the counter-pens. Blowing apart the tail feathers of a fine goose, he was inserting the pens one at a time up its backside.

'A pen, Mrs Scaynes-Tile?' he would be saying deferentially in the New Year, putting it into her appreciative hand.

His account hovered around the ten-pound mark. This was because he scorned the bank as he scorned its clientele, and kept any surplus funds under a loose wood block in the hall of his house.

There were customers who lived at a distance; once local, but moved, leaving their accounts behind. Bertie regarded them as special nuisances, in constant correspondence about their money and beyond reach of retribution. He would take their addresses with him on holiday, often driving far afield to find their homes and make water on their gateposts by night. Future letters about dividends or rights issues brought him reflective pleasure.

Otherwise the excursions were more limited, yet wide-ranging for the time. Though married to the roly-poly and fortunately placid Dorothy ('Doll-gel', in the vocative), he travelled alone, to nearby, never local pubs. His costume for work or leisure was unvarying. Blue serge suit, knees and elbows glinting, trousers too short; brown trilby worn very straight, brim turned up all round, striped band. Boots. His motion was all angles. Swift, purposeful. The laugh a gap-toothed cackle, gaspingly infectious. The bank closed, and Willie's domestic oak safely sported, I would roll on the floor at his wilder flights of fancy: painful bouts never to recur on that scale in the world of professional humour, where jokes are assessed as funny or not by sober rule of thumb.

The pubs were his hides. He watched people, from his solitary corner over his single glass of port. He had mechanical gifts. Once when I called on him in the matter of a saxophone repair I found him, greased to the elbows, reassembling a car engine on the kitchen table, his wife ironing alongside. I condoled with her. Bertie dismissed this. 'Should have been here Sunday. I had the wings off a Crossley, didn't I, Doll-gel? They was laid up the stairs like seals.'

Cars on the road were sparser then, but two of them were Bertie's, both high-nosed old black Crossleys, seldom roadworthy together, owing to continual cross-cannibalisation of parts; or in a dismantled state to admit of some privately devised accessory. One of the Crossleys was always kept serviceable for the night forays, sometimes to outlying Mablethorpe or Boston. Enemies said that he visited an ex-harbourmaster's widow in Boston, but I don't think so. Too much like an involvement.

He ran an unofficial taxi service. Unofficial, since the bank had rigid laws about outside incomes, except for a manager's perks from insurance commission. I doubt if he did it for the money. At any rate it would come a poor second to opportunities for studying, occasionally astonishing or mortifying, the passengers. He astonished the Venerable Bead one evening by informing him that the approaching crossroads had experimental studs in the road, installed by the traffic authorities, causing passing vehicles to set off a warning peal of bells. As foretold, the carillon rang out, though from under the bonnet, Bertie's heel on the secret button. On a cold winter night he drove the local MP and his agent to some political occasion. As no one, not even Bertie, had yet devised the car heater, he did his best for their comfort by means of a paraffin stove in the back. It was not in a prime state of maintenance. At journey's end the politicians, in innocence, stepped out blackened to the eyes.

This was a lovely thing. For some days afterwards he dwelt on it contentedly, repainting the scene for me, as we looked out over the market place from our desks. 'Strokin' their jaws all the way. Big important talk on pig subsidies.' He passed a hand over his facial knobs and nodes, rehearsing the spread of sooty discharges. 'That must have been good, when they strood into the meeting.' He hadn't waited to see that. 'I droove right orf.' Doubtless to a peal of bells.

Not all his fun was anarchic. From that window on the world, when banking was slack, he invested passers-by with imagined secret lives. Even this, it's true, sprang from a conviction that humanity had been created for his amusement. 'Not one perfect specimen, Barley-boy' – contemplating the passing pageant. The more we looked, the more it was so. Strange shapes, eccentric gaits, faces racked by unguessable preoccupations. At such times, had Cleopatra sailed past in all her dignity when the flow was really on us, we should have clutched each other, helpless with laughter at the shape of her ears.

He fastened his wildest, and for me most enduring fancy, on The Swinger, an elderly man with a rolling walk, arm swinging out from his short, square trunk in a rhythmic arc oddly at variance with the rest of him. I had noticed this figure from time to time without particular interest. So had Bertie, no doubt, long before the thick double-breasted jacket and shiny-peaked cap fired his imagination.

'That's sad,' was his establishing comment. 'Waiting for a ship. Seafarin' man.'

The fantasy built slowly during my last month or two at the branch. (I was only exposed to Bertie for a year. But indelibly.) The Swinger's past life of storms and wrecks was pieced together. Whaling. Good money once, long squandered in the spice-heavy bars of exotic ports. Restless now. Out of his element.

'It's the arm. Catches every gust. See how it turns him there, swings him clean up North Street? There he goes, hull down.'

It became vital not to miss him. On days without a sighting Bertie would fear that this had happened, confiding as we called over the paid cheques at the end of the day, 'It's been right for him. Stiff breeze. Cobb's awning filled out.' He sniffed the office's close air. 'There's the whiff of his sternsheets still.' During longer absences he would cheer up. 'I reckon he's signed on, Barley. Away orf. Bangkok.' Then sadness again. The Swinger was always back. There were days when one of us spotted him and not the other. Urgent signals behind Ginger Willie's back, or an excuse found to hurry to the window and glimpse the last flap of sleeve, bellying him round the post office corner into the Angel yard.

It all became realer than real, at any rate for me. And made more real the shock of learning from a third party, just before I left that place, that The Swinger had been a council employee as long as local memory served, following up reports of faulty toilets.

Clover, who of course had always known this, sustained the fiction at long distance for a year or two. Sometimes at later branches, when I examined the endorsement on a cheque cleared through Horncastle, the sketch appeared of an arm, in thready pencil. Not good, but plainly swinging: with a straggling note, 'Seen him today.'

If Bertie Clover was one of a kind, so was Jesse Baggaley, of quite another kind. In memory I treasure them both, though they wouldn't have had a word or an idea to exchange with each other.

Jess had a room over his father's Horncastle pub, the New Inn, which was older than it sounds. The room was book-crowded under its black, tilting beams. I think of a fire always blazing, between battered leather chairs that had to be scooped free of heaped magazines to accommodate Jess and a listening friend, slumping deeper on the exhausted springs, the light dying, the empty beer-bottles in the hearth, and Jess talking.

I don't know how I found the time. What with theatricals, dance bands and the bank I couldn't have had much. But I spent a lot of it in the second chair. Its springs sometimes took a double beating. This was because of a tax-collector's daughter on my lap, an association less chilling than it now seems in recall. There were times when we lost the thread of our host's pronouncements on life and literature. I have wondered since if he noticed, and how much. He would bring us round now and again with a bellow of barrel-chested laughter, writhing his jodphured legs – he rode big old clobbering horses, and jodhpurs were his habitual leisure-wear.

He was of the earth earthy, the Lincolnshire earth particularly. Had stories of old battles fought through neighbouring woodlands until they were, I remember the phrase, "oss-belly deep in blood'. But he was also of the intellect intellectual. Some concentration of chromosomes had driven him to read and read, learn and learn.

I think of him endlessly talking. Mighty nose with the skin tight over the bridge. Blond hunks of hair flopping. And ideas and allusions and facts and fantastications tumbling out. I think of them tumbling. In fact, they came in agonising spurts. He had a stammer. Could temporise with meaningless punctuations. 'I mean. . .I mean. . .I mean,' veins swelling until they must surely burst. But to get out something that really had to be said was a crippling exercise.

'I mean. . .I mean. . .B-by God, n-now! Look at B-Burton for a m-man!' Then in a spurt. 'Used to eat twenty eggs for breakfast. I mean. . .'

Yet I had almost forgotten the stammer.

Which Burton would that have been, Sir Richard or Sir Robert? I hadn't even known there were two, perhaps not one. But I knew nothing. I must have been about twenty-two, Jess three or four years older. I hadn't even heard of Thurber, Benchley. Jess's piled and scattered magazines included the heavy issues of *The New Yorker*, then a mere child of ten or so. He would have been drawn to the quality of it. How had it come his way? To a speck in the flat waste of Lincolnshire? I didn't ask myself, nor what he made of 'The Talk of the Town' and its parochial Manhattan references. It didn't matter. You couldn't keep anything from Jess that had something to say and a style to say it with, from E.B. White to Robert Bridges. I didn't know any Bridges. 'Oh, yes,' said Jess, and after a hideous strain on the veins began to quote. 'Whither, O splendid ship, thy white sails crowding, Leaning across the b-b. . .I mean. . .the b-bosom of the urgent West.' After a few attempts he got out 'urgent West' again, wide-eyed, inviting a shared wonder at the words poets got their hands on. 'I can do wi' it!' he would shout. His highest term of approval.

He could do wi' people and things ranging widely, from Dashiel Hammett to Arnold Bennett, Laurel and Hardy to Shackleton and Scott: nature, the soil, the French Revolution, village cricket. I don't remember his batting. Perhaps he was no good at it. But the bowling image is sharp, the thundering approach, the boots somehow seeming to curve upwards at the sole. Wicket-keepers stood well back, but still flinched and missed.

Well. So we couldn't only have met in winter by the fire. There would have been no political, perhaps not even historical, feelings about the French Revolution. Just that the characters and events had a seizing zest. It comes to mind because we wrote a play together about the French Revolution, which he had to explain to me first. What became of those three fat acts, ribbonbound in thick white card covers? Its hero was Danton, who had never come my way at school: its title, *What Other Pleasure*. Shakespeare, he said, but I've never been able to trace it. Shakespeare had come my way, even at school, but not with the yield of

random and ferocious quotations that were always struggling out
of Jess. Sometimes repetitious, as we slumped in the chairs. 'For
G-god's sake let us sit upon the g-ground' – the chairs were pretty
near the ground, or anyway the floor – 'and tell sad stories of
the. . .I mean. . .of the d-death of kings.'

In the next forty years we only met twice. He came to my
wedding, bringing gifts of pewter tankards and threatening the
seams of his morning suit. And long afterwards I was up there
making some speech, but he was ill then.

When he died his son asked if I would do a local paper obitu-
ary. Unlike the run of such assignments, it was easy. There was
nothing, with him, that had to be discreetly left out. Did I say in it
that he had been the first to show me, perhaps try to read, 'They
told me, Heraclitus, they told me you were dead. . .'? Probably
not. Cut the sentimentality. I may have been tempted. It did have
the line, 'We tired the sun with talking, and sent him down the
sky.'

Oddly, I don't remember *Punch* among those magazines. Perhaps it was there, but meant nothing to me then. It would be
there later. Not because I had sent him a copy with something of
mine in, but because he began to get verses into the paper
himself. They went on for a year or two, our names appearing
within nodding distance of each other in the indexes, and then
stopped; partly because editorial policy towards 'serious' verse
was changing, partly because the war was here, making an
irrelevance of rural rhymes, such as Jess's.

> *My father's father*
> *ploughed this land;*
> *his father's father*
> *thought and planned*
> *to get increase*
> *upon the yield*
> *of his forefathers*
> *from this field.*
>
> *I think each furrow*
> *means a year;*
> *when eighty's done*
> *I'll not be here.*
> *And I'll be bound*
> *before I came*
> *my father's father*
> *thought the same. . .*

Several of them appeared on full pages, with framing illustrations. The early drawings were E.H. Shepard's, when hard-nosed verse contributors of the time called the page 'Shepard's Pie', and vied to furnish the filling. Then Leslie Illingworth took over, just as observant and evocative a draughtsman but with a greater robustness of line.

Jess wasn't there long enough to earn any initials. 'J.B.' beside 'J.B.B.' would have been amusing. But of course confusing.

During the friendship, or that fragment of it spent in each other's physical company, I suppose I took Jess in much the same stride as I took Bertie Clover, old Ashton and the luckless Trouncer, even Ginger Willie; not to say the tax-collector's daughter. They were detail from a landscape with figures, of interest in their different ways.

But I see now that Jess educated me. Neither consciously nor directly. Just by the distilling and showering of bright, undislodgeable particles. He was an auctioneer's clerk in the local cattle market: and content, so far as I ever knew, with that.

Five

THEATRES OF WAR

In 1937 I burst on London. It's easy to remember my age, then and now. Ten years younger than the century. Banking proper was rid of me. The Editorial Department was not exciting, but at least, on *The Dark Horse*, I was living by the word, if it only described, under Branch News, the presentation of a brass-bound log-box to a retiring manager, and his speech of thanks expressing the hope that his successor would receive the loyalty and support which he had himself enjoyed. I could hear Bertie's cackle between the lines.

In London I could never find my way anywhere, and haven't improved much since. Worse, I have the assured look that makes people ask me for directions. I must have put enough old folks on wrong tube trains to fill an eventide home.

But I somehow found my way to St Pancras People's Theatre. Someone must have taken me, hoping to recruit me into the company. More probably I had desired to be recruited, and presently was.

It was a rum set-up, the child of actress Nancy Price, who wanted to bring the theatre to the people, at seat prices starting strangely at sevenpence and rising to a giddy half-crown. She pursued her aim so resolutely that curious theatre-goers who were not 'people' in her cherished sense, but arrived slumming in actual evening clothes, were turned away at the door. The house was in any event not spacious, and members of the company who were not appearing in the play of the week occupied much of what space there was (presumably not even paying sevenpence, I don't remember), before rushing round the back to tell the cast that they had been wonderful, darling.

Resources were slender. No sets. We played in curtains, somehow strained and pleated to admit of necessary doors and windows. The wardrobe was sparse, but infinitely adjustable under ingenious needles. A few feet of gold piping on Christy Mahon's reach-me-downs from *Playboy of the Western World*, and next week they encased General Robert E. Lee, shooting up Harper's Ferry in *Gallows Glorious*. Trollope crinolines from *The Small House at Allington* became full-sleeved Russian pyjamas for *Tovarich*. Wigs were a desperate scramble. Late in raiding the box, you could be left with the least favourite, known to all as Little Nitty. Myself stuck with that, I could only speculate for comfort that it might once have been worn by Maurice Evans, André Morell, Michael Hordern and others who got their first heady whiff of the make-up box at St Pancras (patron saint of the young).

It was there that I met Phil. We fell in love and were married for forty years. As in me, the urge for self-expression was strong. The drama called. With her, it always had. In the days when reputable amateur productions gained the attention of professional theatre critics, they had written enthusiastically about her appearances with the Bank of England's dramatic society. I never saw them. Before my time. But she had the cuttings. Even allowing for a reviewer's lowered expectation on such occasions, it was clear that she had more than an amateur talent. Her chief gift was a voice of richness and adaptability, which could pitch the sad Welsh lilt of Gwenny in *The Late Christopher Bean* or command as Lady Bracknell. It was a legacy from her mother, a concert contralto of some merit, whose records she would occasionally play. Considerably pre-electric, their effect was muffled, but there was a noble set of pipes there, booming forth the staple 'Abide With Me' or 'The Lost Chord' in the hollows of the Royal Albert Hall. But she had never overcome the terrors of facing an audience. Alcohol was for a time a friend, then a destroyer. In my early days at the Savage Club I found old singers who remembered her. Robert Easton, I think. Norman Allin certainly. I never met her. The nearest was when we took our son Toby, about a year old, to wave to her at the window of some grim place. There was a reason, medical or psychiatric, why they were not to be in a room together.

Phil should have been an actress. The ambition smouldered lifelong. A year in repertory might have burnt it out. There was never a way of knowing. I arrived, then the war, then Toby.

In the end, all was tapered into the Talking Book service of the Royal National Institute for the Blind, a late fulfilment in its way. She read scores of books, her whole heart in each. Many survive. After her death I was still getting her letters of thanks and praise, sent on from the RNIB, and had to ask them to desist. I never heard any of the tapes, which would once have been easy, though not now. Time. I never had the time. Busy fellow. I wish I had made it. I wish she could have read the letters.

The voice I first heard was Lancashire. Strictly. Not just your all-purpose North Country. It was Sally's, in Walter Green-wood's *Love on the Dole*. Apt, we thought, looking back, when we came to set up house with not much more than a pair of curtains and the canteen of cutlery she'd received on abandoning the Bank of England to marry me in 1939.

Years afterwards, all hope not yet abandoned, she wrote to Maurice Evans, by then a master of the great classical roles in New York. A last despairing cry. He answered at some length, and kindly, in a letter full of wise discouragement.

Most part-time Thespians manage one production a year: per-haps a couple – while the society lasts. Temperamental in-fight-ing soon folds up most amateur groups like deck-chairs, and can have whole villages not speaking to each other. At St Pancras we did a play a week. Temperaments were frowned on by the two lady producers, one tall and academic, the other short, wispy, ever urging us to 'feel it here, dear' and claiming to have been three years in *The Garden of Allah*. If we weren't playing, we were rehearsing. Discipline was fierce. Miss a rehearsal and you were out. Phil and I would have liked to be in the same plays, which seldom happened, as any such sentimental considerations, themselves deplorable in that dedicated world, could have dis-torted the casting.

When the cast-lists went up in the green room there were cries of agony and joy. The agonised, unselected for the forthcoming attraction, were fit to take their lives. The joyful left by fast bus for French's, in Southampton Street, to grab up a copy of the play. At the bus-stop for home they avidly counted their lines, falling into an actor's stance, weight on one leg, the other a pace forward and bent, surprising the rest of the queue with arcane mutterings, the sudden outflung gesture.

It is to be assumed that we were all earning a living some-where, somehow, in the unreal theatre of real life. I don't know how we fitted it in, particularly as some of us seemed to be fitting in other stage engagements in the rare St Pancras crannies. My own were varied. A nod to Lloyds Bank, in some historical presentation about Warwick 'the Kingmaker', of which I don't remember much, except a contempt for the ready-made gran-deur of the sets and costumes, a sharp contrast with the true working theatre. And without the reminder of documentary evidence I would have said that I had never trod the boards of the Scala in *Night Must Fall*, under the mysterious patronage of Baroness de Goldsmid da Palmeira, all proceeds to the Polish refugees. You forget these things.

But here is the programme, and there am I. Twice. Lord Chief

Justice in the prologue and Inspector Belsize in the play. Though Nancy Price rarely showed up at her own distant outpost (in 1938 she would have been busy with her interminable run in *White-oaks*) she must have kept an iron hand on us: my name is asterisked and footnoted: 'By permission of St Pancras People's Theatre'. Surely as near as you could get to being a pro without actually getting paid. Further down the cast list, as Mrs Bramson's comical cook, was Daisy Nichols, later changed to Dandy, and better known to viewers as Mrs Alf Garnett. Somewhere there's a picture of us. Her in her fur tippet. Me in my cascading inspector's moustache, a necessary adjunct in case the audience thought I was still the Lord Chief, unexpectedly invading the body of the play.

All proceeds did not in fact go to the luckless Poles. My watch, cigarette case, cufflinks and wallet went to persons unknown, nipping in from Charlotte Street while I was on stage passing sentence. Representing, as I was, upholders of the law in both roles, I thought this cheeky, and ran about backstage in full-bottomed wig and underpants threatening to sue the manager. Nothing came of that. But it was a lesson in distinguishing Theatre from Life, something I was having trouble with at the time.

Then there was music. I suppose I wrote my score for *The Love Of Ming-Y* (patronage of H.E. the Chinese Ambassador) in the bank's editorial department, between instalments of the continuing Mr Pitkin saga and accounts of managerial retirement rites. In faintly parallel circumstances, T. S. Eliot may have roughed out *The Waste Land*, or Wodehouse *Leave it to Psmith*.

For the Chinese Ambassador, at the Phoenix, Charing Cross Road, I was in the orchestra pit. I don't know where I got the players from. It was a biggish band. At least eight. Nor do I know how I got involved in writing a Chinese musical, nor whether the Ambassador was there because I'd written it, or I'd written it because he was going to be there. Equally mysterious at the time, though I now know that they do these things, was why a cast of genuine professional actors should have been up there on the stage doing it, for some good cause now forgotten, and perhaps too, with a disingenuous eye, and hope burning bravely, seeing the chance that a one-night Sunday stand would flare into a run.

Gwen Ffrangcon-Davies sang the lead, and did me melodious credit, though after some rehearsal misgivings on my part. I wasn't used to the self-conserving professional approach. Her run-throughs had been in a husky mutter, powerful pince-nez on a nose wreathing out cigarette smoke. She was beautiful on the night. And terrifically Chinese. So was the music. I conducted from the piano, with clever simulations of gongs, and though critical reaction was disappointing, to the point of being absent, one of the actors liked the score so much that he took it to America and lost it.

I shrugged. It was tough on the world of the arts, deprived of a second *Chu Chin Chow* like that. For me, what of it? I was already at grips with my book and score for the 1938 St Pancras pantomime. Again the orchestra pit. The piano pit, rather, under straitened musical availabilities. At least we raised two pianos. John Furness played the other, soon to throw up his musical career for TV producing. Was it *Dick Whittington, Mother Goose*? A conventionally loose adaptation in whichever case. I think Michael Mills was in it, who also became a television princeling, though later, producing scripts of mine at Thames, he couldn't remember, and pardonably. Cecile Chevreaux played something, if my own memory serves, and probably Margery Mason, both destined for stage, screen and radio. I know that Phil, hating it, was Fairy Sunbeam, with a coronet of milk-bottle tops and a star-topped tinfoil wand. But casting was casting. You took it on the chin.

Up to the time of the Munich crisis, we had taken no account of shadowy offstage disorders. Eventually the Fuhrer's voice, harshly insistent on costly blackout materials, penetrated even to St Pancras and blacked us out for good.

It left a gap, soon to be filled by other considerations. Oh, the war, yes. But by 3 September 1939, my third *Punch* piece had appeared.

On Wednesday, 31 August 1938, I had counted twelve copies of that week's issue from the bookstall at the Bank tube station and handed over the money. Six shillings the dozen. Quite an outlay. And a big enough deal, I should have thought, to prompt the man behind the counter to ask the reason for it. He didn't. If he had, and I'd told him, it would probably have been a disappointment. He was flanked by a billion words. No matter to him how any of them got there.

They knew about it in Lloyds editorial department, having been shown, not with too casual an air, I hope, but I can't remember now, the acceptance slip which had exploded on me the week before, signed 'T. J. Childs' in a clear but unstylish hand. Rejection slips, in fact not many, had always come from the Editor, naturally not signed at all. It still strikes me as odd that the acceptance should have come from the printing works, Mr Childs being (and adding after his name) FOC, Father of Chapel. This was in itself odd, or so struck me then, not knowing that printers worked in chapels.

Back at the bank with my twelve copies I all but missed the moment. The weekly issue then had no list of contents, though they appeared, covering six months, in the last number of June and December. (One wonders how many readers held little unsigned gems in their heads all that time, impatient to discover whose they were.)

So I leafed through the editorial pages, in those days clinically separated from the advertisements. I started with the squibs of 'Charivaria' and ended with the book reviews. My article wasn't in.

I was sitting there with my twelve copies, so much expensive waste paper, when Clifford Witting came in from the office next door. He was plump and breezy (and soon afterwards to leave the bank, some time before I did, to write detective stories and other books, including a handsome life of Stamford Raffles). He knew about me and Mr Childs. I wished he didn't.

'They've made a frightful balls-up with your article,' said Witting, looking unusually grave for him. He was a postal subscriber, but had to catch his train before the post arrived. He said his wife had telephoned.

'She says your piece is in all right, but the fools have put A.P. Herbert's initials under it.'

These jokers. They should know that the humorist has no sense of humour where his humour is concerned.

I was in enough shock already to take him at his word. Even if readers thought my own words were just another 703 by APH it was better than nothing. At least I would know different. I went through the pages again. There it was. I still don't know how I missed it. A mind in confusion. It wasn't as if I had never seen my typewriting made print before. No doubt I had never really believed that the print would be in *Punch*; and, when it was, just couldn't accept it, had no idea what it would look like.

Psychiatrists probably have an -ism for it.

My friends were pleased for me; my mother, father and sister impressed, but proudly unsurprised. Father could not have been more gratified by my choice of medium. *Punch* in those days had its old respectability. No sex jokes, beyond perhaps something quiet about the philoprogenitiveness of rabbits; no cartoonist's gags about Christ walking on the water. Had the paper not been favourably referred to in the reminiscences of Dean Hole? (Even

some years later an Air Ministry corporal, delivering my posted
weekly copy, said, 'Here you are sir, your clergyman's comic.')
Perhaps the boy was framing at last.

'Just think,' said Phil, looking at the five-guinea cheque for that
first article – 'if you could get one of these a *month*!' It was some
time before I got another (though in fact the magazine was
weekly). But the war paid dividends. Between getting into uniform in 1940, and out of it in 1946, I had reaped some 150 entries
in the indexes.

The first uniform was the Home Guard's. Shapeless denim
smelling of linseed oil and not in those days a fashion fabric.
Exploits in this costume made my first-ever *Punch* collection into
a book. The second, the RAF's, was soon to make another.

There had been an element of gallantry in volunteering to be an
airman before the due date of call-up – or so it might charitably be
read. I had heard rumours, however, that favours were bestowed
on those eager to serve before they had to. Wars breed rumours.
This one, like so many, proved unfounded. It was also coura-
geous, some might think, to accept service as an RAF policeman.
Phil thought so almost immediately after I emerged from the
recruiting office. I had not wished to fly. The recruiting sergeant
was more than amenable on this. I imagine that an Air Council
Instruction had newly reached him, stressing the thinness of the
disciplinary arm. 'It isn't bloody aeroplanes what's going to win
this war,' he said. 'It's bloody bullshit.'

We had our first car, a leaky, bald-tyred Standard. It had cost
sixteen pounds, and mostly fired on only three of its four cylin-
ders, often continuing to do so, from some mechanical quirk
beyond my grasp, after the ignition was cut. But it was a mark of
our climb in life. I told Phil of my choice as we drove off. It was
not, I said, aeroplanes that were going to unhinge the Axis. She
was lovingly impressed, even to the point of suggesting, as we
overtook, though slowly, a walking airman dragging his kitbag
behind him in the gutter, that we should take him aboard. He
hesitated, looking at the car, but got in. She told him her husband
had just joined his Service.

'What as?'

She told him.

'Yes,' he said, unwrapping a Lyons' Individual Fruit Pie, the
staple delicacy of a thousand NAAFIs. 'We threw our bugger in
the emergency water tank Sunday night.'

It brought the war close to us both.

RAF Christchurch, where I spent my first probationary period,
had one aircraft, a grass runway, something hush-hush to do

with radar, and four policemen, as yet untrained. We performed such simple duties as the poling of outgoing swillbins in quest of smuggled food cans. No living accommodation. I was billeted, alone, with Mrs Cooling. Landladies were back.

She was one of the shortest women I ever saw, and Rose Cottage was spotless as far up as she could reach. We hit it off at once. She gave me a room of my own, put flowers in it, laundered and fed me ('Nice bit of conger today, Mr Boothray'), cleared a table for my typewriter and was a dragon of defence against the world outside.

Even at first, when I was going to the war eight hours a day, this was good. I wrote busily. Soon, owing to the slipping of some administrative cog, more and more unfledged policemen began to arrive at the station. The sergeant running the guard-house was hard pressed to fit us into his rosters. Tours of duty were reduced. From eight hours on and sixteen off to six hours on and eighteen off. Still the reinforcements piled in. Four hours on, twenty off. It came down, in the last few weeks, to a mere two-hour daily stint at the war, with a very real danger of forgetting to go. This eventually happened.

One morning, in dressing-gown, slippers and full creative flow I realised, after a preoccupied time-lapse, that voices had been raised at the front door, Mrs Cooling's dominating. She was still indignant when she brought my coffee and sandwich punctually at eleven. 'Some old sergeant come pounding round. You don't want that riff-raff. Told him you was busy. Is that all right, the salmon and shrimp? Couldn't get your anchovy.'

The charge could have been anything. Desertion, even. In fact it was nothing, a smile of fate intervening. By the time I reported to the guardhouse, braced for the blow, the day's mail had been distributed. 'Letter for you.' The sergeant's manner was unexpectedly mild, handing it over. The envelope had a coat-of-arms on the flap, and '10 Downing Street' beneath it. Bottom left front, to leave no doubt, PRIME MINISTER, in big plain print.

'Ah,' I said, tucking it calmly away. I guessed the contents. One of Mr Churchill's lower-echelon aides was acknowledging a presentation copy of my collection of Home Guard exploits. As the formation of that remarkable body had been a Churchill notion in the first place it had seemed right to keep him posted. Besides, I had given him a favourable mention in the introduction. There is no compassing the cheek of the young.

The sergeant, saying nothing at the time, must have spoken elsewhere. I was out of Christchurch the same week, after a muted audience with the station commander, rare for an aircraftman, second class. He said nothing much either, but wished me luck and gave me a speculative look with the firm parting hand-shake. 'Mole' was not then a word with its present sense. But whatever he called it in his private thinking, he didn't want one.

I went to RAF Uxbridge to learn to be a RAF policeman. Before long I wired Phil with instructions to get my evening clothes out of store, parcel up and dispatch soonest. I wished to appear at my best, compering the camp concerts and playing for dancing in the officers' mess.

Against the general stream of thinking, I have always argued that nothing has ever been remedied by ridicule. I have to yield in one instance. My first concert script at Uxbridge featured a run-ning gag about the state of the East Camp ablutions, of which the CO, in the front row, knew nothing, never having been up there to tread slime and hunt for a bath-plug. The gratifying upshot was the quick posting to Iceland of the sergeant in charge, who had never got up there either. He was a craggy regular, and had a word with me before leaving.

Despite the hazards of police work I was never thrown into an emergency water tank. This was because I never did any police work, and not only on account of musical and theatrical pre-occupations, time-consuming though they were.

After eight weeks' instruction in the policeman's arts and wiles I went into my ninth as an instructor, with commensurate titles and dignities: the cheese-cutter hat, the acting corporal's stripes, the black-red-and-black brassard formidable on my sleeve. 'Out of darkness, through fire, into darkness' was the old sweats' reading of the design, with gaudier adjectives interposed.

My own instructor, 'Red' Rhoden, an intellectual Communist, a linguist and superior chess-player, whose name I was to come across in peacetime in connection with the Hastings Tourna-ment, had adjusted his approach to his pupils with similarly colourful example and illustrations. On the drafting of a charge-sheet: 'It's no good putting, "When on active service, using insubordinate language to the Commanding Officer." What you put is, "When on active service, saying to Squadron-Leader Corcoran, "Go and ----- spiders you son of -----."" His lecture on prisoners in custody, and the need for constant vigilance, included the cautionary tale of an NCO i/c cells who had sent a prisoner outside the walls to wash a bucket. 'Never seen again,' said Rhoden. And, after a well-timed pause, tossing the chalk in his hand, 'Never even washed the bloody bucket.'

The insubordinate language specimen gathered force from including the CO's real name. Not the one I have used. He was in civilian life a car salesman. Used cars, it was said. I would have thought in more refined regions. Berkeley Square or Piccadilly, rather than Great Portland Street. He was an imposing figure, or sought to be, and had his uniform hats bespoke tailored with a larger peak than the common run. Preferring the seclusion of the mess, and the company of a glass, he was not much seen by the courses of student policemen, though his name was held over them as an image of wrath to come.

His main public functions were to welcome an incoming course, or godspeed an outgoing. His addresses often caused bafflement.

'Attention for your Commanding Officer!' screamed W/O Dresser, an impassive six-and-a-half-footer lately a hotel commissionaire but claiming to have served in youth with the Coldstreams. He was always referred to by Rhoden as 'the pin-head guardsman.' The course having sprung to its trembling feet, the CO mounted the platform with controlled steadiness, bringing his eyes carefully to the front.

'Well, men, you have been here for eight weeks. . .'

Or, 'Well, men, you are going to be here for eight weeks. . .'

The bafflement arose from his frequent confusion over whether the men had just arrived or were about to depart. A gymnasium full of newcomers, their kit barely stored, were thrown into mental disarray on learning from an unimpeachable source that they had been around that place for two months. Or, having been around for two months, that they had just arrived.

Don Dresser caught nobody's eye. The rest of the staff as the words rolled on, stern, measured, hopelessly off target, tried to do the same. But a flickered glance was bound to get away. If only between Rhoden and myself.

Rhoden read *Punch*. I was now reporting weekly from my particular theatre of war. Details were prudently fudged, but he had spotted the source. We welcomed each other to the observation post, and its detached view of the antic scene, where feuds raged over class-room allocations and chalk issues, mutinies threatened over snap gas-exercises timed when students were in their last frenzied dash for the goal of graduation. When revised timetables were rained upon us by the Chief Instructor, a peace-time poet and educational theorist, many didn't speak to him for days.

He spoke, as it happened, to the nation, broadcasting late-night verses to strengthen its morale. His rank of Flight-Sergeant, as announced, did much for this. I remember a not bad line on bomber crews. 'Wing-tip to wing-tip, five miles high. . . .' Like me, he had never left the ground.

The closed world turned even more closely in on itself when the Academy (Rhoden's word always) left Uxbridge for a bleak outpost near Blackpool. The war had not greatly interfered with our studies at Uxbridge, but at least there had been the occasional noisy reminder that it was in progress. Here, hard by the bomb-free, still funloving resort (no illuminations, but the swings and roundabouts bravely carrying on), the world forgetting, we were by the world forgot. Vera Lynn never came to sing to us, nor Clifford Curzon to play. ENSA passed us by.

So far as I know, the history of the RAF Police School has yet to be written. Certainly its part in toppling Hitler has never been explored by TV comedy writers, perhaps the only pocket of wartime action to escape. A rich vein there, not least in the motley collection of brassard-wearers. What guiding principle had brought us together, none could tell. All we had in common was having nothing in common. There seemed to be a lot of lawyers, officialdom making no distinction, perhaps, between the judicial and executive arms of the law. Two of the lawyers wrote a book together, chapter by chapter in turn, and sold it. We had a provincial theatre manager, skilled in trick billiards shots; a cinema organist from Nottingham; an animal-trainer who should surely have been in dog-handling unless his occupational claim was false – a view which gathered acceptance when he failed to discourage the CO's Alsatian from lifting its leg over the fire-buckets and getting fatigue parties into trouble.

More credibly misrouted was a dental mechanic. After several attempts he gave up his fight for remustering and gained much kudos for his lecture on the rules of evidence, notably in cases of rape. He taught by rote. Fellow-members of the faculty, passing his open windows, heard a deep, rhythmic chanting.

'So all together again. When is the offence established?'

Chorus: 'When actual penetration has occurred.'

'And again. When?'

'When actual penetration. . .'

Instruction then proceeded, still in antiphon, on the several kinds of evidence. Real, documentary, circumstantial, hearsay, eye-witness. The last not easy to come by in rape cases.

We heard nothing more warlike than a practice-range rifle-crack. In charge of this exercise I once received a memorable rebuke from W/O Dresser, the pinhead guardsman. 'It's no good telling them to keep their sights 'orizontal. 'Orizontal with what?'

All this developed the actor in me. I was acting the airman, the policeman, the educator in however limited a field. Above all, the upholder of discipline. I threw myself shamelessly into that – in retrospect shamefully. I bounced my ego off the captive audience; at its desks, in its barrack-room, on the parade ground. I could strike terror with a tirade against bent cap-badges, the iniquitous use of string instead of laces in a PT plimsoll. As if I cared. Have we all a sleeping tyrant inside, just wanting a pretext to storm awake?

'Never to shout at the pitch of one's lungs again,' I wrote towards demobilisation time, itemising unforeseen regrets at being out of uniform. It was an exhilarating outcrop of brief authority.

I had in mind a morning of engulfing fog on the square, when I about-turned my men at its nether edge and sent them quick-marching away. They at once vanished, even their boots silenced. Something or someone then distracted me, until I realised that the boots, somewhere out there, were still marching, must by now be about to pass through the cookhouse. Theirs not to reason why.

I drew a deep, stinging breath.

'A-bout. . .tah!'

Nothing. Neither sound nor sight. No crash of glass and crockery, which was something, but the distance was great, and audibility poor. It was a long half-minute before they pounded out of nowhere within a yard of my cheese-cutter; they would have mown me down but for a smart order to mark time.

A triumph over fearful odds; we old veterans dwell on such things.

None of these roles really fulfilling me, the drama proper presently beckoned. The Police School production of *Journey's End* (Captain Stanhope – Sgt Boothroyd) was so well thought of, particularly by the cast, that we toured it round the bomber and fighter stations, showing the boys what real war was like and taking the bread out of ENSA's mouths. We beat dents into our steel helmets with the back end of fire axes, deepening the scars with No. 5 greasepaint. Temperaments had asserted themselves early. With the arrival of the costumes, I had to stand up firmly to the Adjutant, who was only playing a walk-on but meant to walk on in the best breeches. My victory was bad for discipline but good, I still think, for the play.

We were a fine company in the end, if terrified. The din was nerve-shattering. The off-stage grey hordes, or effects department, gave us all they had, the roar and bang of their thunder-flashes leaving the Alamein barrage nowhere. Even the CO stayed awake on opening night, and I had no compunction, as the valiant Stanhope, in putting up my MC ribbon for act two. The third act dugout collapse was still to come, and though it had been devised by an orderly-room clerk claiming to have been something at Pinewood Studios its genuine sandbags could fall anywhere.

There seemed to be no shortage of policemen now, if indeed there ever had been. They streamed in, scruffy, reluctant and bemused, and streamed out a fine body of frighteners; having in my case clubbed together and given me a wallet, the course spokesman blushing prettily and shuffling his blinding boots. I reaped enough wallets to set up in a leathergoods business.

Much of what I had written under Mrs Cooling's guardianship went into a second book, *Adastral Bodies*, notes and comments on Air Force life at rock-bottom level. Its only satisfaction for me, at the present remove, is that I signed a copy for a god. Hard on publication, an Olympian party of top police brass arrived from the Air Ministry to inspect the Academy, spear-headed by a Group Captain APM (Assistant Provost Marshal), an eminence to stagger the mind. My fame had clearly spread, since he begged a copy of the book. I was touched and delighted and proud, and threw in the bonus of an autograph.

For a suspenseful week or two I waited to hear how he liked it, but never did. Later, commissioned and at the Air Ministry myself, keeping an eye on the nation's security from that high place, I came across the book under my name in the subversive suspects file. I was well situated to remove it, but suppressed the impulse, less from a sense of duty than a reluctance to spoil the joke. It could still be there, now microfilmed for posterity.

The Air Ministry sounds grand. It sounded grand to me. I had a stake in the war, signified by a brief-case with the Royal Cipher in gold outside, though nothing inside but this week's *Punch* and next week's proof.

I also had the new, smooth uniform, and a Crombie greatcoat, affected even in milder weather. Without it, the absence of wings over the breast pocket was too apparent. I received my first salute in Regent Street, actually in the course of coming down Austin Reed's steps. A magical moment, and I threw off my nonchalant response to the manner born.

I was not, of course, at the Air Ministry. I was at Air Ministry. The custom of dropping the definite article, at the same time inflating the institution in some way hard to define, may have started there, as the TUC now describes itself as 'Conference.' I once debated with Barbara Castle at the London School of Economics – can such things be? – who brought off a fine double: 'I am a member of Cabinet, I am at the heart of Government.' It annoyed me very much, and I still couldn't say why.

Nor was I even at Air Ministry in the full Whitehall sense: our headquarters were in Moorgate. The building had been taken over from the Eagle Star insurance company shortly before I moved in as personal assistant to the Provost Marshal. I once called his attention to the inscription in stone over the entrance: 'STAR CHAMBERS.' 'Mm,' he said. 'I think we'll forget that.'

He would. He was a good, kind, tolerant and beautiful man. Owen Washington de Putron. Air Commodore. I wrote about him a lot, but never got the chance, in that sort of piece, to speculate on what sinuosity of service planning had landed him up in that unlikely job. Or, to descend a few notches, how I landed up in his outer office, where often his superiors in rank, yea, even to Air Marshals, made brave small talk until my buzzer buzzed and I ushered them in on to the carpet. There was no talk of any size when they came out again. I escorted them to the lift in their silent pain.

The PM, which here never meant Churchill, must have had a steely streak. I never saw it. To call him beautiful means handsome as well as gentle within. Tall, sauntering, a pipe-smoker with none of your gurgle and suck and tap-tap-tap. The reflective 'Mm' was frequent among his few words. Sometimes a murmured 'Excellent', often standing for 'Thank you', as on finding his desk lighter refuelled. This was a bulky brass artefact in the shape of some figure. Britannia comes to mind. During my first week it kept appearing in his out-tray. Deducing mere absent-mindedness I kept putting it back on the desk. He just wanted it filling. He would feel it assertive to say so. He had matches in a drawer. I should catch on eventually.

I became efficient in such matters, notably in unjamming the zip of his tobacco pouch, whether in the out-tray or handed back over his shoulder in aeroplanes. They used to say that it took nine men on the ground to keep one man in the air. I kept him going single-handed, though we were both on the ground much of the time.

The part suited me. I enjoyed playing it. Especially scenes in which high officers, wanting me on their side as an intermediary, showed me well-advised respect. I developed a fine blend of power and deference. 'Well, sir, I can certainly raise it with him, but–'

My green scrambler telephone was a treasured prop. I was Michael Redgrave, Trevor Howard, an unflurried finger on the secret button. 'Should we go over?' My best profile to camera. It was handy for confidential negotiations with other Messes over the Algerian wine shortage, or the proposed swap of a half-dozen scotch for a half-dozen gin.

We had no proper Mess there, only a small bar. When Toby was born in 1945, this saw my celebration of proud fatherhood. It was attended by the PM and others, including Wing Commander Dangerfield, a crisp man who used the word 'speediest' in all memos, and was transmuted to Wing Commander Perilmead on the printed page. 'Cheers, then, sir,' said the corporal barman, much my senior in years. 'He'll soon be twenty-one.' This was so. And you could soon double it. The PM presented a christening robe of fine lawn, how acquired in days when nothing was acquirable I never knew.

They were also the days of the flying bombs. These had inconsiderately begun to fly into the south-east at the time of my posting from tranquil Blackpool. I had a week's notice. Time, I told myself, for our matchless boffins to find the 'answer'. I had largely avoided conventional high explosives, though once, when I was still a civilian, a nearby consignment had me downstairs at the brandy before Phil got a leg out of bed.

Not much detail had been released about the V1s, but enough for me to wish equally quick reactions from the scientists. They failed me.

On the night before reporting to Moorgate I was put up in some small hotel, I think in the Marylebone Road, commandeered as a staging post for such transients. It lacked luxury. A sergeant seemed to be in charge. Up in my room, intent on a healing sleep against the morrow, I had heard what seemed an exceptional number of taxis, proceeding along the road outside by fits and starts. I came down again to ask about breakfast. The sergeant, who for some reason was wearing his helmet, saluted smartly.

'Sir?'

'Sergeant, about breakfast.'

'Here's another sod,' he said, and dived flat behind the reception desk. There was a not too distant detonation.

After a day or two the ear became attuned. Taxis and flying bombs made quite different noises if you listened. You listened.

Despite their criss-cross taping a few windows had gone when I reached Star Chambers one morning. 'Excellent,' said the PM, when I pointed out the kite-sized dagger of glass stuck through the seat of his chair. A comment, no doubt, on his having luckily, like myself, arrived a little late at the office that day.

It would have been a bad way for him to go. I suppose he was about fifty. I only recently found that he had been badly wounded as an infantry officer in the earlier war – but went through all four years of it – before being one of the first to fly when the RFC, predecessor of the RAF, came into being. I know it was said that he was a dashing flier in the old Hendon air displays of the twenties. Perhaps it took the same sort of courage, yet a different sort, to be a top policeman.

He retained for the controls of aircraft, though by now his eyesight was a little dubious, an enduring itch, a matter of anxiety for me when we flew about together to Greece, Egypt, Crete, Italy, Palestine, Iran, Iraq. I prayed for strong-minded pilots who would stand on their rights when he intimated that he would like to go up front and take over. Even such lower orders as flying-officers or flight-lieutenants, however severely outranked, were entitled to resist such advances.

They never did, the weaklings. Disquieting spells resulted: there were sensations of flying sideways; emergences from low cloud over inhospitable terrain. Once, circling Heraklion, I thought all was lost. It looked for a few chilling minutes as if the pilot proper, a mere boy, was going to let my revered chief put down on the strip. Or have a sporting try. It was a relief when the PM himself decided against this, though leaving it late. The boy seemed pleased too.

There was a curious sight on the abandoned field of Monte Cassino, real warriors long gone, though not before lining-up in immaculate parallels, as if for inspection, the shattered wrecks of military vehicles, rank upon rank of twisted scrap. I heard the order in echo. 'Get this mess straightened up, Sergeant-Major. Can't leave the place in this state.' 'Sir!' The knife-sharp salute. 'All right there, some of you men.'

We flew to many areas of battle, but we were always there after the battle had moved on. Not by design: it was just that by early 1945, the worst was over of the war I never saw. This did nothing to diminish my air of having participated. It took nobody in. Dashing briskly up the steps of Shepheard's Hotel in Cairo, as if I had the whole of the desert campaign behind me, what I had behind me was a man in a tarboosh crying, 'Guide, sir? You want a guide?'

We saw the pyramids. Somewhere I played the piano by moonlight. This, I always say, was in Farouk's winter palace. Thinking it over, it seems unlikely – but then, as all agree, it was a funny old war.

Equally unlikely, I must have been in charge of getting us from one place to another. We seemed to make it, I can't think how. 'I want to go to Habbaniyah,' said the PM. It would be an inspection of some kind – the local RAF glasshouse, guard-dog displays – this wasn't a holiday, after all. I showed my draft signal for approval. 'Excellent,' said the PM. 'Is that how you spell it?' It wasn't, but we got there: by some particularly alarming aircraft which gave me bad moments on take-off, when the pilot suddenly threw all his energies into a frenzied pumping. I should have been forewarned, I thought, that his undercarriage had to be raised by hand. My confidence in navigation techniques was also undermined. Then, as now, I assumed that we were magically, or at least scientifically, beamed to destinations. But over the wastes of Iraq the pilot and co-pilot kept looking out of the window. They were not barred off from their passengers in those things. You could hear them discussing whether or not they ought to be seeing landmarks down there. The Tigris, the Euphrates, a dried up salt lake. 'Well, something, for God's sake,' said the co-pilot, who suffered from air-sickness and kept retiring to the tail of the plane.

We were invited, in Habbaniyah, to dine with a local sheik. 'Ever had sheep's eyes?' asked the PM, always indulgent about his personal assistant's preferences. Whether he was served this delicacy (or had expected to be – I wasn't the only one sporting a sense of humour) I never discovered. Afforded a benevolent loophole I elected to go into Baghdad for the evening instead. Only forty miles in a scalding jeep, insects the size of matchboxes splattering on the screen.

The romance of it! Baghdad! Those dark, mysterious, spice-laden alleys, behind whose high, barred windows. . . 'What would you like to do, sir?' asked my sergeant-driver, parking the vehicle and removing its distributor-head. It was hard to know. 'There's a good film on,' he said, helpfully. We saw Bob Hope in *My Favourite Blonde*. But at least, afterwards, something of the country. In a flaring bazaar I bought Phil a pair of truly beautiful silk and embroidered pyjamas and saw them parcelled up for posting. What eventually arrived was a bundle of tawdry rubbish. The sergeant should have warned me: it took some explaining.

The PM felt none of my own romantic stirrings in those faraway places. He had been there before. For me, particularly in Palestine, the names alone had a wonderful ring. I thought what Father and Mother would have given to see those holy spots: Bethlehem, Nazareth, Galilee, snow-capped Hermon, the old and the new Jerusalem. At Nazareth the PM would remember that an old fellow-warrior had run a maintenance unit there. . .

Cana reminded him of a court of enquiry about a stores fiddle. . .
he had once had engine trouble over Hermon in a biplane,
thought it was a Gloucester Gladiator. . .Mm.

At Galilee, for a moment, I thought his sense of ancient time
had surfaced. The place, he said, always did something to him.
He hitched his khaki drill shorts. 'All the goodness,' he said,
'seems to go out of the elastic in my underpants.'

I said it was probably something to do with the water being so
far below sea level. I'd got the wrong sea, of course, but it wasn't
a bad comeback for someone in shock.

All these things, and many before and after concerning him I
wrote in *Punch*. Other officers from time to time referred to them,
but until our only meeting after the war, when I paid a sincere
tribute to him at a highly-ranked dinner on his retirement, he
never did. Though he would have been exceptionally well placed
to add further to my dossier among the subversive suspects.

On my disappearance to the war Phil had returned to the Bank
of England; not to the solid grandeur of Threadneedle Street, but
to a hutted camp in Hampshire, with some large clerical division
that could be out of London without disruption of the nation's
finances.

We seemed to meet painfully seldom. In memory, it was
always winter in Hampshire. She was lodged in a gamekeeper's
bleak cottage. We interleaved the bedclothes with newspapers.
At the rationed four pages a paper it needed plenty to be effective. We found – or she did, always good with ideas – that by
holding very close, and breathing very deep, and exhaling very
slow, some trickle of circulation could be aroused and sustained,
until the time came to emerge, gasping visible steam, for morning
ablutions from a jug of icy water.

Somehow, sometime, Toby was begotten in that place. Amor
vincit omnia.

In one of the worst winters I drove there, probably from
Uxbridge. I don't know where I got the petrol. Legally, no doubt,
as an officer of the law. The decrepit car remained my pride,
despite its fitful mechanisms. It just made it, but entered a snow-
drift with a bodeful groan and never regained consciousness. She
was businesslike about it, and after I had returned by train sold
the tyres for six pounds, which we both thought pretty good, all
things considered, especially the state of the tyres.

As of the Police School, there is an unwritten story to be told of
that outcast Bank society. Or to be scripted. It was another closed
order of a kind. Boredom, privations, separation from loved
ones, feuds, jealousies, unlikely liaisons established.

Phil established one of these, of a purely practical nature, with the resident manager of a renowned firm holding the camp's catering franchise. Partnered in the local darts league at the village pub they beat all comers. His admiration for her unerring flights into the treble-top caused him to take her aside after one evening's famous victory, and formalise his respect in a confidential hint: 'Never touch the mince.' She said he was not a demonstrative man, and a loyal servant of his masters. She knew what it must have cost him.

In 1946, after the war and nearly seven years of marriage, it was time to set up home together. First find your home. We tramped the streets of Dulwich, Twickenham, Hammersmith, carrying between us, by plastic cot, our heavy and late-walking son.

Punch was then still appearing with its Richard Doyle cover, where the dog Toby, in frilled collar and feathered hat, gazed out morosely from his perch of bound volumes. It would have been my idea to give our son a dog's name. Phil may have had reservations. But she went along.

It was in Hammersmith that we had the first place of our own, the toppest flat in a liftless block. It could have had a lift if the builders hadn't used the profitable shaft space for another eight flats. We had pooled our all for a key and curtains, and our all included the war's dividends in the shape of helpful *Punch* guineas. So some must have been worse off, if not those in the Key Money game.

This was a vital part of setting up a post-war home, and was to some degree legal, but beyond that not. In order to rent furnished, that is, one had to buy the vacating tenant's key for some official maximum figure. If he thought this inadequate, which was the prevailing thinking, he pushed it up as high as the market would bear. The added amount was outside the law. In my place the transaction took place inside an ABC teashop. There I palmed the extra £400 or so under the table, since government agents might be anywhere, to our predecessor and benefactor, I believe a Mr Shangri. Shangri but no La.

'Furnished' bore a loose interpretation. For us it meant the kitchen curtains – shortly to be augmented, as creature comforts, with the canteen of cutlery and our wedding presents. These, under imminence of global conflict, had gone into store on arrival, sight more or less unseen. There were surprises. A wealth of coffee-sets. A camel's-stomach table lamp. At least practical were half a dozen gaudily illustrated fish plates, necessarily all-purpose. Not fussy about food I never took comfortably, all the same, to eating rationed rectangles of corned beef from pictures of dead mackerel in living colour.

Now would be a good time, perhaps, at last to thank the donors of all these things. This courtesy had had to be shelved in late 1939. There were other preoccupations. But it should have been observed before now.

Six

FUNNY THING HAPPENED

ANY SHORT WORD in italics still jumps out at me from any printed page. Probably just an emphasis, a book title, a foreign borrowing. But it could be *Punch*: if so, claiming eager attention. Even at the cost of finding its context disparaging. On the whole, writers writing about the paper rather than for it – though they may, like the once rejected Charles Dickens, have tried – favour the disfavourable view. They fail to draw blood as they once did, but raise a painful bruise even now.

The *Punch* article is a special trick. Less so than it once was, in A.A. Milne's time when, as he said, a rejection had nowhere else to go but the waste-basket, since no one else used that sort of writing. Its style and range have broadened, though still less than successive editors have sometimes planned. Breezing in with new ideas and new people to broom out the old dust and the old contributors they have often found the last, anyway, presently required to reappear and settle again, performing more or less as before.

It looks easy. But that's the trick. It is sometimes tempting to explain the difficulties of working it. But no. Not for the reason that the magician guards his secrets, but because the association with the magazine is private and sensitive, and no fodder for light chat at drinks parties. One would as soon offer revelations about the matrimonial bedroom. There are decent reticences. And could you in any event explain how the rabbit gets into the hat? Let alone comes out of it, which even the weekly old-sweat contributor has never himself quite grasped.

It was different at first. I wanted to tell the world. Though surely the world knew already? I felt it must. On the strength of one short, anonymous piece, it should be admiring me in trains, at bus stops, nudging its friends and saying, 'You know who that is.'

Rejections had come from the Editor, with regrets but unsigned. Mr Childs's signed acceptance gave me a line of communication. He loomed large for the next year or two. There was often a time-lag between a submission and a rejection. What had happened? Had either or both been lost? The submission perhaps accepted, but the formality of acceptance overlooked?

I used to have talks on the phone with Mr Childs. He was a gentle creature. I felt I could brave him out. To have telephoned the Editor, or indeed anyone at 10 Bouverie Street, would have been unthinkable. I don't say I didn't sometimes think of it, but drew back from such presumption.

The week would drag by. Nothing. On the pretext of idly taking the air I would ambush the postman. 'Anything for number eight? Save you the trouble.'

He would flip through and hand me, if anything, my SAE, thick with the bad news. But I had already identified, could identify at twenty feet, the precise placing of the stamps, the typing style of my geometrically centred address, the manilla's creases, now flattened, in exactly equal thirds. All representing that resolute professionalism, echoed in the contents of clean, clean copy, which is never the mark of the true professional. He has confidence. No number of deletions and amendments and marginal scribbles will obscure the value of what he has to say. My hope was, and often continues to be, that having nothing to say worth saying, it may be carried by the pure beauty of the page.

Years later on the *Punch* staff, charged with sieving outside contributions, I saw the error of this. It was the impeccable typescript that sank on sight the hope – ever present with editors, though not widely credited in outside circles – that here at last was a bright new talent. Anything worth having would more probably be atrociously typed on both sides of the paper and a machine apparently salvaged from a junk-yard.

But my own obsession with the visually appetising grips me still. I have changed titles before now, hell though titles are, to make sure that the byline, typed beneath, leaves an even number of spaces at each end. I always type my byline. The professional dashes off his written surname in a corner.

It was Mr Childs who told me that Mr A.P. Herbert, anyway at that time, wrote by hand on pages torn from exercise books, sometimes in pencil, often with an added message to whom it might concern: 'And leave my damned punctuation alone.' It wouldn't have done for the new technology.

The old was bad enough. During my eighteen years in the office I stayed away from the printing works whenever possible. Its soulless hum and clatter offended against the recollected anguish of writing. Worse, there was the risk of hearing that week's article being read back to check the setting.

The dirge droned on. 'New para cap T the man comma turning quickly comma seemed upset colon cap I wondered why stop cap H he said comma, open quotes. . .'

I knew nothing as yet of these goings-on until I was asked to the paper's first annual party, an accolade indeed, where a girl told me she read every word I wrote. Extravagant but delightful. She turned out to be the girl the printer's reader read to.

The telephone talks with Mr Childs took a more or less standard form. Exchanged enquiries after each other's health. A mention of the weather. Then, 'I just wondered if you happened to have anything of mine there?' Sometimes I would pretend to have remembered something wrong that I had meant to change. But in time I dropped this. Though by word or tone he never hinted that he saw through me, I knew that he must. He would go away and look. There was the sound of machinery, but I already sensed that it was printing nothing of mine that week; as Mr Childs, returning, confirmed in his grey, uninflected voice.

I met him once. During my early days at Uxbridge I somehow found that he lived there. I was asked to tea. The room was small. Nothing of *Punch*. Choked with a lifetime's trinkets. His wife, having poured tea and handed biscuits, withdrew to leave the men together. Exchanges were sparse. But his name, unlike many others encountered since, and with greater claims to fame, has never faded.

These secrets, probably in drink, I once confided to Bernard Hollowood. (Fellow contributors can say such things to one another which could scarcely be told in other company.) This would have been some time before he edited the paper. He had a severe, thinking face. It could suddenly light up with a smile of great sweetness. When I told him of my oblique approaches through the FOC, this happened. I at first took the illuminating smile as one of amused disbelief. In a way it was. I had actually been in the habit of telephoning old Childs for news of the loved one? It was incredible. Bernard had done it too. Had also ambushed the postman. Had even – and surely no one could have done this but me – been so torn with passion that when his posted copy of the paper arrived, and he knew there was nothing in it of his because nothing had been accepted, threw it aside without even sliding off the wrapper.

Had he, I now wonder, not having asked at the time, had his first cheque photographed and framed? I had. It must still be somewhere in the house, though no longer hung where visitors couldn't miss it. They usually did, I think. I may occasionally have had to take it off the wall and show them. They would be speechless. Not with envy, admiration, amazement. Just nothing to say. What was there to say, for those beyond reach or under-standing of the spell? It was as if an accountant had invited me to gush over a model tax return. I don't hold it against them. Not now.

I have a few original drawings where people can't miss them, but still do. Ronald Searle, Norman Mansbridge, E.H. Shepard, Russell Brockbank, Robert Sherriffs, some Langdons and Emetts. They are mostly survivals of the days under the editorship of Kenneth Bird ('Fougasse') when an artist and writer were sent off in double harness to cover odd places and events – Brighton Pavilion (an odd place indeed), an orchestral rehearsal, archery competition, Palais de Danse, the Mr Universe Contest (my title, 'Came the Brawn'), the Farnborough Air Show, that sort of thing. They afforded me my only experience as a proper journalist; something to write about, as a change from my usual nothing.

Otherwise, the visitor sees little to betray my obsession, though two recent acquisitions sometimes take the eye. These are doorstops. For years they had been purely practical, two Mr Punches in white-washed cast-iron, handy to pick up by the curl of the cap. A couple of summers ago, Bill Hewison, then still the paper's art editor, and his wife Elsie, also an artist, came to lunch. They each picked up a doorstop and took them away, later to restore them in the old hunchback's full colour livery, impeccably and lovingly done, transformed from pressed-out commercial hulks into things of beauty.

There are, of course, the bound volumes in red and gold, accumulated half-yearly, getting on for a hundred of them now. Visitors can hardly miss them, but the only comment I remember was made recently by my American grandson. 'Did you write all those books?' I had to say no. Just that I had written something in all of them. But nice to be asked. Childish to want to be.

Top on the left is the volume of significance. July-December, 1938. I suppose it contains about three-quarters of a million words. Including seven hundred and three of mine. When even I was tired of reading them I must have counted them. Where the signature would have appeared, had I been 'R.M.', 'A.P.H.', 'E.M.D.' 'H.F.E.' or 'A.A.', the figure is inscribed in a pencil ring, on the page of my surviving unbound copy. Did I think, perhaps, that this was a magic number, to be noted as an editorial trigger to future acceptances? Such superstitions were not unknown among other aspirants of the time besides Hollowood, as I discovered during later speakings of minds. They shared my quandary over single or double quotation marks as factors in acceptance or rejection. A 'z' as opposed to an 's' in a verb-ending might well tip the scale. We worried about margins, line spacing, paper quality. What of the covering letter? To send one could smack of ingratiation. Not to, of calm assumption.

There were theories about the ideal day for a contribution to hit the editorial desk, though we probably didn't then know who sat at it, let alone that it was E.V. Knox who weekly signed himself with the Greeks' lamenting cry of 'Evoe'. But someone, up there, in remote and awful judgement, might have benevolent lapses: on a Monday, perhaps, fresh from his day of rest. Or a Thursday might be better, when the incoming tides of laughter had broken over him and receded, leaving him at leisure to recognize something special.

I loved every one of my seven hundred and three words. Also the two in the title. 'Willow Pattern' wasn't bad for an early dip in that maddening bran-tub. The piece was hung on Hutton's 364 against the Australians at the Oval the week before, and pictured the confusion in the Wisden office as they feverishly up-dated the records. So it was not only about cricket, very English – *Punch*, after all was very English – but about immediate and topical cricket. I see now that it was bound to get in. Also that if Hutton had made no runs, or even a mere hundred, it would never have been written, and I might never have got in at all. I didn't get in again for thirty-six weeks. I don't know how often I tried, probably not too often, but persistently enough for editor's regrets to give way to editor's letters, though Evoe hardly spread himself on these. One which I can quote from memory without difficulty, read in full, 'Dear Sir, I think chickens may be said to have been done.'

It shows the sort of areas I could have been plunging about in without Hutton's guiding influence. I met him long afterwards at a Savage Club guest night, and confided this bond between us. It would have been agreeable if those Yorkshire-proud Biggins could have seen us hobnobbing.

As befitted a knight, which he was by then, he received the information courteously, though without undue excitement. Mention of 1938 and the Oval could only have meant a record 364 to him. It had another but equally enduring significance for me.

I never got to know E.V. Knox well. Perhaps few did, beyond those in his immediate circle and, to a degree, those who worked with him in the office, which I never did. He had been gone five years by the time I joined the staff in 1952, but would sometimes return for a Wednesday lunch at the Table, and still contributed intermittently. R.G.G. Price, in his *A History of Punch* (Collins, 1952), the author modestly insisting on the title's indefinite article, paints a wonderfully observed portrait: the dry, donnish figure betraying nothing of the fun battened down inside, nor of the 'warm, shy heart'. His letters of rejection were terse only because of his feeling that men of words, dealing together, needed only the minimum of vocabulary. More would be as much meaningless claptrap as the commercial 'Assuring you of our best attention at all times'. Recipients would understand, reading between the lines. Between the words, almost. It was some time before I learnt that if words, however few, accompanied a returned article ('Dear Sir, I think the plot's not bad, Yours very truly') they disguised a hint to amend and re-submit. The code took a little breaking.

He wrote to me only twice at any length, much longer the first time, with a two-page volcanic tirade against wartime censorship of the paper's contents. It was not a matter I had in any way raised, but it must have been obsessing him. Perhaps he discharged his rage on all correspondents that particular day.

Between this letter and the second I had called on him by appointment. It was ridiculous for a valued contributor not to have met his editor. By then at the Air Ministry, I had made earlier pilgrimages to 10 Bouverie Street, but on inspection visits only: to contemplate the sacred exterior where, over the door, a larger than life Mr Punch posed on a stone balcony, daring me to enter.

Even entered by arrangement the building had an awesome air. I expect that was my imagination. It was graceful inside, and had the feel of a small manor house plonked incongruously down in the middle of London. The 'Sergeant', a stocky figure in some sort of anonymous uniform and emanating no mirth, led me up the curving staircase – gilded finials to its balusters – under portraits in oils, probably of Mark Lemon and other early incumbents – to the hush of the editorial corridors. Somewhere behind those closed doors next week's laughter was being processed with proper gravity.

Evoe's door opened on to smoke. Some of this was from the grate, where the modest fire fumed damply; the rest from his cigarettes, whose smouldering butts, according to Price, he pitched about at random until the management, after a few waste-baskets had gone up in flames, persuaded him to accept a metal bin.

He sat at a very small desk, which was littered and spilling with paper. This was to continue in use through the editorship of his successor, Kenneth Bird. Then Malcolm Muggeridge, succeeding in his turn, gave it one look and threw it out in favour of an opulently huge replacement, also demanding other refurbishings: some painting, a change of curtains, an improved carpet. 'Ask for everything the day you move in,' he stated as a tried principle, 'because you'll never get anything afterwards.' Editing should be seen to be done. It was typical of him that when art editor Russell Brockbank was one day expecting a caller likely to put some non-*Punch* work his way, perhaps in advertising, Malcolm said, Brockbank's own accommodation being on the lean side, 'But see him in *my* room, dear boy. Much better. I'll clear out until you've landed the fish.'

At least I was glad about Evoe's cigarettes, matching my own addiction. During a later interview with the non-smoking Kenneth, no ashtrays provided, he snatched to safety, in the nick of time, a small valuable picture awaiting hanging. It was framed with raised edges, and my cigarette poised over it for stubbing. I joined the staff as a result of that meeting, but things could easily have gone the other way.

The encounter with Evoe had no drama of this kind. Of any kind. We had nothing really to say to each other, I don't think he was quite sure who I was or what I wanted. As to the last, I wasn't too sure myself. Perhaps just to get past the building's defences – like a girl once kissed, and even left at that, it would never again be entirely unapproachable.

We may have touched on the progress of the war, its end then in sight. I seem to remember his account of what his army son, somewhere overseas, was contributing to final victory, and I had nothing much to come back with, in terms of my derring-do as personal assistant to the Provost Marshal.

There were long silences, once broken by the Sergeant to add a small coal to the small fire, a welcome diversion. My impression, possibly false, is that *Punch* was not mentioned. I felt embarrassed, but only realised afterwards that so did he, lacking any facile, perhaps by him despised, machinery to put me at ease. I recalled, feeling no easier, that it was to this austere personage I had sent articles on chickens and God knows what other topics that might 'be said to have been done'.

I had been glad to get into the building, but was just as glad to get out of it.

In some way, nevertheless, I must have drawn encouragement. The second of his longer letters dealt with an apparent request to 'sign' my contributions after some four or five years' anonymity.

'Dear Boothroyd,' he began (at least an improvement on 'Dear Sir'), 'You wrote to me some time ago asking that your initials should be used under your articles. There is no reason why you should not have this distinction (if it is one).

'So many were permitted by my predecessor that it is difficult to take a line about this. It used to be a sort of favour conferred after long service. Now it is principally a matter of confusion to readers. . .'

He went on to list some of the initials that were confusing readers already, several with 'B's in. A nom de plume had as many disadvantages as advantages. If I wished to sign, I must be 'ingenious and original about it.' He didn't think B.B. would do. Mine very truly.

He had scribbled at the bottom, 'I don't think there's any J.B.B.,' perhaps feeling he had not otherwise been of much help.

This I deciphered as permission to put J.B.B. under my articles. (The J is for John.) It meant much to me, if nothing to anybody else, and I thereafter took a superior view of other contributors still anonymous, their blunt-ended pieces just stopping in the air. Who were these people?

The initials had their drawbacks. For a long time any book of mine had to have 'J.B.B. of *Punch*' under the author's name, suggesting that the paper was better known than I was, and carrying me into authorship on its back. Nothing could have been truer, but still. And BBC announcers, when I began broadcasting, always felt it necessary to introduce me as 'Mr J.B. Boothroyd'. Initials were no indication of gender. Listeners must have the ground prepared. But it could take the light-heartedness out of 'light-hearted' talks, which were often going out live in those days and running to a now inconceivable fifteen minutes, most of which I spent shaking off the portentous effect of the introduction.

On the other hand, the initials were my only toehold on the rocky climb to any sort of recognition. When Malcolm arrived, fresh from the *Daily Telegraph* and the thumping by-lines of Fleet Street, he lost no time in according full names to all contributors. I still kept mine at J.B. Boothroyd. Had I made it Basil, readers could be asking who I was, and what had happened to poor old J.B.B., probably swept out by the new Muggeridge broom?

In the end it was through radio that I made public the Basil, always for some reason a private embarrassment. Several long-running programmes, and chiefly four or five years fronting

something called 'Monday Night at Home', emphasised the
stuffiness of being introduced as a Mister. And Bernard
Hollowood, moving into the editorship, said that if I was Basil on
the air, why not on the page? So this happened. And the management said, why not a plug on the air, as Basil Boothroyd of *Punch*?
So that happened too, and is the main reason why chairmen at
dinners introduce me as the Editor, more lately the ex-Editor; and
usually, with lively chairman's wit, get in a reference to Basil
Fawlty or Basil Brush, or both. I join in the delighted laughter.

Bernard himself, before Malcolm brought in the full names,
had signed himself 'Hod'. His initials were A.B.H. They would
have come too confusingly near those of a fellow contributor,
signing A.P.H. Alan Herbert himself, though no enemy of ac-
claim, was content with 'A.P.H.' to the end. So was Evoe with
'Evoe'.

Evoe's shyness took several forms, among them an uneasiness
at praise. On one of his last appearances for lunch, I ventured –
by then a Table member myself and feeling on more even terms –
a commending word on his piece that week. I think it was about
dustbins, or something else that might be said to have been done,
though not as Evoe would have done it, with what R.G.G. Price
calls 'a kind of mad poetry'. He heard me out gravely as we all
stood on the editorial landing waiting to go down to eat. Lost for a
response, he was saved by the appearance of a typist or secretary,
bound for one of the offices with a sheaf of papers. He drew me
into a doorway and said, 'Why do they get all the best-looking
girls in the advertising department?'

As at our first meeting, the conversation then floundered.

But, with other unlikely (for different reasons) admissions, he
let me into the pages, a matter for enduring gratitude. I wrote to
him when he retired, saying this. His reply, for once in handwriting, was warm but unexpectedly full of doubts about his decisions. 'How could I know whether I was right or wrong?'

Now looking back, unwisely, at some of his decisions in my
favour I think he was wrong quite often. At the time I thought it
was the rejections that had deceived his judgement.

Looking back is a mistake. Did you write that rubbish? Six
months ago? Ten years? Laboured, unfunny, missing all sorts of
points, it beats you how it ever got into typewriting, still less into
type.

Your this week's piece, on the other hand, is a triumph. Flow-
ing, compact, tailored. That will wear off. Give it six months and
it will wrinkle and fade. The triumphant element, in any case, lies
mainly in having once more worked the trick: once more, despite

the assailing doubts and fears: and the conviction that this time, as so often dreaded in months and years gone by, you really would have to give up, call the office, and tell them to give the page to someone else. The fact that you have never done that, though this week you were nearer than ever before, does nothing to comfort you. And it won't do anything next week, either.

For the born writer all may be different. I think of Anthony Powell, whose twelve astonishing 'Music of Time' novels were followed without pause by four volumes of autobiography. Malcolm, streaming out in all directions, sacred and secular. Words their natural element. Of my younger contemporaries, Benny Green, who falls out of every paper you open, and is hard to miss if you turn to the World Service in the sleepless small hours, or roam the shelves of the public library for something on jazz or cricket, Wodehouse or Fred Astaire. Benny says he reckons to send a thousand words out of the house every day, and that doesn't count those he's piling up inside for hard covers. Sheridan Morley, for a long time *Punch*'s theatre critic, hugely carefree and genial, could keep four other weekly columns juggled, in the intervals of averaging a book a year, attending first nights in London, Chichester, New York, occasionally visiting China but returning in time for the next stint on radio or TV. Miles Kington, appearing to live permanently at the stroll, is writing a column a week for *Punch*, five a week for *The Times*, and gigging about the country playing bass fiddle with 'Instant Sunshine' – and without noticeable interruption of these pursuits will stroll off to Peru to make a television programme about its railways.

It would all upset me less – puzzle, perhaps, is more the word – if the work showed any sign of the pressures. It doesn't. Their words are bursting to get out. No desperate dredging and quarrying. From Bill Davis's editorial room the sound of his typewriter had the regularity of machine-gun fire. To avoid delays, he had his sheets of paper gummed together, bottom edge to top. No hold-ups in the production line. It was sometimes a bore if the *Daily Mail* rang up for an urgent article when he was in the middle of a *Punch* piece, but it could be fitted in, even if it meant an hour with other work suspended.

Hearing that busy rattle, when I was in the next room trying to construct a ten-line 'Charivaria' paragraph, it didn't do to recall that Bill, born in Germany, had come here at the age of sixteen with no English (having, as he once disclosed, sold his Hitler Youth uniform as a souvenir to the first American soldier he saw). He had not only learnt English but, with perhaps pardonable limitations, English humour. Once, on an office outing to Boulogne, one of those excursions still practised at *Punch*, echoing the old times when the staff already liked each other enough to be together outside the office as well as in it, we received a civic reception. The Mayor of the town read a speech of welcome, referring to the brave, dark days when his countrymen and ours had 'stood together against the common foe'. Bill, as Editor and immediate recipient of the tribute, was the first to smile.

David Langdon's comment, when Davis's origins first became known, was, 'We have ways of making you laugh.' Alan Coren, broody – as who is not? – over a rejected contribution in the days when he was already in the office but not yet Davis's deputy, flung the thing back on his desk, and philosophised, 'Well, you can't expect a sense of humour from a man who spent his formative years selling rats in Hamburg cellars.' Both remarks were unfair. Funny, though. It's hard to be fair and funny. Bill himself would probably have laughed. But gone grave again, on the need to knock off a couple of articles before lunch.

I once asked Margaret Morley about her husband's blinding proliferacy. She said, 'Yes, but you see he never re-writes anything.' My thoughts readily flew to my work-room floor, strewn with false starts: and false continuations, all those heaves on to the top of page 2, each a triumph in its own right until it runs into the long grass and stalls halfway down.

How did I get into this business?

Still, there is a perverse satisfaction in having banged out millions of words on anything from the history of the tram to Abraham Lincoln without betraying that I looked up the whole lot in books, thus fooling most of the people most of the time – to the point, indeed, where some of the people whose specialist territory is invaded write to debate with me as an equal on, say, Mozart's relations with the Esterhazys, or the quickest way up the Eiger. (I'm not sure that Mozart actually had any relations with the Esterhazys, now I come to think. I should have to look it up.) This is flattering but a nuisance. It was last week I wrote about Mozart or mountain-climbing, and knew all about it then. It has served its purpose and gone. This week I'm on the disappearance of the European ibex. I do sometimes wish I knew something about something. The thoroughly steeped one-subject man is to be envied, with his sure grip, and free-surging output, on wine, gardens, baby care, home maintenance, foreign travel or the motor car; envied not only because he always has something to say, so needn't worry how he says it – if you can hook them with the What they don't care about the How – but always knows what he's going to write about, namely foreign travel, home maintenance, baby care, gardens or wine. Or the motor car. Since many of these come round regularly, notably new gardens and new babies, with new crops of consumers available to receive all the old information, he treads the easy familiar road.

Specialisation is the thing. This was pinpointed for me one day by John Hillaby, natural historian and famed walker. He was just back from some conference where one of the speakers, he reported, was 'an expert on a particular flea that lives up the arse of a rare tropical finch'.

For the humorist – defined in the OED as 'a facetious person', and it would be nice, but difficult, to come up with something better – all human life is there. Instead of making things easier, which might be supposed, this has the contrary effect. What to pick? How to know whether a promising topic, such as an unusual wealth of earthquakes (is God trying to tell us something?), or an experience nearer home with a bees' nest in the roof, can be relied on not to lose its steam by the second paragraph?

Hammer on is the only way. Are you saying anything worth saying? Dangerous to ponder that. Is it funny? You don't know. Facetious? Very likely. Would you prefer to be a writer of political leaders, assembling the hard facts on the world crisis of the week, and beginning your last paragraph, 'One thing is certain. . .'?

Not really. But I do envy the all-purpose man. Or woman.

One of those go-ahead press ladies once called to interview me on, as she had said in a preliminary letter, my 'creative concept' as a humorous writer. It seemed polite, before she pushed the recorder button, to ask something about her own areas of the printed word. These proved discouragingly various. Fashion, cookery, dogs, an advice column. It was quite a list. 'Of course,' she ended, 'I do humour, too.'

Just doing humour is enough for me. At times too much.

Seven

PUNCH DRUNK

IT'S HARD TO fix the year, but it would be soon after the war, 1946 or 1947. Waiting at London Bridge for that notorious No. 13 bus that never comes until it comes in a convoy of five, I saw a man with an attaché-case initialled H.F.E. I would still be on my way, in those days, to Lloyds Bank editorial department, by then hived off from the dignitaries of head office into a small top room in the Borough High Street. I had been contributing for some years, but apart from the solitary meeting with E.V. Knox I knew nobody else at *Punch* – knew, that is, in the sense of having met any of them.

This was a great opportunity.

'You must be H.F. Ellis.'

'Good heavens,' he said. 'I wish I were.'

Like the real H.F.E., of the familiar initials, he was nice.

That he knew what I was talking about, and even whom, was no surprise to me. It should have been. The odds were heavy against picking on a reader at all, let alone a fellow-admirer of the real Humphry Ellis. But I still cherished the idea that to write for *Punch* was to address the world, and its regulars were household names, anyway household initials or pseudonyms. On Wednesdays, publication day, the nation would storm the bookstalls. What were they all saying this week – A.P.H., H.F.E., R.M., V.G., H.K., 'Eric', 'Evoe', 'Hod'?

There had already been passing disillusionments on this, as when some 'contact' for a feature article would say, with the handshake, 'So you're from *The Punch?*', wondering, it often seemed, why his organisation, whatever it was, should be getting the attention of a boxing paper. I wrote this off to ignorance. Rightly. At least most people (all, to my thinking) knew about *Punch*. Not one in a thousand knew what or who was in it.

Richard Mallett was the first I met. His crazy pieces over 'R.M.' had a special appeal. Their darting, surrealist flights were something I would have dearly loved to do, but knew I never could. They were only a part of his work. He was the paper's film critic, his notices models of exact assessment, particularly with the run-of-the-mill product. Anyone can praise the good and damn the bad, but to be fair to the mixed is hard work. Now that television smothers us with films, all highly spoken of in the programme note come-ons, it is a wonderful time-saver to turn up Richard in a *Punch* volume of the time and learn whether the offerings are riches or rubbish. (Though the out-and-out rubbish he was apt not to review at all. Too easy. Sitting ducks.)

I persuaded him out to a pub lunch, perhaps only pub drinks, I forget. This was on the strength of some slight correspondence. He was in the office, and would have perhaps written to say that some title I had used had been pre-empted by a hierarchical superior: or with a gentle intimation of error. ('I think you need "dousing" to suggest extinguishing. Isn't "dowsing" water-divining?") Unlike other publications, which were ruthlessly unfeeling, this one never cut or changed without reference to the writer.

It was to be an ordeal to meet him. What should I say? He would dazzle me with mad fireworks. I sought support from my own editor, Tom Gilbert, of that great organ of banking opinion, *The Dark Horse*, and took him along too. He was better read, would know the books that Mallett parodied, the parody being one of Richard's brilliant forms. Besides, an editor in tow gave me status. Besides, again, I should be showing the grand circles in which I was now beginning to move. No bad thing. On the whole a liberal boss, Gilbert had sometimes got a little tetchy when I forgot to attend a Chief General Manager's retirement rites but was scrupulous with advance warnings of required time off for a *Punch* stint on ice-hockey or the College of Heralds.

The problem of what to say proved not to be mine but Mallett's. As I learnt in years to come, he never said much. Words and their arrangement called for ponderous deliberation, at the typewriter and alone. What flashed on the page, the lunatic conceptions and images seeming to spout spontaneously, he had assembled in slow agony, like marquetry work or a tessellated pavement. I have made some play here and there with my own difficulties. Compared with Richard I was an Anthony Powell. To form sentences for mere speech, therefore, was not what words were for – or about, to use a present idiom which would have had Mallett's eyes bulging with an enraged exophthalmic glare. Were they to be so used, they needed to be selected with care before delivery.

It was all a surprise to my editor and myself. I don't know

whether he had ever read any Mallett, but in any case I would have prepared him for a glittering experience.

Richard affected subfusc suits, whose trouser waistbands came so high up the chest that you wondered where he found short enough braces. The hang of the jacket was always impaired by newspapers and notebooks sticking out of the pockets. In cold weather, when a greatcoat, similarly burdened, was superimposed, there was no chair he could get into without a degree of disrobing. He walked slowly, warily, slightly leaning towards his objective, likely either to be the *Punch* office or his flat across Fleet Street in Fetter Lane, a three-minute walk only, even for him. One wondered how he got to the cinema several times a week, before subjecting himself to what he called 'the tyranny of the weekly article'. His progress up the office stairs was a thing to see. On the theory that the ascent would be eased by throwing his trunk forward and adjusting the centre of gravity, he moved upwards like a gorilla, knuckles trailing.

All this, on the day of the meeting, still remained to be known. He sipped his small, neat Irish whiskey. We sat behind our beers, awaiting some manifestation of comic genius. Nothing. On the contrary, it was Richard who had the quiet air of expectancy. Would some topic be originated? Somebody say something worth a note in any of his more accessible notebooks?

Long afterwards, at later meetings, even if it was only a matter of looking into his room at Bouverie Street, I formed the habit of preparing two or three things to talk about. Phrases that had pleased me, titbits of personal predicament and adventure that might amuse. He was readily amused, given to tears of laughter if you worked the thing right; these he would mop with the handkerchief which, when rarely preparing himself to venture on the spoken word, he would twiddle endlessly between his hands, as if about to produce a sudden design, a rabbit, a napkin in the shape of a sunflower. But it went back into his pocket with no achievement of this kind. He knew by heart inscriptions on monuments. The long one on Cleopatra's Needle, a reverberant account of its adventures, was a favourite. And he was much taken by that on the plinth of a general's statue in Trafalgar Square (is it Napier?) 'Erected by public subscription, the most numerous contributors being Private Solders.'

He had been in the army only a month or two at the beginning of the war, but long enough, before being invalided out, to enjoy the subtleties of that.

The invaliding out had been because of epilepsy, the *petit mal*. Again, of course, I knew nothing of this until later, when I found people in the office, or at lunch, were always watchful for an onset. They knew what to do about it. This didn't amount to much, beyond trying to see that he didn't hurt himself when falling: though Richard Price – a great friendship was struck up between the two – discovered that the other Richard, well in character, had done nothing for years about up-dating his drugs, and some improvement was made.

It was a bitter affliction. In full health I think Mallett would still have found writing difficult and slow. With this thing hanging over him all the time it must have been hell to get a word on paper at all. But nothing he wrote ever suggested anything but a care-free bubbling.

Living alone, mostly being alone, not a gregarious spirit, he was naturally bound to suffer what he called 'one of my little blackouts' when no help was near. He would sometimes appear in the office with a facial bruise, but no comment, either from him or the rest of us. Except that he came in one day, bruised but jubilant, having been picked up as a drunk and put in a police cell for the night. It would not have been like him to carry any explanatory document, altogether too self-regarding. The incident brightened his life for some time. His handkerchief twirled dizzily as he relayed the news to all rooms on the editorial floor.

He had one of his little blackouts towards the end of the already rather disappointing session in the pub that day. That was the effect, I believe, for him. A blank. Consciousness returning. A quite short period of taking his bearings. Tired afterwards. Then apologetic, as if for a lapse of good manners.

For the onlooker, as he knew, the attacks were alarming, especially if not primed for anything of the kind. Gilbert and I were very alarmed, and returned to the office not saying much.

Twenty-five years later, with another two thousand films discussed, and many intermittent wrestlings with prose and verse, as intricately constructed as a watch, he had an attack crossing the Haymarket and was run over and killed.

Preoccupied as ever with words, his last verses in the paper had discerned people in headlines that the sub-editors hadn't put there:

> Man Held (a Swedish novelist, of course),
> Dawn Swoop, once more of all her mink bereft,
> Gem Grab, that girl impatient for divorce,
> Those two Dutch crooks, Van Holdup and Van Theft. . .

Richard Price (whom I should have been calling R.G.G.P. by

now) wrote his obit, avoiding all the usual clichés for the other Richard's sake. Though 'much loved' must have put itself forward.

If the man at London Bridge had been the other Humphry Ellis, he would have been, as well as a classical scholar modestly disguised, a writer of the classic *Punch* piece in the 'Evoe' tradition, an ex-Rugby winger and later an acclaimed authority on the game and the paper's Literary Editor during my early struggles. For some reason or other he was doing theatre criticism when my own first article appeared, and since the pages faced each other the initials H.F.E. were burned into me deeper than the rest.

Parts of his notice also registered powerfully. He felt that *The Fleet's Lit Up* hadn't been too witty.

Let's have a joke –
'My father was eaten by cannibals.'
'That's tough.'
'No, he was tender.'
We simply roared. Some people on my right repeated it to Auntie, but they were so overcome with laughing themselves that they could hardly speak, so she missed it after all.

It is a deprivation for the *Punch* gang that they can't always roar with the rest. This gets them a name for having no sense of humour, and being stand-offish.

Ellis now lives in a Somerset village, no longer writing for *Punch*, but still, enviably, for *The New Yorker*. We exchange funny bits by correspondence. He distils the occasional items from the *Somerset County Gazette* ('a paper that you perhaps do not always see'). I last sent him an unusual letter I had received from Taunton, asking if he could recommend a suitable response, since he could easily go and look at the address from the outside and form some conclusions about my correspondent.

The letter said, in full:

Dear Mr Boothroyd,
I am writing to tell you what a marvellous man I think you are. I wish you the very best of health, luck and happiness.
                    Yours faithfully,
                            Mark Linegar

He responded without delay: ('Anything to rid myself of your revolting enclosure.') He said he 'was not often in Bloomfield Close', which was the address given: but the telephone book

listed an E. Linegar at No.7, and he imagined my admirer to be a
son of the house.

'As to the form of your reply, I think he would appreciate a
poem, e.g.:

> *I've been searching for years*
> *For a good rhyme for vinegar*
> *And at last it appears*
> *Thanks to you, Mr Linegar.'*

Richard Mallett had often complained that there was no rhyme
for silver, and was apt to worry about it. But vinegar (or Linegar)
is no pushover either.

It was Ellis's idea that I should join the editorial staff. I had been
a banker for twenty-five years, and writing for *Punch* for half of
them. It was almost too late. I was forty-two. I was never strong
on initiative, and without his it would never have crossed my
mind to make the leap. I owe him much, even allowing that had I
stayed in the bank I should now have been long retired and
sumptuously pensioned. But probably dead.

He sold me to Kenneth Bird, by then moved into E.V. Knox's
chair, to edit the 'Charivaria' page, for half a century the opening
collection of bite-size bits and bobs, comments on curious press
items, but mainly short topical paragraphs with smart pay-offs,
at first illustrated by Douglas England, later by Kenneth himself,
indeed for long after he had abandoned the editorship. The
whole shoot had to be ready by mid-week for the artist to see and
decide what he wanted to draw. This made topicality an interesting problem. Readers weren't going to read until a week after
that. Would some news item hold that long? Would an introduc-
tory reminder be necessary, making tedious the early sentences
and lengthening the paragraph cumbrously? It was a matter of
long or short focus. Something in the daily papers that took my
own fancy as a flint to strike a spark off might not have been read
by anyone else, in which event helpful groundwork had to be
laid. Matters of general knowledge and concern could be
plunged straight into: it could be assumed that everyone knew
about Eisenhower's landslide into the White House, even the
discovery, off Madagascar, of the thought-to-be-extinct coela-
canth, or our atom tests in the Monte Bello islands (1952 was the
year I moved into the office). A couple of sentences would do,
one of them preferably funny. But it took more to build up to a
punch-line on something I'd spotted, God knows how, in a sheet
of amendments to the *Post Office Guide* ('After "daggers" insert

"fresh and dried fruit"), which I see I headed, not too imagin-
atively, 'First Aid Hint'.

Never fond of newspapers, I grew to hate them, gutting a
dozen a day as I panned for a grain or two of gold.

Humphry saw all the paragraphs, granting or withholding
approval. He could see how to sharpen a clumsy failure into a
success, or clarify an obscurity by substituting just the word to
catch the light. He schooled, encouraged, comforted, praised:
not only over those maddening paragraphs but my ordinary
articles, which somehow got written as well, at home and usually
late into the night. My room at the office was too full of smoke,
curses and screwed-up re-writes of abortive small jokes to favour
any longer constructions there.

Ellis believed in editing, getting the best out of writers, which
Evoe, on the whole had not. Evoe, perhaps, was the last of the
school which gave the impression, as someone has remarked,
that the paper 'seemed to be produced by a few gentlemen in
their spare time'. Humphry attacked the business of being funny
with a proper seriousness. Unlike Evoe – and indeed Kenneth,
who, as an artist, was more inclined to edit the artists than the
paper as a whole – he welcomed interviews, and would invite
promising new contributors, perhaps only on the strength of a
couple of articles, to call on him and talk. After one such visit he
came into me in a state of shock, having just seen the back of a
promising undergraduate, whom he had asked, after the pre-
liminaries, if he would care to consider contributing regularly.
'I'm not really all that interested,' had been the astounding, the
heretical response. Humphry could barely bring himself to
repeat it. "'Not that interested.'" His distinguished, rather
Holmesian profile, was solemn against my window. 'Not
interested?'

Punch was his life. Not in the self-centred sense that it was
mine. The paper was the thing. After Oxford (Magdalen; '1st cl.
Hon. Mods.', said *Who's Who*, '1st cl. Lit. Hum.'), only a year as
an assistant master at Marlborough had intervened before he first
wrote for it, and he was on the staff two years later in 1933. He
was twenty-six. He missed by a year the editorship of Owen
Seaman (Shrewsbury, Clare College, Cambridge), so his immediate influence was Seaman's successor, E.V. Knox (Rugby,
Corpus Christi), whose family was crowded with bishops.

I had a right to my awe, not only for him (who will be surprised, if he reads this, to learn of it), but back and forth over all
those academic people, from those I never knew to those I
worked with later and some I work with still. The more or less

straight hop from university to *Punch* had long seemed the recognised thing. Hopping from a bank was freakish. I felt the
freakishness. It was all in my own mind. If it was ever in anyone
else's it never got out. I'm sure it wasn't. Not in Peter Dickinson's
(Eton and King's), not in Eric Keown's (Cambridge, I think,
whose signature was 'Eric' and nature a model of sweetness), nor
in Bernard Hollowood's – though Bernard, I fancy, born in
Burslem, would have thought Oxford and Cambridge a touch
toffee-nosed and highfalutin. Still, London University, M.Sc.
(Econ). Educated, above my own level of failed attempts at Part 1
of the Institute of Bankers examinations. Similarly with Richard
Price (Dulwich, and Jesus, Oxford).

Living nearby, he is my quickest and cheapest source, at the lift
of a receiver, for whatever bit of information I want to pass off as
my own this week; the function of the Master of the Rolls,
perhaps; a brief plot breakdown of *Edwin Drood* or last year's
Booker prize; the purpose of the Crusades; or which English
Queen died of dropsy. His *Punch* field is the wild fantastic, which
may partly have accounted for his bond with Richard Mallett.

Gravely, into a faltering conversation, he enjoys dropping an
unexpected pebble ('I've been wondering about a commercial use
for sleet') and standing back to observe the spreading rings: or
will volunteer a scrap of family reminiscence – how his uncle, in a
single morning, both saw a piano fall from a second-floor window and trod on Alfonso XIII of Spain. He is disinclined to add
detail. Take it or leave it.

At the *Punch* Table he is a listener rather than a talker, which
goes strongly against the general trend. But if the talk veers off
misguidedly on some error of fact he is likely to interrupt with a
dutiful correction. The footprint found by Crusoe was *not* Man
Friday's.

Mallett never said much either. Once when Lord Hailsham
was a guest, when guests were rare (he was writing for the paper
at the time), Richard suddenly took idiosyncratic exception to a
remark about Greek verse which he regarded as sweeping, and
flew into quite a passion, before subsiding as suddenly. His
comments were mostly quiet asides. 'Through their veils,' he
murmured, when someone rhetorically asked how women in
pubs could drink port-and-lemon. He spent much of the meal
manipulating a retractable metal tape-measure to capture distant
salts, peppers or sugars, and was not too pleased if they were
politely passed across just as he was within wavering reach of
success.

I was three years in the office before joining the Table for the

Wednesday lunch. I have misgivings about giving the word a capital T. Not that I don't think of it like that, even now. But it suggests that other people do. Most of them don't. Why should they? Those who know about it don't know what it is, or what goes on there, and are apt to refer to it as the Round Table, making some hazy connection with the Algonquin in New York and the table the *New Yorker* men once used to gather round. Possibly with Arthurian legend.

Alan Agnew, the paper's proprietor, wrote with the formal invitation. If I felt I could accept it 'there are no privileges and the only onerous committments are that you should present me with a signed photograph of suitable size to be framed and hung on the line in the Dining Room and also in due course to carve your initials on the ancient table.'

Small T. Despite that, and two of the same in the middle of 'committments', I felt I could accept – and framed and hung the letter in my own dining room, where it attracted the usual lack of attention.

The photograph had to wait. It had to be something special. Eventually I had it taken by a rather special photographer. It was very bad. Or perhaps very good. Subjects and their likenesses differ on that. For the last thirty years' lunches I have tried to avoid its eye.

But I couldn't wait to do the carving. When I did it, I overdid it, not to be outshone by those who had carved their initials before: Thackeray, Tenniel, du Maurier, Phil May, Charles Keene, John Leech, Bernard Partridge, A.A. Milne, Ernest Shepard, Alan Herbert, Illingworth, Mallett, Ellis, Knox, 'Fougasse'. No one seeing the table was going to overlook 'J.B.B.'. Implements not commonly being provided for the exercise, I brought a jack-knife from home and dug deep, though not as deep as my embarrassment when I stood back and looked at the vainglorious result. I might have invented the paper and been running it single-handed since 1841.

For weeks afterwards I would steal down periodically with a bottle of ink and try to dim the glare. The deal surface* drank thirstily, but with small effect. The shout of self-satisfaction persisted.

People may ask whose initials they are one day, but they won't miss them.

*Thackeray's verses celebrating the high old times at the dinners, as they then were, were called *The Mahogany Tree*. Never trust a writer with facts.

Milne complained that his own 'modest and monogrammatic "A.A.M."' was taken for Anthony Armstrong's (long a contributor, but for some reason never a table member). This was Milne's fault. His monogram was light and neat, but too ingenious. By crossing both halves of the M, making them into A's, he extinguished the M altogether, leaving an apparent A.A. In fact, this was only compounding a confusion between the two men's contributions on the printed page, so that if A.A. wrote about cheeses or golf-balls it was often A.A.M. who was showered with golf-balls or cheeses. However, some wartime verses of Milne's about running out of marmalade did attract a lot of marmalade, this time correctly addressed. Reader response of that kind seems to have waned in more recent years. I once got a bird-table, which arrived impenetrably wrapped, a mystery and later a surprise, but I think it was the result of a broadcast.

When George du Maurier was invited to carve his initials he gave much thought to their placing, finally picking a spot as near as possible to those of his revered fellow artist, John Leech – who had added, though initials alone are difficult enough, his personal symbol of a leech in a bottle. Prince Charles, a hundred years later, also went beyond the bare essential of a 'C', with a fair representation of the Prince of Wales's feathers.

I put mine as near as I could get to 'H.F.E.'.

The du Maurier incident comes from a book of his letters, edited by his granddaughter Daphne. A passage in her introduction runs,

We who are offered today a so-called wealth of literature from the bookstalls of stations and airports, pulpy pages known as digests or potted shorts, find it hard to understand the part played by *Punch* in the latter half of the nineteenth century.

It stood alone, the only weekly paper of its kind.

A gibe at the government from *Punch* in 1870, and worried members of Parliament would be discussing the fact in the lobbies the same day. A cool criticism of a picture or a book, and the luckless author hung his head in shame.

I only quote this, which may go over the top a little, but has a substance of old truth, because vestigial shreds of these grand notions still hung about the place in my early days. Especially about the table itself, where the Wednesday lunch, now almost entirely convivial (only partly because it is now on Fridays, when the paper has gone to press and the week's anxieties are eased) had as its main business the discussion and decision on next week's political cartoon. The country, or the world, would be told, in stern pronouncements, how to go on, or where it got off, in such matters as Aneurin Bevan's loss of the party whip, French leadership confusions, Khrushchev's denunciation of Stalin or the signing of the Turco-Iraqui pact; all of which, with much else in the wider field, seemed as remote to me then as it does now. Though I do recall doing a 'Charivaria' item, on politically con-fused France, warning tourists not to go there for fear of being asked to form a government.

I used to end the page with a verse, often as smart and informed as they come. One of these, I see, combined a seeming interest in world events of 1955 with a stubborn old fancy of mine – that the poet Burns, when stuck for a Scottish idiom, would invent one to suit, and none of us Sassenachs the wiser:

> There some wad be to ca' Berlin
> The pouther-keg and a' that,
> Or blame the doolful' plight we're in
> On Chiang Kai-shek and a' that;
> Waesucks! on dinsome joys to feast
> Wi' Bulge and Khrush and a' that;
> The weird is in the Middle East,
> Amman's Amman for a' that.

Thirty years on, it's discouraging to see how little I achieved with my bold assaults on the follies of the age. All survive and flourish, from oil-pollution and apartheid to stultification by TV and the same old nuclear arms race. Not to say the Middle East.

Putting the world to rights was easier at the typewriter than at the Table. My spoken word never added much to the debates.

One of the few members who said less was Leslie Illingworth, who would have to draw the picture, and became thoughtful about impending artistic problems. It was all very well for the rest to plump unanimously (the decision had to be unanimous) for a rebuke to John Foster Dulles, failing to recognise the latest Israel-Egypt crisis: its further decision to show this by making Dulles an ostrich, head buried in the desert sand, would pose some diffi-culty at the drawing-board.

Illingworth, as always, came through undaunted, where even a Tenniel or a Partridge would have been daunted. Though Tenniel, it's true, had been set a tough task by Carroll with the oysters in *Alice*, which the text required to be given legs and footwear. Still, they didn't have to look like anybody. Idler car-icaturists, doubting a captured likeness, run to initials on briefcases, or trouser-cuffs where worn. Leslie would never have descended to this, in any case tricky with ostriches.

With Dulles the ostrich he didn't quite bury the head. Just most of it. What remained was nevertheless unmistakeable as both bird and statesman.

He was a beautiful Welshman, beautiful in the beholder's eye, though not, it was said, in his own, having the lineaments of an immensely genial monkey, with eyebrows like hedges and a radiant prognathous grin. He shared with Eric Keown the gift of making everybody feel they were the one person in the world he wanted to see. Of his gifts as an artist he was simply unaware. On one cricket afternoon, as we changed into our mostly borrowed flannels in Ernest Shepard's house, it looked as if Leslie was never going to get changed at all. There were Shepard drawings round the walls. He couldn't be got past them. 'Just look at that, mister!' (His form of address always.) He might never have drawn a line.

His own work, faultless to other eyes, he quite often found disappointing. As an expression of private dissatisfaction he would leave off his signature. It was hard enough to find when it was there, demurely buried in the darkest corner.

He was a frequenter of El Vino, where he bought champagne for all. It was a commonplace that nobody could ever buy any for Leslie. We tried. The battles for the bill were regular and futile. In the end we gave up. All Fleet Street had given up long before. 'It's paid for. On my account, mister.' And his glass raised in something not quite a toast. An incantation. 'Have no sense of sin.'

Some people, aggressively open-handed in this way, are an embarrassment. With him there was nothing to do but laugh and put your money away.

The failure on my part to enliven the cartoon discussions soon didn't matter. Under the Muggeridge editorship the discussions themselves were wiped out. They had sometimes gone on for hours. Malcolm, partly from the impatience of a daily paper man schooled to racing the clock, partly from a broad iconoclastic streak which saw the whole procedure as an archaic ritual dance, decided to dispense with it. Not immediately. At first he would just arrive with his own idea for the subject, quite clear in his head, presented with his own brand of laughing persuasiveness always hard to resist. A few vigorous spirits might put up a fight, but in the end submitted. It cut down the Table time considerably, which was further reduced when he decided that by conferring with the artist before lunch, telling him his choice of subject and hearing how it was proposed to be drawn, he could take the editor's end of the table with the main business of the meeting already settled.

Not surprisingly, some older members were uneasy. This was Malcolm speaking, not, as in the past, *Punch*.

The voice was different, sharp, direct, gleefully malicious. Its owner had been doubtful about taking on the editorship, and may well have been swayed by the idea of playing with a wonderful new toy, a blowpipe and an armoury of wounding darts in the hands of a bright and mischievous child. He loosed them off with zest. It could only have been his idea, when Eden finally succeeded Churchill, to have him depicted as Graham Sutherland had just depicted Churchill in the famous farewell portrait: the bulk of the suit, the same slumped pose and fadeaway legs; but from the low collar and bow tie the new leader's head emerging, unconfident and rabbity.

Often what upset poor Alan Agnew, at the management's end of the table, was the bad taste of it all. Like other Agnews and other Bradburys (the paper at that time was still in the private ownership of Bradbury & Agnew, as it had been for eighty years, and of Bradbury & Evans for fifty before that), Alan had been brought up to the gentlemanly life, and believed in gentlemanly behaviour. Sometimes if I sat next to him at lunch he would talk matter-of-factly about the old gracious days when the family carriage and horses were entrained for Scotland and the shooting. And I would listen with understanding nods. Pretty well my own background, really, though I left that to be assumed.

Malcolm didn't believe in gentlemanliness, certainly not for *Punch*, which in his view should be a snook-cocking guttersnipe. That was how it had begun, before cheeking its way into social acceptability and then assuming a kind of spokesmanship for the well-off middle classes. It should return, he thought, to putting its fingers to its nose, ringing door bells and running away.

He laughed at his loudest and most desperate when the management took pained exception to his attacks on Khrushchev and Bulganin during their historic visit of 1956. Was this courteous? Were they not our country's honoured guests? Oh, dear. He wiped his eyes with joy. If the Russians were ever to visit our country in force, the Bradburys and the Agnews would be the first for the salt-mines. It was just his kind of joke.

He had a theory that the owners were puzzled by humour; more accurately, by its mystery as the commodity from which their incomes had so long been derived. This made them unhappy, Malcolm said. If it had come from something tangible, such as steel or property or airlines, they could have understood, felt more at ease with themselves. Money from jokes was a difficult concept for them. It seemed to work all right, but in some indefinable way was unsatisfactory. They woke up every morning worrying about it.

Thus would Malcolm run on at the editorial conferences, in the intervals of sparking off ideas like a Catherine wheel and taking laughing phone calls from the famous. Not yet a celebrity himself, his time as a TV sage still to come, he seemed to know everyone who was. This was something new. A man from the real world, with India and Moscow and Washington behind him, and an exotic Intelligence war, from what amounted to spying in Lourenço Marques to 'rescuing' Wodehouse (from the French, though indirectly the British) in Paris.

Those phone calls shook me. Names I combed from the newspapers as targets for one of my witty shafts were just names in the papers to me: Malcolm had dined with them last night. They were staying with him next weekend. They were genuine live people, telephoning. Ambassadors, press lords, social and literary lions. Hanging up, he would as a matter of politeness identify the distant subscriber before getting down again to business.

It was impressive. One morning, the celebrity flow more disruptive than usual, even Malcolm showed a touch of exasperation as the phone rang yet again.

'Jesus Christ,' he said, lifting the receiver.

'It can't be him,' said Bernard Hollowood.

Malcolm's vocabulary was highly-decorated at that time, and contained expressions 'not even in *Partridge*', as Price recorded in his *History*. After an early session at the print works with the new editor, seeing the pages to press, Humphry Ellis came back in astonishment and outrage, yet half wanting to laugh. 'It was beyond belief. Words like [he quoted the words, with something of my father's discomfort over that special constable's night cry] were flying round the place like bullets.' Adding reflectively, 'A thing unknown in Sir Owen Seaman's day.'

Malcolm enjoyed his own naughtiness. Deflating the Table became a favourite diversion. Though the meal had never been a gastronome's delight, indeed it remains part of the tradition to remark disparagingly on what is offered, he knew he was pushing things by declining to eat any of it and sending out for sandwiches. Alan Agnew, in controlled dignity at the other end, remained expressionless. Even the bad words passed him by, who had probably never himself uttered more than a 'damn'. I can't remember what we talked about over the brandy. Trivialities, probably, or what Malcolm, scornful of small talk, would regard as such. 'Well,' he once broke in cheerfully, looking at his watch and pushing back his chair – 'shall we fuck off?'

Only Ellis had anything to say, and that after a pause. 'If you have to put it like that.' Quietly very angry. Apart from Malcolm's laugh, which could redeem most situations, but not this, we dispersed in silence.

Father's contentment at my association with the Clergyman's Comic would have been seriously ruffled. He would have been happier to hear of later occasions when, though at long intervals, I would still sometimes see Malcolm at his home down in Robertsbridge, reclusive now but still laughing, though claiming eagerness for the release into the hereafter. He was apt to be organising sacred essay competitions for the Church of England Children's Society, seeking my services on the panel of judges. We talked under photographs of Malcolm and Mother Teresa, Malcolm and the Pope. Though the last, on second thoughts, my father would probably have preferred to be turned to the wall.

His editorship had long receded. Only four years or so of his life, but still from time to time the subject of laughingly disparaging references in speeches and broadcasts and the papers. A vale of tears. . .'the time when I once had the misfortune to edit a so-called humorous magazine. . .' Well, the joke about *Punch* not being funny was always the joke about *Punch*. Repeated in one form or another by Malcolm it aroused much fury in Bernard Hollowood, his successor: to the point, even, where he wrote asking for it to be dropped. Malcolm was knocking his friends and colleagues, who were still trying to run the thing.

The reply was predictable. 'But, my dear boy. . .' How could anyone suppose any but the kindliest and most charitable intentions in any references to the 'old mag'? Nothing was further from his thoughts than. . .

No doubt he believed it, but there was some strange worm eating away inside him. Long after his retirement I met by chance on Paddington station Anthony Powell, whom Malcolm had brought with him into the office as Literary Editor. They had been great friends. Somewhat obviously, my opening line was to ask if he saw anything of Malcolm these days. It didn't go at all well, Malcolm apparently having written a stinking review of one of Powell's later books. Again there had been correspondence. Again Malcolm had been amazed that any exception should have been taken by the author to what was only the friendliest, the most well-meaning and admiring. . .

But relations had been broken off all the same.

From the contributors' point of view, anyway those whose

work he favoured, he was a better editor than might be supposed. He had no end of ideas, but never insisted on them if the
writer failed to kindle. In my case, and perhaps not only mine,
the kindling was a matter of seeing that they could be done, and
how they could be done, rather than taking fire, or feeling particularly enthusiastic, about their subject. They would often be
attacks on Malcolm's personal and peculiar targets, delegated
with much laughter as usual. Sometimes, at the typewriter, you
wondered just how he had beguiled you into taking them on, but
you were somehow on your professional mettle to bring them
off.

These were not wholly admirable exercises. I am not proud of
mine, looking back. Gilbert Harding, then a notable public figure, ringing me up one day with caustic comments on a powerful
but ill-founded attack I'd made on him, called it 'venal'. And spelt
it for me. It was the sort of thing to be expected, he said, from
some hack on the *Daily Express*. But from *Punch*! His rage modu-
lated into grief. He was right. But Malcolm had laughed a lot,
which for once was not sufficient reward. I told him about Harding's call and he became compassionate, if only towards me, by
now in a state of remorse and trembling. 'You must never let
them upset you,' he comforted, an arm round my shoulder.

Years later, finding I had to meet Harding in a radio studio, I
felt deeply apprehensive, and still remorseful. It seemed better to
raise the affair before he did. At first he had difficulty in recalling
it. And then, 'Oh, that was a long time ago.' A kindly, vulnerable
soul, under the public hectoring.

From that occasion, though we met at other times, I treasure a
spontaneous epigram from him. It was one of those days, familiar to all broadcasters, where nothing in the studio went right.
The green light wouldn't come on. The producer's talk-back
wouldn't work. The producer himself, young, pale and nervous,
and not the man to handle any programme with Harding in it was
soon being referred to as 'that cream-faced loon' when Harding
thought the microphone was off, but of course it wasn't. Things
were bad all round, right up to the point where he took a draught
from the statutory studio water jug, which by bad luck hadn't
been renewed for a day or two.

He spat it out.

'This must be the water,' he said, 'that Reith put his teeth in on
the night of the Abdication speech.'

I drew in my horns a bit after he had helped me with my
spelling over the phone. Malcolm sensed that I was not happy,
though ignobly willing, to butt around at people whose only

offence was to have been in the news that week. The word 'venal' had stuck. So although my more natural line, of domestic predicament and the general small-change of living, came near to infringing his ban on material 'about Celia and the washing-up', and qualified for the stigma of 'old *Punch*' which he was so resolute in throwing out in favour of the new, I relapsed into it. And still somehow got printed with plotty little squibs about bees in the roof, motoring dramas, plumbers.

How this came about I don't know. It's possible that Malcolm, as somebody once said, had no power of rejection, or had come to see that to change the paper's character entirely would be less desirable, in terms of readership figures, than he had at first imagined. He had certainly learnt one difficult lesson, that it was necessary to admit work that he didn't himself think funny – indeed, raising laughs for their own sake, what we called in the trade 'absolute humour', was horrible to him – because he was assured by some of us that it was. Or perhaps I am thinking of his later period, when television increasingly wooed him away from the office. Though I should really reverse the direction of the wooing. He saw that the cathode-tube was the coming thing, and said once in so many words that he was determined to master it. This he did, becoming famous and hated. And so long as he kept one foot in the office, in fact long after he had removed both, the staff were often called upon to defend him against the rebounding disapproval of shopkeepers, window-cleaners or their own private circle. Television only had one channel, and everybody watched everything. Except Malcolm himself, who never owned a set and still does not, but got no end of fun out of decrying the medium that enriched him. I found him easy enough to defend, if only with the assurance that the TV persona was not the real one. Yet in part I suppose it was. Chiefly it concealed a generosity of spirit in personal contacts, and the spell, the kind of charm, in the sense of bewitchment, exerted at close quarters. Easy to hate the man you hadn't met, but five minutes' exposure would change all that.

When Richard Price had difficulty adapting to the new *Punch* it was Malcolm who suggested that he should write the history of the paper. And Price, in his last chapter, though not hesitating to be fearless about the faults of the régime, put his finger on a point easy to miss:

> The first thing that struck many people about Muggeridge was his approachability and his kindness. It became an absurd situation when infuriated traditionalists wanting to find a sym-

pathetic ear for complaints about the new Editor thought first
of 'Malcolm', who was quite ready to discuss himself in the
most detached way.

In the matter of my continuing to appear in the paper –
elsewhere, that is, than on the front page – any leaning towards
mere frivolity was well countered by the heavyweights he had
brought in his train, either actually into the office or as contributors to be regularly called on. Anthony Powell, Claud Cockburn,
John Betjeman, Lord Kinross (better know as Patrick Balfour, but
I liked the lord, myself). I don't mean that they were heavyweight
writers, but men who had knocked about the world, Betjeman
perhaps excepted, and could take an informed and sophisticated
view of it.

When Cockburn and Powell and Muggeridge consorted in the
editor's room a strange music came out of it. They all seemed to
make their upper-class noises from somewhere in their sinuses,
weaving up and down in tight nasal tones, often in simultaneous
or at least overlapping concert, though with the punctuating
bursts of laughter pitched in high unison. Hard though I had
worked on eliminating my Nottinghamshire, I knew that only
the best schools and universities could do this for people. Malcolm's own tones (so much detested by the millions of viewers
who viewed him all the same) may have been to some degree an
affectation, or the result of having talked much with people who
talked like that. Just my theory. I don't know. If his beginnings
had not been exactly humble, it seems unlikely that the voice had
begun as a natural top person's.

Christopher Hollis was another daunting importation. Eton
and Balliol. The voice was different, but of immense power and
harshness. Though no longer an MP, when he once took me to
hear a Commons debate he was rebuked by a white-tied usher
just for the wattage of his whisper.

They accepted me as one of them. In saying so, I sound as if
they were patronising, which is patronising of me. But I didn't
understand their jokes. They seemed to respond to remote trig-
gers. One of them would mention the name 'Nehru', or some
phrase like 'Continental Sunday', and the others would be helpless. They had led varied and colourful lives, compared with my
own. Had seen, and saw, the funny side of things I knew not of.

They all seemed to write quickly, proliferously, effortlessly.
Claud, particularly (who mysteriously inscribed one of his books
to me 'with the profound admiration of one good professional for
another'), would sit down and write anywhere. One day I went

to lunch leaving in the typewriter a page with only a couple of lines on it. Returning along the corridor I heard a burst of heavy typing and found him at my desk. Coming across a handy machine with paper already in it he had rattled off the start of some piece of his own, but on glancing at the page was now looking uneasy at its failure to run on from the lines I'd left there.

However, he'd been out to lunch too.

Malcolm asserted that Claud, an old friend, believed all physical ailments curable by whisky, claiming that once, as a guest of the Muggeridges, he had somehow dislodged a heavy handbasin from the wall which fell on his foot and broke it. He went to bed with a bottle of Scotch and was fully recovered in the morning.

Cockburn was also said to be adept at securing money from publishers on promise of work that either didn't get done or hung fire beyond even a publisher's liberal interpretation of contract dates. And that he once attended some party at Hamish Hamilton's with his young son in tow. The lad had recently been given, and was wearing, a western costume with guns. These, with a cry of, 'Stick 'em up!' he thrust into the publisher's back.

'Who are you?' said Hamilton, turning and looking down.

'I'm Claud Cockburn's boy.'

'I might have guessed.'

Again, it was probably a Malcolm story. If a story was to be told, even in print, his respect for truth was not absolute. In his account, or one of them, of the Wodehouse affair, he claimed to have advanced in Wodehouse's defence that German Intelligence, nurtured on the exploits of Bertie Wooster and fellow-Drones, had parachuted an agent into the Fen country wearing spats. 'This unaccustomed article of attire led to his speedy apprehension.'

The last time we met I asked him if this had in fact happened. He was laughingly evasive.

Anthony Powell was brought into the office as Literary Editor in Malcolm's train. I knew his pre-war novels, *Afternoon Men*, *What's Become of Waring, Venusberg, From a View to a Death, Agents and Patients*. They had left their mark, clearly. I quote without a reference: even remember, I believe, the opening sentence of *Afternoon Men*, though my copy has long been lent and lost: ' "How often do you have to take it?" said Atwater.' Some sort of medicine. Beginning books, beginning any writing, is tough.

It was exciting to shake the long-admired hand. He was at that time well on towards the halfway mark with his monumental *Music of Time*. Strange to shake the hand responsible for the earlier books: stranger, by hindsight, or perhaps just more gratifying in terms of a brush with fame, that responsible for the latter. He in turn showed a pleasing interest in my banking career, though, as it later proved, for practical purposes. He was then working on the first of his three novels on wartime army life, and wrote, in his 1982 volume of autobiography:

> Another adroit *Punch* writer to help with specialised information was Basil Boothroyd, who, having worked in a Lincolnshire bank in his early days, would supply just that smattering of professional jargon necessary for indicating the civil life employment of Territorial officers, nearly all of whom came from banks. For a novelist to obtain such arcane trimmings, anyway in just the form needed, can be unbelievably difficult. Although there may be many bank clerks (or any other particular group) by no means every professional can provide from a given background the instances that carry conviction.
>
> Boothroyd himself always retained a touch of the *Three Men in a Boat* trio, escaped from their London bank for a weekend, having a high old time on the upper reaches of the Thames. One could well imagine him in the straw boater and high straight collar of the period. [He] possessed musical aptitudes; once humming for me Vinteuil's 'little phrase', which, isolated and interpreted in such an individual rendering, deserved at least a few thousand words of Proustian analysis.

So for a long time I was palisaded by great names. What did the wise, confident and renowned, speaking out of the wider world, think of me? Stephen Spender, William Gerhardi, Randolph Churchill, Robert Graves, Graham Greene, Stella Gibbons, Stevie Smith. . .? They wouldn't get far, I felt, into my pieces about troubles with the central heating, or cleaning out the cupboard under the stairs. Truth to tell, though, I didn't always get all that far into some of theirs.

I always read Malcolm, until he began to tail away and appear more before the cameras than in the pages. It's easy to forget – or never to realise by people knowing him only as a face and a voice – the quality of the writing. Lucid, graphic, compact. I must ask him some time, should we both be spared, if he is one of the lucky ones who finds it as easy as it looks.

His real-world background still impressed. Reviewing the first volume of De Gaulle's memoirs, he wondered how that complex figure, having at last achieved supreme power in France, 'could find nothing to do with it except allow the discredited, ramshackle Third Republic to be reborn. Why? I once put this question to him directly. . .'

Did he get as much satisfaction out of putting questions directly, on *Panorama*, to lesser figures? Salvador Dali, Brendan Behan?

We would ask him, on the morning after, what such people had been like. They had usually been ghastly, dear boy. Dismissed. I only remember in any detail an account of the confrontation with Behan. Programmes were live at that time, and the playwright had reached the studio 'over-fortified' (a BBC euphemism of the day). So much so that almost up to transmission time the producer, Michael Peacock, had been urgently pacing, undecided whether to proceed or cancel.

In the end he took the plunge. 'We'll do it,' he said to Malcolm. 'Just one thing. If he says the word c---, don't laugh.'

Malcolm laughed. I mean in telling the story.

I missed him when he went. I think we all did. Possibly excepting the management, now doubting their wisdom in seeking to invigorate the paper with an 'outside' appointment. His introduction of those big names, his general brisking-up of material, born of an insistence that the paper should be this week's paper and not any old week's, may have injected new vigour. But for Alan Agnew, hopes that he would 'do something about the circulation' were unfulfilled. In fact he did something about it, but not what the management had in mind. Perhaps the high residue of middle-class, middle-aged readers (as opposed to today's, more or less classless and their average age in the thirties) weren't ready to be shaken up so disconcertingly.

At least I played my own part, keeping still-faithful readers comfortably in touch with the world of commuter trains and jobbing gardeners. But branching out, too, into other parts of the paper. I reviewed books, was pretty stern with most of them. When Richard Mallett or Eric Keown was away I would take over the film or theatre criticism. I have said it is a mistake to look back, but it can be horribly interesting. What strikes me now about those notices is their unwavering self-assurance. After the opening night of *Waiting for Godot*, I told Samuel Beckett that if he wanted to get anywhere he should make up his mind whether he had anything to say, and later gave Harold Pinter the same advice about *The Birthday Party*.

No one was safe from me, the man who had co-written a play about the French Revolution. I told Shakespeare that *Troilus and Cressida* was 'a heap of rubbish' (a phrase luckily, or industriously, got from Dryden, writing three hundred years before). I

Broadcasting. (BBC curtains in poor taste and covering no window)

With Ian Carmichael (bearded for a play)

Punch party. *Front row, l to r:* E.H. Shepard, Bernard Hollowood, A.P. Herbert (bespectacled), E.V. Knox, Leslie Illingworth, Humphry Ellis; *middle row:* Kenneth Bird ('Fougasse'), Norman Mansbridge, David Langdon, Leslie Marsh, Richard Mallett, Basil Boothroyd, John Betjeman; *back row:* Eric Keown, Russell Brockbank, Alan Agnew

Punch dining room. With Ernest Shepard. And seemingly at home with oysters

Alan Coren makes me laugh. *Punch* office

A Ronald Searle drawing for my *Punch* room. The inscription reads:
'Dear Basil, Here's company and an ever watchful pair of eyes to
keep you huddled over your typewriter. A regular reader perhaps...
Yrs Ronald S'

Peter Dickinson, my oldest friend

At Robertsbridge. June and I with Malcolm and Kitty Muggeridge

didn't think much of *The Comedy of Errors*, either. He had been too clever by half, I told him, with his two Dromios and two Antipholuses, and if he looked at it again he would see that the plot didn't actually work. I gave the producers what-for. John Barton, for one, whose Stratford *Troilus* seems to have been performed in the near nude. 'Torso and Cressida', I see I called it, witty, and raised other objections: 'Why does Agamemnon wear a straw hat, Aeneas look like Haile Selassie, and everybody call Hector "Heck Tor", as if he were going to be climbed any minute?'

The players I was pretty lenient with, perhaps feeling an exhibitionist affinity – wasn't I myself playing a dramatic critic? – and therefore lacking, like Malcolm Muggeridge over articles, the powers of rejection. I did once rebuke somebody in the role of Claudius, in a Mermaid *Hamlet*, for not having his belt-buckle centred. Still that would just be my dress sense coming out.

But the rest of the Theatre must have been relieved when my stand-in stints were over, Richard Mallett and Eric Keown returning to restore fair play. I only once heard from a victim: Terence Rattigan, writing at length, and deeply wounded, honestly wounded, by strictures on some later play of his. I felt small and guilty, and wrote back saying so. This would have got me drummed out of the Critics' Circle if I'd ever been in it, and I would have left without regret. Here was a man who had given me great and wonderful joy in the past (which I trust I also said), and here was I, dressed in a little brief authority, peppering off my popgun from safe cover. A ghastly trade.

Perhaps more of the creative should write to critics. Or fewer read them. 'You must never let them upset you', was all very well for Malcolm. I lacked his sturdy hide.

The film world also ignored me, except for a single romantic response from Hollywood, to a friendly mention of Linda Darnell. She wrote in green ink and a rounded hand. My clipping would be kept forever against her heart, with the photographs of her little ones. Scientific scrutiny might now expose this as a piece of prudent PR by her agent. If so and nevertheless, I was pleased to be taken in at the time.

But show business and I had not been strangers, even apart from distant St Pancras and the one-night Chinese musical.

We have to go back a bit. Further than I thought. It must have been about the time that Tunis and Bizerta were falling to the army, and the dams of the Ruhr to the bouncing bombs of my own chosen Service, then involved, as far as I was concerned, with struggles to the death over Police School timetables. Despite all this, Phil and I achieved a rare get-together in London and went to the Prince of Wales Theatre, agreeing, as we came out still weeping, that anyone who hadn't seen Sid Field had never seen a comic worth the name.

I would have said, except for the conflicting documentary evidence, that this didn't happen until after the war, when people were settling down again to serious matters, but the document is dated in the middle of 1943, a letter from Field, with the form of address, 'Dear Sgt', so I hadn't even taken my first salute on Austin Reed's steps.

The writing, very regular and schooled, humanised from actual copperplate by an occasional flourish, goes on, straight to business,

> I have kept your script because I can use some parts of it. Will you please let me know your figure for same and I will forward it per return.
> If you have any other material I should be happy to read it.
>   Yours Sincerely
>   Sid Field

Well, who remembers him now? I can't remember much myself, even of the first impact that made me want to write for him. I see him desperate behind the bars formed by a set of decayed tubular bells: as the Cockney wide boy starting with alarm on being menaced by the shoulder of his own overcoat. Then there was the famous golfing sketch, his anchor piece, which he had played for years in the variety houses of the Midlands, before being enticed, a tower of insecurity, into the West End. I told him once that I had seen this sketch done by some other comedian elsewhere. I expected an explosion. But nothing. Field, no doubt, had himself acquired it from some vague source, without asking what the figure was for same and forwarding it per return. Somewhere still, I expect, on the ends of piers in the summertime, other straight men are delivering Jerry Desmonde's line, 'You have to make the tee with sand,' and other comedians failing to approach Sid's outrage on the comeback, 'I'm not going to drink *that* stuff!' It doesn't seem much, but you aren't hearing the Sid Field sound.

Perhaps it was indeed nearer the end of the war, or after it, that he used anything of mine in later productions. Or some parts of it. Field, for all those years the sure-fire comic golfer, with guaranteed laughs in guaranteed places, was in torment with new material. Would my comic photographer or week-end painter work for him, without the injection of old and tried scraps and snippets from earlier successes? These were usually of startling irrelevancy. His singular technique disguised this from the audience, but for me, sitting there, now a Man of the Theatre, it was alarming. At a last rehearsal, in impresario George Black's office over the Hippodrome, I would have seen the script pretty well savaged, and resigned myself. On the opening night even that 'final' version would be further distorted, usually at points where I was poised to appreciate another of my best lines that went unspoken.

Field was a simple man, privately very glum. He did not, in the common cliché of clowns, want to play Hamlet. He wanted to play a clown assured of his laughs. He listened unhopefully to the outline of any new venture. My proposal to seat him at a mighty Wurlitzer (still in vogue then) depressed him deeply. As I faltered on with what I saw, the spreading, illuminated console, the manipulation of the stops with unexpected results, he remained silent. It was only when I got to the acrobatic potential of the pedal keyboard that his face lit up. 'Ah! I get my foot stuck.' Not all doubts dispelled. But enough for him to use it. Or parts of it.

I think as long as anything of his ran, with anything of mine in it, I was on a fiver a week. He couldn't have made a lot himself. He died before the golden apples began to fall from the television tree, his shining talent clouded by doubts and fears.

He kept on his make-up table a framed letter from C.B. Cochran, a bigger name, even, and more versatile impresario than George Black. It advised him to pay no attention to his good notices, only his bad ones. Sound in principle. But if Field had gone against it, ignoring the bad and feeding on the good, it might have done more for him than that other resort to confidence, the awful bottle, that ended him as it had Phil's mother.

George Black's principles were more practical. Once, during my short sojourn in the tinsel world, I asked him to give of his wisdom in the matter of stage lighting. I was either interested in this, or affected to be, or hoped to put an informed edge on my dramatic criticism, perhaps taking to task some director for hashing up the Banquo's ghost scene.

It was in Black's office that I sought his views. He had a large model theatre set out there, and placed a stubby hand in the middle of the stage. 'That's where the buggers are. That's where you want your light.'

There is theatre and theatre.

Also cinema and cinema.

I have tried to remember how I got involved in my level of cinema, which was low, both in budget and brow. Somehow I landed on the fringe of the J. Arthur Rank empire, far-flung even to some small studios in Highbury. I should need a map and guide to find the place now, but I know taxi-drivers were excited at going there, and slowed down yearningly as we passed the football stadium. My directions beginning 'The film studios. . .' held no comparable magic.

My period of taxi rides to Highbury could perhaps have come about through Peter Butterworth, probably met with in some radio studio. An amiable, intelligent comedian (whose wife, Janet Brown, similarly endowed, became one of Margaret Thatcher's most acute impersonators), it was certainly he who suffered the leading roles in my early scripts.

These were for comedy shorts, the juvenile audience in mind. I have since often been saddened by those children's television programmes in which grown actors undergo trial by paint, soot or kindred ordeal to divert the young; and have as often expressed doubts on the actual diversion content at the receiving end. I am told I am wrong in this, and that an adult with a white-wash bucket stuck over his head affords joy beyond compare.

(By chance at the time of this writing I am in charge of my youngest step-grandson for the evening. He supports my theory. In both our interests I had video-taped an hour or two's entertainment on the above lines. After watching enough to satisfy good manners, eight-year-old Sam substituted the tape he had arrived with, an oldish James Bond.)

Right or wrong, I dispensed much the same treatment for the hapless Butterworth. He was to have a merrier time later in the adult, rather than 'adult', stream of Carry-On films. Well, they may have been a little 'adult' here and there, but none of the scripts, so far as I know, made him walk out to sea off Shoreham until nothing was to be seen but his floating hat, or miss his footing as a grocer's boy and fall into a barrel of treacle. Anything for his art, Peter said, but that sequence had taken three days. On two of them he had had to start work by resuming his glutinous clothes. Studio authorities had been adamant that nothing but real treacle would look like treacle on the screen.

The mistress of these Highbury revels, J. Arthur Rank's representative on the spot, was an unexpected figure, scholarly and grey. Mary Field had gone through the documentary and educational mill from continuity girl to director, had lectured the world over on children's cinema, examined for the British Board of Film

Censors, advised UNESCO, headed the Children's Film Founda-
tion, reaped many awards and honorary degrees. So she must
have known what was good for the young. She was gentle with
my innocence, exercising practical restraints. 'I think,' she said
once, looking up from my pages, 'nothing with too much *water*,
don't you?' This probably didn't refer to the English Channel off
Shoreham. That could be handled. Studio water was different. I
withdrew my flooded supermarket idea, with Peter breast-strok-
ing down the aisles amid bobbing cereal packets.

It must have been about this time that for some reason, money
not to be ruled out, I agreed to write an advertising film, I think
for an oil company, and having no thought in my head except to
set the action out of doors, hammered out the first line: 'Scene, A
Beach at Alassio.' Months afterwards I met the producer. The
film had gone well, it seemed, particularly enjoyed by the technicians and cast. 'We had a great week in Alassio,' he said. I was
impressed, but ungenerously annoyed. For the same number of
letters typed I could have packed them off to Torquay. Or saved
one and made it Whitby. I would have preferred to have got Peter
Butterworth to Alassio for a week.

After Highbury, there was Denham. Real studios. That great,
now vanished spread. I claim responsibility for two of the worst
feature-length films that ever came out of it. I know their titles
and readily suppress them, revealing only the actor's names,
Jean Kent, Patricia Roc, Nigel Patrick, Stanley Holloway, Miles
Malleson, Guy Rolfe, as an excuse for commending their courage
and dedication, equal to Peter Butterworth's, if responding to
other challenges.

A nod should be spared for Earl St John, the producer-in-chief,
a heavy man, understandably humourless. At our first meeting,
one of few, I was surprised to see his spacious office walled with
Punch volumes, from the first, 1841, to that time, which must
have been the mid-1950s. He didn't keep them for the jokes, I
could tell that, so asked why. They were the only certain record of
British period costume for more than a century; not just decade to
decade, but year to year; Phil May, Du Maurier, John Leech, and
other of those faithfully representational cartoonists, would have
been pleased. They would have like him to enjoy the jokes too,
but you can't have everything.

A volume to come round a couple of years later was never
added. It contained my account of the studios' falling under the
hammer, a nine-day sale of everything from three thousand
assorted cornices, a boat-rocking machine and many glazed
house-fronts, to four-wheeled broughams and (Lot 2849), a bam-

boo open frame circular ape cage. I wrote in sadness, real or feigned.

The empty theatre, the stripped stage, the fairground after the fair has moved on, these are notoriously evocative images, as none knows better than the movie-maker himself. In Denham's great caverns, at one time or another, Ralph Richardson staggered sun-blinded through the desert of *The Four Feathers*, David Niven rode up the monstrous celestial staircase of *A Matter of Life and Death*, Laughton lived the private lives of Henry VIII, and young Jim Hawkins listened for the tapping of the blind man's stick. Now the silence, the darkness and the emptiness, where light and colour and splendid confusion have reigned so long, seem more affecting than in any other forsaken arena. . .

I had even then thought it best, though listing other productions from that place, to keep quiet about mine. A danger still hovers. Insatiable TV could still fill time with late-late re-runs, Great British Film Disasters of the Fifties. People wouldn't know that 'Screenplay by Martin Lane' meant me. But I should. I had adopted the name for no other reason than that we show-business people did that sort of thing. But was wiser than I knew, evading all responsibility. I remember thinking the false identity rather smart at the time. St Martin's Lane was theatre country, Irving's statue at the bottom end.

Eight

MINISTERS OF MIRTH

FOR THE NEXT thirty years or so (one throws off these figures) I left stage and screen to get on without me. *Punch* and a lot of broadcasting were taking up all the time I had. But writing for television means offers one can't refuse. It was adapting, rather than writing, in my case. A small distinction. There is as much writing in adapting as there is in writing, and of a more worrisome kind, since any heaven-sent flights of personal fancy are so much waste matter. In translation from one medium to another they have to be suppressed.

With 'A.J. Wentworth, B.A.', for Thames, I soon saw more complicated worries. The original work was Humphry Ellis's, a book collecting his *Punch* series on English preparatory school life. The episodes, founded on his own experiences, when briefly teaching at Marlborough long before, revolved round Wentworth, a huff-puffing senior assistant master in constant trouble of his own making.

This was one of the complications: that it was the author, my hero and friend, who thirty years before had guided my frightened feet along the corridors of Bouverie Street. His feeling for the printed word, and the only word that would do, was well known to me. It played a great part in his delicate effects, all things understated, some not stated at all.

With a stranger this wouldn't have mattered, or would have mattered less, and would have been less inhibiting. I had already done an adaptation of *The Diary of a Nobody*, and that had had its worries. But the Grossmiths were dead, and beyond a rising up to complain of garblings. I saw that these were going to bedevil any attempt to get Wentworth off the page. Television, for comedy especially, doesn't lend itself to the subtleties. It would be silly to suggest that Humphry didn't realise this. There were bound to be failures of expectation here and there.

It was clear from the first that structural damage would have to be inflicted. Episodes in the book, rounded and complete, would not run to the needed half-hour on the screen. There would be uprootings and transplantings from one to another, wrenched in my own words to at least simulate continuity. And multitudes of my own words – how near could I get to the Ellis? – where passages of description must be turned into dialogue. Could I achieve this, even on paper? Given that, there was still another chilling hazard, that the comedy, whether the true Ellis or my counterfeit, could, in the playing, cross the fearful borderline into farce. And I hadn't started yet. Humphry had been lucky not to see an earlier adaptation by persons unknown, sent to me by Michael Mills as a possible source of additional plot material. One scene showed Wentworth in the suspected rape of a boy's visiting mother. Horrors.

Michael (long ago of St Pancras People's Theatre) was alive to at least some of my apprehensions, and later to lots of Humphry's. I wrung two assurances from him. First, that there should be no studio audience, appreciating nothing 'but inexplicable dumb-shows and noise', to laugh in the wrong places and too loudly, a response always going hand in hand with free seats; secondly, that I should be by-passed in all correspondence between him and the author, of which I correctly foresaw plenty. Our friendship could strike and sink.

Things hadn't been made easier by Humphry's touching faith. He was fully alive to the problems and wrote to me, when the project was only a cloud on the skyline, 'If it were anybody but you doing it I wouldn't look at this proposition. Can even you get over the fundamental difficulty and leave the main character – for whom I have a certain fondness - recognisably as written? I dare say you can. "You're a clever chap", as old Charles Graves used to say in his mellower moments.' (Charles was *Punch* Assistant Editor, 1928–36, and uncle of Robert.)

Michael Mills respected both these undertakings, but notionally breached the second by sending me copies of their letters. Humphry's forebodings grew darker on seeing a completed script.

Even the stage directions stirred his apprehensions.

Page 24. The instruction 'General pandemonium' is getting a bit too near Will Hay for my liking. A little excitability on occasion, by all means, but no pandemonium *please*.

Michael's replies were patient and reassuring. With the other hand, so to speak, he was patiently reassuring me. 'Now, don't get fussed,' he would begin, proposing cuts, additions, amendments. And finish on page three, 'Don't be anguished.' I was not to 'take to heart' either his or Humphry's strictures. All would be well in the end.

He emerged with credit and honour. Besides spreading sooth-ing balm on us both he had other minor preoccupations: budgets and schedules to wheedle, sets to get designed and built, actors to audition, including hundreds of boys, exterior locations to hunt out, a school to find which would not only suit for Ellis's 'Burgrove', but welcome the cameras and lend its pupils for crowd scenes (he found one that further had the initials 'BS' on its caps, a bonus for the wardrobe department). Apart from the occasional eruption at the end of a long studio day, he remained master of all confusions and frustrations – the latter at one point compounded by a strike of carpenters, who were on £22,000 a year and complaining. Meanwhile, seeing stacks of photocopied scripts one day in his small office at Teddington, I realised that, with 'A.J. Wentworth, B.A.', only half through, he had been engaging his spare energies and time on parallel complexities for something quite different, his next programme.

Still, I had my own troubles. A couple of Wentworth scripts got through before Humphry felt enough anguish to by-pass Michael and write to me direct, displaying his awful bruises. I haven't kept his letter. I hope he hasn't kept my reply. Both came fiery off. Both flouted a useful rule of life commended to me, as it happened by Humphry himself, many years before: when some-thing enraging arrives in the post, put it aside marked 'Do not answer for three days'.

In this case we put further correspondence aside for some time, allowing our bristling nerve ends to settle. The breach healed, but for a horrible moment we had gazed into the abyss.

You could see how Gilbert and Sullivan didn't always hit it off.

Another anxiety concerned another friend. In a widely applauded Wodehouse TV series, Mills had earlier directed Ian Carmichael as Wooster. Shortly afterwards I wrote some thirty episodes of 'The Small Intricate Life of Gerald C. Potter', for Ian to do on radio. They ran for six years or so, from, I think, 1975 onwards.

They not only bonded our friendship, but caused me to receive at the hands of Sir Harold Wilson an award, or perspex object, with no money attached. At least for me. I daresay Sir Harold got a little something. We were photographed together, and I would have kept my print if it had shown me looking more suitably cheerful as a perspex winning comedy writer. But his speech had depressed me, its emphasis heavy on his launching of the Open University, and on radio's other vital role, for the old, frail, bedridden and otherwise disadvantaged. It came home to me that I was occupying valuable air time with domestic flippancies between Ian, as earnest but unsuccessful author Potter, and sparkling Charlotte Mitchell as Magnolia Badminton, his scatterbrained but best-selling wife. A melancholy had seized me. I was feeling old, frail and disadvantaged. Besides, those are tense occasions, as the doomful envelopes are slit and the names drawn out. This one was no less tense, since the award organisers, Imperial Tobacco, had organised it in an auditorium flagged with 'No Smoking'.

Oh, well, radio, people say. But if fewer are now listening, radio is still as difficult to do as it always was: in many ways more satisfying than television if you feel you've done it right, whether at the microphone, the typewriter or the control panel.

But Ian still wanted something from me for television, and had also kept in touch with Michael Mills, with the understanding that if Michael found a promising idea landing on his desk he should get on to me about it. This is how Wentworth landed on mine, and I treated it from the start as something for Ian, trying to see and hear him as Humphry's middle-aged schoolmaster.

Actors suffer more than most from the merciless march of the years, particularly if long cherished in the public mind as age-proof light comedians. This was Ian's opportunity to modulate into middle age. He could have done it. But I couldn't get any picture of him. The lines just stuck on the page. They had to be Wentworth. But also Ian, who on the radio, playing well below his age, had spoken thousands of my lines that couldn't be less like Wentworth's. So I couldn't hear Wentworth either.

There entered a further complication. It emerged, from those dim, labyrinthine corridors behind all stages and screens, where money and contracts and options rush to and fro in ceaseless commotion, that Arthur Lowe, who had read the Ellis book on the radio, owned some sort of stake in it as a 'property'. He was disengaged, was looking for a series, wanted to play Wentworth, was cast, and Mills was delighted. There had, after all, been no contractual obligation to Ian Carmichael. But I felt a moral one: perhaps just one of friendship. It was Ian who had started this thing, at least partly to do something for me, and was now to end up seeing somebody else in the part. That's show business. But I wasn't in show business. I hadn't developed the armour. It worried me.

What worried me as a related complication was that whatever I wrote for Arthur Lowe would have to present Arthur Lowe, if his then large flock of followers was to be pleased: in this I could lose

Wentworth. Had Wentworth not been the creation of Ellis, who would be watchful and vulnerable over unfaithfulness, this would have mattered less – audiences probably wouldn't know A.J. Wentworth, B.A., from Nicholas Nickleby. But they wouldn't tolerate an identity change in their esteemed and bumbling Arthur.

The lines stuck. Now they had to be right for Wentworth, Ellis and Lowe. And, of course, for Michael Mills. He had placated Humphry on most counts; for instance on a challenge to the age of the boys in Wentworth's form IIIA, who were older than Humphry had seen them. This was because of stern legal provisions on permitted employment hours of child actors. Above a certain age they could be kept in the studio longer. And studio time was precious as always, technicians religiously observant of their own employment hours. I would be horrified, up in the director's gallery, when Michael, seeing the digital clock with five minutes to go to the down-tools, would decide to scramble in one more take before the minutes showed their deadly .00.

Actors not being, in Michael's words, 'precision instruments', the one take was often not enough. Just near enough. It meant that some patch of dialogue that had cost me an hour would lose a gem or two. And not only from racing the clock. Others disappeared because Arthur, much loved for his bumbling throwaway, would sometimes bumble and throw away where I could have wished otherwise. Michael's own care for the words, though respectful, was subject to erosion from a different cause.

Harry Andrews was playing the Headmaster of Burgrove. Splendid actor, modest soul, his enormous height gathered emphasis at rehearsals from his unvarying attachment, by a lead, to a very small dog. He was among my legends, of the Old Vic, or the Royal Shakespeare. Buckingham, Bolingbroke, Enobarbus; elsewhere as Allenby in Rattigan's *Ross:* memorable in Shaw, Chekhov, films without number. It seemed a presumption to put my words into his mouth.

Sadly, after reading my first script, Michael begged me to put as few as possible. The memory was going. The actor's nightmare.

It was distressing, infinitely so for Harry. But the rest of us too found our toes compassionately curling, as the words petered out and left him either silent or grappling with improvisations. Most of his scenes were with Lowe, the Head and Wentworth in yet another disciplinary confrontation. While Harry struggled and improvised, Arthur bumbled and threw away, and Ellis and Boothroyd sank without trace. Often the four of us were only got on to the screen after the salvable bits of many takes had been stitched together to achieve a passable comprehensibility.

I don't think I disburdened any of this on to Humphry Ellis. And who else would know or care?

This is too long, as Polonius says of the first player's tedious Trojan tale. There were two unexpected after effects. When the work was finally unspooled on the public it topped 'Coronation Street' in the ratings. And some time afterwards it was sold for transmission in Saudi Arabia. I wonder sometimes what they made there of Humphry's classic of English preparatory school life in times gone by. And how the dialogue stood up to Egyptian dubbing, or more likely sub-titles. I somehow couldn't hear anyone dubbing Arthur Lowe.

But the repeat money suited my conscience. Under the usual terms of such contracts, though I've lost this one, sales to America yield something like two hundred per cent on the original fee paid, declining thereafter on a sliding scale for elsewhere. The oil-rich Saudis paid one per cent.

Miles Malleson, actor, musician, dramatist in his own right, adaptor and translator for the English stage of Molière and Turgenev, later to crown his achievements by appearing in a 'Martin Lane' screenplay at Denham, was one of the first eminences I met on being elected to the Savage Club.

Or not so much met, on that occasion, as saw before my very eyes, in the catch-phrase of fellow-member Arthur Askey. Eventually we would chat at the bar as one literary man to another. Or I would chat with Mark Hambourg or Benno Moiseiwitsch, if not as one pianist to another. No violinist, I was spared inhibitions in chats with Max Jaffa (predictably known in the club as 'Juicy'). Henry Williamson would sometimes turn up from Cornwall, for ever branded with *Tarka the Otter*, and gloomy, it was said, over the more subdued reception for all his other works.

He would have had to be pointed out to me. The place was full of famous faces, voices (in my first week I lit a cigarette for Tommy Handley), and famous names whose faces I didn't know. Newly back from a holiday cruise with Phil, I told a neighbouring member at lunch all about ships and how they worked. We got on well. The club's Hon. Sec., Alan Wykes (*The Snake Man*, and a long list), happening to pass, I sought an introduction, even if it was a bit late. Alan, who knew everyone, and loved them, was surprised. 'You mean you don't know old Cecil?' I exchanged a formal handshake with C.S. Forester, whose ship-wise

Hornblower had been my bedside hero for years. Still faintly in shock, the name Hornblower went from me. I said instead how greatly I had enjoyed the film of *The Indian Queen*.

'African.' The circumstances reversed, I couldn't have resisted the correction either. He said he thought Indian Queen was a village in Cornwall; but went on, over the cheese, with reminiscences of Humphrey Bogart and Katharine Hepburn. It paid to be cautious at first. Once at the big centre dinner table I nearly came unstuck with a light, uninformed remark about nuclear energy, but checked on reading, from his open spectacle-case, that the member opposite was Professor E.N. da C. Andrade, FRS. He had practically invented the stuff.

Everyone seemed to be somebody. I never remember running into Augustus John or Edwin Lutyens or Gerald Kelly, P.R.A., but there was always a risk. Somerset Maugham came to the club's centenary dinner in 1957, but was usually at a safe distance in St Jean-Cap Ferrat. A mixed bunch. Bud Flanagan next to Alexander Fleming in the members' list. Me next to Arnold Ridley in the bar. I felt an affinity there. We would discuss our hard times, not an uncommon subject with us actors, and had I not once played in his *The Ghost Train*?

His own times were to become less hard. Ah! the magic box. Here was a man with a lifetime's theatre behind him, plays uncountable written or acted in, but fame and fortune awaiting his appearance in *Dad's Army*, as the one-gag private with a urinary affliction. But *The Ghost Train*, surely, must always have been money in the bank? Hardly a night, for half a century, when he wasn't collecting royalties from the amateurs? But no, as it turned out. He had sold the play outright to French's for a hundred pounds. I was aghast. He bore no resentment. He had never, he said, needed a hundred pounds more badly in his life.

The Savage Club's unwritten rule is that, whoever you are, you are nobody once you're inside. It is observed. I was just a little slow in realising it, despite a unique claim to distinction. I think the word unique must stand. The membership categories are rigid: Art, Drama, Science, Music, Literature and (more recently, since lawyers seemed to be getting in under Literature) Law. I must have been alone in getting past the qualifications sub-committee as a practising bank clerk. *Punch*, no doubt, was a help. At a later time, sitting on the committee and hearing the hair-splitting deliberations (was advertising copy literature?), I wished I could have been there when my own name had come up in 1946.

My sponsors must have put the case well. David Langdon

proposing. James Hadley Chase seconding. Further support from a group-captain publisher I only met once, declaring he had known me long and well and I was no man to be blackballed. Not a figure of speech, that. Those fateful spheres really were dropped into a timeworn wooden box. Langdon's declaration was comparatively genuine. We had been fellow-warriors. As squadron-leader editor of the *Royal Air Force Journal* he had commissioned articles. I remember my Dickens parody in a Christmas number, and hope nobody else does. Wing-Commander James Hadley Chase I hardly knew. There had been some storm about him in the Commons teacup, a new appointment in RAF Public Relations being thought unsuitable for the author of *No Orchids for Miss Blandish*. It had glancingly touched my own Air Ministry department, I can't think why. Nothing came of it.

In 1946 we were all still in uniform. Was the Committee swayed by such an array of gallant lads? Our ranks were interestingly graded, from my (acting) flight-lieutenant to the unknown group-captain. Assembled, and the formalities observed, we should have been saluting each other. I would have liked a photograph of that.

Langdon had one of his drawings in his Ministry office. A nervous airwoman, up for promotion and tussling with the stock question about the service's commissioned ranks. 'Pilot-officer, flying-officer, flight-lieutenant' – and onwards and upwards – 'air vice-marshal, air marshal, air chief-marshal, Marshal of the Royal Air Force. . .[a wild guess]. . .God, I suppose?'

It summed up my feelings. Marshal of the Royal Air Force Lord Tedder, GCB, also became a member of my club, no doubt under Literature (*Air Power in War*, 1948). I don't recall our meeting. But then I would have steered clear, despite the unwritten rule. James Hadley Chase, whose real name, Rene Brabazon Raymond, had the ring of the perfect pen name, disappeared to France, then Switzerland. He never went to America, where *No Orchids* had been so profitably set with the aid of dictionaries of American slang and maps of American cities. I remember his complaining of broken nights as a family man, when nothing would quench the baby's howls but being wheeled round dark London streets in a pram. His *succès de scandale* with Miss Blandish set up one of those writer's fetishes. All subsequent books had to have five-word titles. *A Lotus for Miss Quon, A Coffin from Hong Kong*, and, in 1980, *You Can Say That Again* – he was lucky: he could. He seemed a quiet man.

The Savage had always been well studded with *Punch* people, from the engraver, Ebenezer Landells, who had a large hand in founding the paper and, to some degree, the Savage itself, through Phil May, Shirley Brooks (its second editor) to later and present times with Alan Herbert, Ernest Shepard, Ronald Searle, Langdon, Russell Brockbank, Thelwell, ffolkes, Norman Mansbridge and others, dare we say, too humorous to mention.

So I didn't always have to talk to atomic scientists or Moiseiwitsch. I did try not to play the eight-foot Steinway grand if Moiseiwitsch was within earshot rather than up in the card-room playing poker with Hambourg and other cronies – where, it's said, Hambourg one day rushed excitedly in to say that a film was being made about Beethoven, and he was to play Beethoven. 'Who's playing the piano?' said Benno Moiseiwitsch, studying his cards. It sounds true.

But there were times when the place was empty on a late afternoon, and the mellow tones were not to be resisted. I had an understanding with John, the barman, to warn me if any proper pianists came in, but he failed me once. I was well into my arrangement of 'Ain't Misbehavin', which even at home sent the dog under the sofa, when I spotted Benno in the shadows at the long drawing room's far end. Nothing was ever said, or at least between us.

Had I become a Savage three or four years earlier I should also have had to keep an eye open for my fellow member Rachmaninov. He and Moiseiwitsch had been great friends, at times performing duets for four hands, in the club's star-spangled Saturday night entertainments. I did once hear Mark Hambourg play on one of those occasions. Very old then. 'Well, you asked for it,' he said. Then the still magical sounds.

The occasions continue, though now on Fridays. It was a sign of growing confidence, out of the bank and thus legitimised, that I allowed myself to be numbered among the artistes. I was never up against Hambourg or Moiseiwitsch, though John Ogdon once, and eminent orchestral members, either on their own instruments or improvised combinations of hose-pipes and watering-cans. It was bad luck to follow B.C. Hilliam with a song at the piano (Jetsam, alas had gone, but Flotsam survived). Or eminent Shakespearians with one of my stand-up monologues. I still hear Henry Oscar, quelling that unruly audience to a hush as he pealed his beautiful bell. 'O, what a rogue and peasant slave. . .' Or what he thought the bard's best, from *Cymbeline*:

> *Fear no more the heat o' the sun*
> *Nor the furious winter's rages;*
> *Thou thy worldly task hast done,*

> *Home art gone and ta'en thy wages:*
> *Golden lads and girls all must,*
> *Like chimney-sweepers, come to dust.*

Or Parry Jones or Owen Brannigan would sing. A Savage choir, dropping everything to grace the last sad rites of a friend come to dust, took a lot of beating. Eight of them sang Sullivan's 'The Long Day Closes' for Handley.

One of the later and most unlikely *Punch* importations, in fact straining likelihood to its limits, was the solitary, ruminant, constitutionally unclubbable Richard Mallett. I can't think whose crazy notion this was. The other Richard, Richard Price, disclaims responsibility. The proposal, even to Mallett, never mind the club, was someone's hopeless misconception. It may have been Russell Brockbank's. The result, as unexpected as snow in August, was that he said yes, so did the club, and it became his home from home – more home than his raw little flat – until he died. Russell and I, who had considered ourselves fairly heavy frequenters, became by comparison casual droppers-in. Mallett was always there, amused or amusing, no longer alone in the evenings, was soon a 'character', and is still so remembered. People at Carlton House Terrace, like those at Bouverie Street, knew just how to handle his little blackouts.

And then, besides, there was always a doctor in the house, usually several. Though the Science category only admits healers with achievements in fields of original discovery or research, they must, like Picasso, have begun with conventional forms before exploring the less comprehensible. Richard was secure.

He shortly adopted or affected a new persona. It was always hard to know whether his crusty clubman was a private joke, a conscious role-playing to accord with the clubland of fiction, or whether it took him by stealth. His testy outbursts on some lapse of facilities or wrong-headedness in Committee decisions were high caricature. When the club moved to King Street, the heart of a Covent Garden whose gutters were at that time still rolling with fruit, he exploded on the first day, when a waiter was unable to produce an apple, his favoured dessert.

'What! No apples? *Here?*'

He went off into a self-deprecating chuckle afterwards, as always. But the waiter had retreated to cover by then, probably sitting down for a minute. None of us really got used to the idea of Richard's becoming a clubman, crusty or not. Perhaps the secret lay in one of many attempts to define the Savage aura. Its

members, someone said, were all people who didn't want to join
anything.

The phrase would have pleased Thurber, a prominent figure in
the Mallett pantheon, who happened to be in London at the time
when Mallett was to chair one of the Saturday dinners. I wrote
and asked him if he would come along there as my guest. As he
seemed much beset by cameras, microphones, interviewers and
other intrusions, I assured him there would be none of this, and
he would run no risk of being called on to make a speech. I don't
think this caused him to decline, but it turned out, in part of his
three-page close-typed reply, that it was the wrong bait. My
phrase, 'No speeches', he said, reminded him of something said
at *The New Yorker* by Harold Ross.

He and I were asked to be guests of honour at Columbia
University, and to receive a small dingbat called a Laughing
Lion. . .Here's the way Ross put it to the man who rang him
up, 'I won't come if I have to speak, and Thurber won't come if
he can't!'

However, he couldn't make it, for other reasons, but his letter
was courteous, grateful, and very, very long. A reason for the
length only became clear at the end, with a suggestion that I
might like to read it out on the night. He was going to make a
speech anyway, if only in his absence.

There was certainly a lot of funny stuff in it. With good names
to drop. How Franklyn P. Adams had said to a drunken, profane
and obscene member of the New York 'Players' (a Savage affiliate
over there), 'This is a gentleman's club, sir, and he may be here
any minute.' I decided not to make his speech for him. A lot of it
would have had to be cut. Who was I to edit Thurber and ruin the
shape?

But it was ripe with ribaldry, as I saw from its opening, 'Away
back in 1938, John O'Hara, the American authority on instant
sex, and I. . .' It went on to recall meetings with Frank Harris,
who had written, in an essay on Ruskin, 'Without the pleasures
of love, life is but a poor inheritance', and confided to Thurber
that he intended to live to a hundred, and continue to enjoy the
pleasures of love by the nightly use of a stomach pump. Next
came something I could have used. How Thurber appeared so
seldom at the Players' that he became known as the unknown
member. When he did get down there and tried to buy a drink at
the bar for other members,

the bartender invariably said, 'You'll have to let one of the members of the club buy the drinks, sir.' I told him that was fine with me, but the other members spoke up and insisted that I belonged to the club too.

But then more difficulties. Called on unexpectedly to speak at the same club.

I gave, in part, a brief set lecture on the short sex life of the American male as compared with that of the British male.

I retold a story that Clifton Fadiman had told me, after he had interviewed Lord Bertrand Russell one day when that great man was, I think, eighty-two years old. Fadiman had asked him what was his greatest pleasure in life at that age, and he looked astonished and said, 'Screwing.' When I told this story a few weeks ago to an Englishman in London, he said, 'Why, Bertie knows how to say that word in seventeen different languages.'

It was a letter of great friendliness and charm, as well as length. I was proud to have it. I have managed not to lose it. Sotheby's might like to have it one day. But too much of it was hardly on Richard's wave-length. Or even his audience's. Though charges of prudishness have never, so far as I know, been brought against members of the Savage, I somehow felt it wasn't quite right for us.

Clubs have a hard time these days, ever retrenching, and this usually leads to their doubling up with other clubs. We doubled up with the National Liberal for some time, which threw Mallett into deep dejection for the first week or two. Not apple trouble this time. He had made a tour of the building with one of his notebooks, and recorded fifty-three pictures, effigies or other representations of Gladstone.

Later, when we moved in with the Constitutional, he was no longer with us to take an inventory, but could no doubt have depressed himself by quantifying the prevalence of Disraeli.

The Constitutional, and therefore the Savage, pleased me by its smart address, in the heart of clubland. I stayed there, it seemed so very right, the night before Prince Philip was to fly me to Mexico. An official note of the arrangements, distributed to me in triplicate at the club, at the *Punch* office and at my home address, said:

Wednesday, 11th February
0800 Mr Boothroyd departs with his hand luggage from the
Savage Club, 86 St. James's St. in a car arranged by the Royal
Mews and proceeds to Buckingham Palace.

0825 The Duke of Edinburgh, accompanied by Mr Boothroyd
and his Police Officer, departs by car from Buckingham Palace.

They were both nice addresses to be involved with, and I quite
understood the palace's problem in drafting the second paragraph. Though always courteous, they couldn't really put me
first. But 'Mr Boothroyd, accompanied by the Duke of Edinburgh
and his Police Officer. . .' would have avoided the suggestion
that I was now, in a new self-importance, taking my personal
security man everywhere. It was tempting to correct the syntax.
'Evoe', it was said, at Owen Seaman's funeral, had passed the
time by proof-correcting the Order of Service. As with Thurber's
letter, again a document of exalted origin, it was not for me to be
captious.

Thurber had been one of *Punch's* first guests after I joined the
Table. Outsiders were then still traditionally barred with a near-
Masonic severity. Two earlier visitors are recorded by Price, in
one short sentence and with that zest for startling juxtaposition
relished over his uncle, the falling piano, and Alfonso of Spain.
These were Garibaldi and Mark Twain. Before my time. I should
have been lost for words with either ('I loved your revolution/*Tom
Sawyer*'), and did little better with Thurber. I had loved his words
by the million, but as I guided a glass into his hand – he was
almost quite blind now – they all left my mind but three. I had
never, I told him inanely, understood what was meant by 'the
catbird seat' in his story called *The Catbird Seat*. The roles
reversed, it would have been just the remark to cause me to leave.
All he replied to the shadowy idiot with his drink, was that he
thought the meaning had been made clear in the story; which at a
re-reading turned out to be so.

Luckily guests of honour sat on the Editor's right, Bernard
Hollowood's at that time, and I could guard against uttering
vapidities by keeping well clear at the other end of the table.
Bernard cut up Thurber's food without, I think, giving offence.
But a hard decision to take. And his guest responded by cutting
his self-effacing 'th' in the table. I never learnt what they discussed. Hardly J. M. Keynes versus monetarism, I imagine,
though Hollowood was at his happiest with economists. Perhaps
Frank Harris versus the stomach-pump.

Somerset Maugham also attended the Table one day in Bernard's time. Like Garibaldi, but unlike Twain, he was not elected to membership. Beyond a murmur on introduction I was not called on to converse, which was good. I could have told him I had never understood why his 'Ashenden' story about a hairless Mexican had been called 'The Hairless Mexican'.

It must have been a year or two later that I had a letter from Kirkwood, Missouri, providing a proud link with Samuel Langhorne Clemens, author of *Tom Sawyer* and other works still in store for me to read. It notified me that I had been elected a Knight of Mark Twain, and was signed by Cyril Clemens, editor of *The Mark Twain Journal*. Here I was in sparkling company. The letter paper carried tributes from fellow knights.

> I well remember reading Mark Twain and it is my hope that my fellow Americans will continue to be inspired by his fine works. – Richard M. Nixon

And in its way more loquitive:

> Put me down ditto to the above statement. – Lyndon B. Johnson.

A further note of appreciation seemed to honour the *Journal*'s editor almost more than its subject: 'Cyril Clemens, a worthy kinsman of Mark Twain, who brought light into all our lives.' – John F. Kennedy.

But we all have our vanities. I showed the letter to David Langdon. He said that he was also a Knight, and knew practically nobody in the humour trade who was not. I remained proud. Possibly because my own knighthood had a distinction. From the terms of the citation, rather waveringly typed, the award was for my only serious book.

Peter Dickinson, when we were together at *Punch*, beat me at chess most working days for eighteen years in the Red Lion, Fleet Street. As elsewhere, our relations over the chess board went well, since I never minded losing and he quite liked to win. He made what I regarded as the right vocal noises, except perhaps for calling a waistcoat a weskit, which seemed overdoing it.

He once gave the only answer to an old and teasing question. This was put at the *Punch* Table by William Davis, the editor of that time. He had the disquieting habit of 'going round' for members' views on anything that came into his head. Rummaging for one's own pronouncement, bound to be exacted as the remorseless sequence unfolded, it was easy to miss other people's. German by birth and upbringing, Davis (inevitably dubbed Kaiser Bill by *Private Eye*) may have had a special interest in the British view of things. Some questions were worse than others ('What is a sense of humour?'). But this one was pretty bad. 'What is a gentleman?'

'Someone who never thinks about it,' said Peter. And didn't even trouble to add the long-drawn 'a-a-a-and', his usual contrivance to stop anyone else getting into the conversation.

Accent and pronunciation, Fowler says somewhere in *English Usage*, is less a class thing than a class-conscious thing. I plead guilty. And still mark a radio script with coded reminders to rhyme my 'bath' with 'hearth', and close up the syllables of cir-cum-stance and sec-re-tary.

It has never done me any good. After my first broadcast the producer was approving, but had a qualification. 'Pity you lost so much of your northern accent. It would have given you character.'

It must be a couple of years since I last saw Peter. It is a rule of life that those best loved are least seen. He had that morning finished his thirty-first book in fourteen years, and was buzzing with the plot of his thirty-second. Also complaining of too much time on his hands. 'After all, I only work a fifteen-hour week. A-a-and. . .'

Long friendships can bear strains. I had to ask him, in friendship's name, some time ago, to stop sending me his books as they flopped off the production line. It was bad for my confidence. I can spend fifteen hours on an article and still hate it.

Peter, however, having come to supper this time, as ever endearingly unkempt and in a terrible pullover – that assurance that needs no backing from outward display – had felt it convenient to bring his last two books, warm from the press, to hand over with a genuinely apologetic laugh and a release from obligation: no need to read them.

Coming to supper that night, and reminiscing, he had a correction when I recalled eighteen years of sharing beer and chess. He put it at about twelve. 'Then I got tired of winning. And we went over to sharing champagne and Philip Hope-Wallace.' This I accepted, give or take few years. We had certainly crossed Fleet Street at some stage, from the Red Lion on the north to the famous, perhaps over-famous, El Vino wine bar on the south. Often in the news for its stern attitude to the drinking woman, who was barred from standing at the bar and obliged to take a demure seat, which resulted in sporadic feminist protests, it was also prim about obligatory ties and jackets for men, to the point of keeping some of these articles to lend to the improperly dressed but otherwise welcome spender.

My recollection is that the champagne would be occasional rather than regular. I think of claret, if that's what I mean. Not brought up to wine, I tend to go by the shape of the bottle. Peter was different, and I was reminded of a characteristic Peterism in El Vino one day, when he asked for some particular wine, and was told by one of the ladylike young ladies that they didn't keep it. He challenged this. 'Oh, but I was drinking it the other day. Pray look again.' He enjoys the old forms.

The girl came back with a reaffirmed negative. After a moment's thought he apologised. She was right. He had been unforgivably stupid. 'I was thinking of the adjoining vineyard.'

Had it come from me, it would have been a joke, a dig at the know-all wine buffs. With Peter it was just a fact. Had it been an overheard remark from a stranger, it would have enraged me as a piece of insufferable exhibitionism, and drawn one of my scorching glances.

I have a good line in these, founded in a pathological disapproval of those behaving in ways different from my own. Trains are the usual scene. Rattling up to London one day, trying to work on something or other, I was tormented by two men talking in what Peter himself called 'the hound voice', bred of a need to make itself heard across the wastes of the hunting shires.

The opening exchange had been bad enough.

'Got any duck on your lake?'

'Rather curious. Only on the small one.'

But they went on. My glances, which should have struck them dumb, went seemingly unregarded all the way to Victoria. There, one of them, courteously giving me precedence to alight, said, 'I hope you didn't mind my talking to my friend?'

It was well done.

Sharing Philip Hope-Wallace must have begun through Peter, who would naturally know him, as I would naturally not. I was at first assailed by familiar misgivings about exposure to intellect. These were to be dispelled.

Philip always had the same chair, at the same iron-legged table, holding his small court. Over it the El Vino management had accorded him a modest brass plaque on the wall. There was something wrong with it, I forget what. Nothing as bad as the name mis-spelt. Some oddity of punctuation? An OBE instead of a CBE? I know the mistake amused him. It would be conscientious to go in and check. But I don't go in since he died.

The side door was convenient. It gives on to the steep alleys down to the Temple Gardens, a short cut to the *Punch* office. An establishment enclave, those gardens. Smooth lawns behind tall railings. The law alone walks there. I used to thread along on the public side, admiring the uniform splendour of the parked cars and stepping aside for the occasional white-banded barrister.

The door was also handy because a peep from outside covered Philip's table. There are places to be peeped into and stayed out of, seeing someone preferably avoided. I would peep in and stay out if I didn't see Philip. He had soon come to hold no terrors for me, despite his eminence in the world of the arts, and his wellspring of anecdote. He was one of those few raconteurs who enlarge rather than diminish the effect by being carried into laughter by their own stories. A childlike joy in having so much joy to impart. Laughing at one's own jokes is generally thought obnoxious. What the generality fail to grasp is that the laughter is not self-admiring, but disowning: praise to the gods for putting the joke into one's head.

He ranged widely, from the private whims of opera stars to exotic experiences of his own. 'Once when I was lecturing in Khartoum. . .' But it proved, as with other *literati* joining the group, that the world of banking, with its rites and mysteries, held a fascination which, in my banking days, had invested the world of letters. I could come back with, 'Once in Lloyds Bank, Skegness. . .' and command his laughter in return.

On Bernard Hollowood's first day I arrived as he was about to enter the Editor's room. I had a flashback to the war, and meetings with fellow NCOs newly commissioned. 'Well,' I said. 'I suppose I've got to stop calling you "Bern" from now on.' I never did. With other *Punch* people, we were contemporaries. Something odd must have been in the air in late 1909 or early 1910. Myself, Angela Milne, Richard Mallett, Richard Price, Colin Howard*, and I think a few more, had all been born in 1910, and had known, under various editors, what it was like to be on the outside trying to get in. Bernard too.

Interviewed in *The Times* when he retired, eleven years later, he

*Howard specialised in the domestic-fantastical, as with *The Port-Fed Stilton* in which the cheese, over-fortified, became dipsomaniac and took over. Angela Milne was A.A.'s niece.

described himself as 'a bit of a batty schoolmaster. And I've had enough of reading other people's essays. And a second-rate humorist, you could say.' There were further self-revelations. The radicalism: 'I've never liked Tories and I'm damned if I ever will.' The egalitarianism: 'No man's worth twenty times another man, it's impossible.' The passionate anti-racialism: 'Have you ever wanted to kill anybody? I sometimes think I could knock off Enoch.' Cricket? Well, of course. (His time at *Punch* was shortened by having played too long, acquiring a ruined knee cartilage that gave acute pain for the rest of his life, and well worth it, he would have said.) 'But don't get the idea I'm a flannelled fool, I'm just your ordinary, average, sportsmad Englishman.' He threw in at the end, 'And you can put down anti-religion and anti-monarchy too.'

Anti-religion? Perhaps just anti-religionist. He was certainly against Pope Paul VI's being against the Pill. Women were as much entitled as men to have fun in bed. He wrote saying so, furiously, under the title 'Sex and the Single Pope' – a thing unknown, as Humphry Ellis might have said, in Sir Owen Seaman's day. But this was one sign, among many, of a compassionate heart, an undenominational Christianity.

Second-rate humorist? If Hollowood was no Thurber, and Thurbers are few, he could still be a pretty funny writer when not too stiffly on a hobby-horse. He could be funny about economics, and the grittier aspects of social and industrial history, neither usually regarded as rich mines of mirth.

The schoolmaster? Yes, that came out somewhat, mostly at editorial conferences, when light topics could lead off into heavy weather. 'Oh, dear,' he would say, half a groan, half a laugh – 'You're plain ignorant, the lot of you.' And we would be instructed in the mysteries: cyclical unemployment, Gresham's Law, the arbitrary distribution of purchasing power, mobility of labour and economic growth.

But he read our essays with care. I won't say that when he gave poor marks, in the cause of duty, it hurt him more than it did us, but it hurt him quite a bit. In his last number as editor my own essay took the form of a farewell letter. It said towards the end:

> The truth is, my old Bern, you're a cryptosentimentalist under all that hard-faced stuff about wage policies and the gross national product. You're sentimental about *Punch*, about editing it, about us in the adjoining rooms, about friends (same thing), about life, about wives and families, yours especially, but in general as well. No flower ever revived more spec-

tacularly under rain than you under a kind word truly meant (all these are truly meant), or shrivelled more miserably under a critical blast. So you knew how it worked the other way. Getting a contribution past you was always a small victory. Getting your applause for it was a triumph and a joy.

None of this, I told him, meant that he was forgiven for making me play cricket against the over-forties of The Hague.

There had always been *Punch* cricket of a kind, mostly sporadic, on village grounds in the game's own country and cradle. This was a rash fixture.

Bernard apart, it was likely that none of us had walked out of a real pavilion on to a fully-mown field and a manicured pitch, to play an all-day match. It had been news to us, and I don't know how Bernard got hold of it, that the Dutch played cricket at all. We were inclined to regard it lightly. We crossed by ship, on a day of brilliant calm, practising a little on the deck with rolled-up newspapers and bread rolls. It turned out that The Hague ran about fifteen XIs. The receiving party when we docked displayed enough Free Foresters and I Zingari ties to fill Lillywhite's basement, heavily overshadowing our own status symbols, limited to the Editor's Staffordshire cap.

Had our hosts been lighter on the hospitality, the night before the game, we might have done better, but I don't really think so. On the morning of the match Russell Brockbank said to their wicket-keeper, 'I'm afraid a few of us are drunk.'

The response was impressive for its command of our language. 'Still, or again?'

Their cricket was also impressive. We batted first. Bernard stayed out there until all but he had fled, including David Langdon, a keen golfer, who took a tee-ing stance, uprooting the off stump with his back-lift; Russell himself, whose game, from a Canadian upbringing, was ice hockey; and the rest of the ninepins.

Our opponents then moved in and wiped us off with all wickets standing. It was quick: all over in time to see the evening paper headline, ENGLAND THRASHED. In Dutch, of course, but we weren't short of willing interpreters. I had a small disappointment, having been privately interested in what would be the Dutch for 'lbw', which proved to be 'lbw'. The Dutch for 'How's that' was also 'How's that'. 'Out' was 'Out', too.

A last note on *Punch* cricket must record an act of heroism at Balcombe, Sussex, where we were batting on that beautiful and interesting ground which slopes gracefully from the pitch, making outfielders invisible unless unusually tall. B.A. Young, well down the order, was serving as umpire at the bowler's end. Hollowood, at the wicket, was on 99 when the appeal for caught-behind rang the welkin. Freddie Young, after a pause barely perceptible, raised his finger. Not many of us could have done that. He left the office shortly afterwards to edit the arts page of *The Financial Times*, but rumours of cause and effect were probably ill-founded.

It was a pity that guests at the lunches hadn't really gained a hold before Bernard himself left. An occasional economist appeared acceptable. Thomas Balogh, I seem to remember, one of Harold Wilson's advisers during the vogue for Hungarian gurus. Professor J.K. Galbraith (*The Affluent Society*), from Harvard, Princeton and everywhere, including a US Ambassadorship to India, who unexpectedly unfolded his great length and made a short speech, or rather told a story, equally unexpected, which had something to do with piles. When it comes to humour, strangers to *Punch* company sometimes don't wish to feel outdone.

Had conventions relaxed earlier, Bernard would have invited cricketers. I think we should have seen plenty, but no. Later, under Alan Coren, we had a Captain of England, Mike Brearley, as amusing and intelligent as one might expect of a lecturer in philosophy. Two Captains of England, in fact. Rachel Heyhoe Flint the other. We were inviting women by then. A thing unheard of in Sir Owen Seaman's day.

It was Bill Davis who really began throwing things open. To some degree he saw the Table as a power-base. This was instinct. I wouldn't say that it was on these grounds only, when *Punch* was acquired by United Newspapers, that he successfully fought to keep the table – that is, the physical piece of furniture – when our new masters understandably coveted it for the board room. But he favoured as guests people of distinction, influence, of personal and practical interest. It would have been idiotic to let slip the opportunity of bidding the great and good to sit on his right hand. They were biddings not often refused. I daresay the same is true for other cultural eating centres, *The Times*, say, or *Private Eye*. But the *Punch* Table is the *Punch* Table.

Bill too would have economists to lunch. Chancellors of the Exchequer, say (if they qualify in the Galbraith and Balogh class). He was expansively at ease with them. Much laughter. But he knew what they were talking about. I wouldn't know what either of them was talking about.

Occasionally I could get my two cents' worth into the heady

talk. For instance with Chief Secretary to the Treasury Joel Barn-
ett, newly back from Washington after shaking down the IMF for
a handout. He had an engaging larkiness about the higher
finance as he flicked the billions here and there across our
smoked mackerel and horse-radish. He was jargon-free and
lucid, and I warmed to his simple arithmetic. How, I asked him,
after those involved deliberations, did he keep anything clear in
his head? He said he didn't try. He scribbled the figures on the
back of an envelope. I enjoyed believing him.

Money men were natural enough guests for Davis, a money
man himself. He had left the lately shattered Germany a mid-
teenager with no English, was on the *Financial Times* at twenty-
one, soon City Editor of the *Evening Standard*, then the *Sunday
Express*: and from the financial editorship of the *Guardian* made
the oblique, spring-heeled leap into the stronghold of the British
joke. One felt it could have been anywhere. 'I might change my
mind in mid-air,' Sid Field used to say, threatening the audience
with a somersault.

But all politicians were welcome. Though for me, as ever,
vaguely suspect. I must have hinted this, surely in the most
general terms, to John Stonehouse, the last of our Postmasters-
General before telecommunications changed their style. He gave
me the direct blue gaze, intent yet amused. 'But why do you
mistrust politicians?'

I didn't know. Still don't. A feeling, perhaps, that they stand
too high above the battle, the distant clash. It would be nice to
meet a Minister of Transport in a bus queue one of these days –
without benefit of pre-alerted cameras, that is, to capture the
stroke of democracy. I strongly recommend the No.13 stop at
London Bridge.

Emboldened no doubt by claret, I once tried to narrow down
Harold Wilson's focus to the individual, not, I hope, described as
the Man in the Street, though wine is a mocker. It was the man in
the street, or at home with his wife, family and tax return, that I
was after. The concept seemed hard for our guest to grasp. Too
simple, perhaps. Or I expect I put it badly. He got away from me
again into the broader thinking.

Table days were then Wednesdays, and I had bad mornings
chipping out enough of my smart little bite-size paragraphs to fill
the front page, by then called 'Seven More days', since fewer
readers than ever knew what was meant by 'Charivaria'. It came
to the same thing. Often too pushed to glance at the guest list, I
would find, joining the gang for drinks in Bill's room, that
Edward Heath or James Callaghan, whom I had just crowned

with a sparkling insult, were in there. William Whitelaw, perhaps. You never knew. Denis Healey, being funnier about something than I had just been about him.

No doubt they had their sensibilities. I remember James Callaghan complaining of hurt Welsh feelings because someone had barracked him at a recent meeting with a yell of 'Bloody Irish peasant!' They all seemed amiable and harmless enough. One forgot what a Home Secretary might have been doing that day with a stroke of the pen.

Edward Heath was apt to be taciturn. George Brown leaning the other way. Wilson grating quietly on. Mostly they were surprisingly communicative, their small talk about things the headlines were blowing up into big talk. High matters, yet discussed rather as if they themselves had no part in them. Still, a Ministerial opinion, even if it might just as well have been advanced by the Man in the Street, gains substance from its source; is quotable. And we were all journalists, at least of a kind. In Bill Davis's case, a very journalistic kind. He presided at ease, laughing a lot, making a terrible mess of his cigar. Other people's cigars seemed all right, perhaps were waved less, missing rapid air-streams. Bill's always seemed to come unwrapped, ending up in the silent movie cliché when a door has been slammed on them.

The politicians appeared to enjoy themselves, forbearing about the cartoons and lampoons we flailed them with week by week, leaving, of course, no wound. Some of their caricatures were in their familiar place round the dining-room walls. I think particularly of a caricature of Heath by Trog (Wally Fawkes, artist, jazz clarinettist), half hiding a thunderous face behind a jolly, laughing mask. Accounting in part for the taciturnity? Probably not. If any of them felt exploited I never heard of it. Their presence enabled Bill, the following week, to write politically without gauzy references to Usually Reliable Sources. 'Harold Wilson told me', was better. 'I told Harold Wilson', better still.

However, all celebrities were welcome, given that their fields were influential. I missed the Archbishop of Canterbury, and no doubt many more, having left the office, though not the paper, after only a year or so of the Davis régime. My free lunches in high company, though still frequent, were intermittent. I didn't miss Margaret Thatcher, who was there the week after her triumphant speech that made her the party's leader. As she told me (this is an easy style to drop into), it took her five hours to write. As I nearly told her, it took me longer than that to write a speech opening a church fête. I was actually thinking how sexy she was.

To say that she was all woman would be an overstatement, but she was enough to have made me wonder since, sometimes, whether gentleman heads of foreign states ever find their thoughts slipping down from their summits. I later suggested to Alan Coren that I might do a parody of *Antony and Cleopatra*, with Brezhnev and Thatcher in the leads. Even Alan, more sensitive than most to the tied tongue of a writer trying to explain how he's going to write something, looked clouded. 'If you think you can.' However, I thought I couldn't. Shakespeare is difficult, without imposing fresh plots, and I certainly couldn't see round the scene in which our Prime Minister applied an asp to her bosom.

But I did recently come across some old Shakespeare of mine: the scene Moscow, a Council Chamber, where Bulganin and Khrushchev are about to be dispatched on their visit to Britain (the one whose discourteous reception by Malcolm had so offended Alan Agnew's sense of good manners).

Enter ROSENKRUSH and GUILDENBULGE tired for a journey.
ROSEN: And so, good Guildenbulge, my twin in embassy, a word privily, ere old antick Voroshilov comes to pipe our imminent passage.
GUILD: And with him that pied ninny Malenkov, grinning like a cheese, plump fingers still callus'd from pats o' the English head. . .

Malenkov had already been over here, and in the Kremlin's view a lot too chummy. On the other hand, the KGB's Serov had also fallen from local favour by sounding off too aggressively: as marked in Voroshilov's closing speech.

                    These base chamberers
Have sore disservic'd us. The one hath smiled,
With marchpane cloying up his beaming jowls
And spoke full idiot-fair to English ears,
Palm-clapping all in moist and cheveril clutch
As who would prove our State a slop-fed maid.
Whiles hath the other wreakful, nut-hook knave
Glinted his gunstone eyes at vigilant lens,
Tilted his ravin'd cap, laid bare his fangs,
And with fierce ostent glowered forth his bile
Till foes who would be friends have read his mien
As our design true-mirror'd. So, these both,
One with false clay, with falser steel the other,
Distort our cause, and treason's fee shall pay:

Withdraw their food cards. Take them both away.

Exeunt SER. and MAL., bound.
Two ordnances shot off.

I was pleased to chance on this, if only as a reminder that I
wasn't writing about garden ponds and gasmen all the time. It
also reminds me that I was the first in the office to unfold an
evening paper with the sad news of Voroshilov's predecessor.
This practically filled the front page with two words. STALIN
DEAD. I was trying to take them in when Malcolm passed and
said instantly, 'It means twenty-five years' peace.' So it has. And
more. Of a kind.

Malcolm and Kitty were in due course to have staying with
them, down at Robertsbridge, the eminent murderer's daughter,
Svetlana. TV cameras periodically attended, capturing the peace-
ful scene. Figures in a landscape. Walks and talks in the Kentish
fields. Kitty's account ran less to such rural pursuits than to the
local shopping. 'She behaved like Royalty.' Indicating her
requirements with a commanding finger and leaving Kitty to
pay. Natural enough. Svetlana had been brought up a Princess, a
Tsarevna, no more accustomed to fret about money than those
other Princesses before her, shot by the Bolsheviks at Ekaterin-
burg as an early step towards equality for all.

Distinguished guests have changed since Alan Coren succeeded
Bill Davis at the top end of the table.

They say the Actor and the Actress keep
The courts where statesmen
gloried and drank deep.

Glenda Jackson or Penelope Keith, radiant with professional
awards. Instead of Willie Whitelaw, Billie Whitelaw. Carl Fore-
man, Mel Brooks. John Cleese, pretty quiet. Dudley Moore,
entirely so. Joanna Lumley, a beautiful icicle. Billy Connolly,
unable to resist a one-man show, perhaps feeling it expected of
him. Vincent Price, suddenly corporeal after all those remembered shadow-shows. (Still, I had once lunched at the Savage
with Boris Karloff, né William Henry Pratt, a thoughtful man
whose hobby was growing prize flowers.) Larry Adler, mouth
organist and raconteur. Like Claud Cockburn's son, he too had
once been dragged along as a child to a grown-up party, where he

was lectured on being kind to his mother by a fellow guest who turned out to be Al Capone. Princelings of the chat-shows turn up. The Parkinsons, Wogans, Hartys. The kings of push-button culture, Melvyn Bragg, Russell Davies, Humphrey Burton.

Sometimes they are writing for us, and they can do it, which annoys me. It should be enough for Barry Humphries to invent his twin horrors, Dame Edna and Sir Les, without being funny in print as well. I curb my resentment. It's hard, even for me, for anyone, to resent Harry Secombe, kindly ebullience his natural state: or Robert Morley, vast and beaming in good suits. He has been intermittent, both in the paper and at the Table, since the latter days of Davis. 'Let's go round the table,' Bill once said, in his let's-go-round-the-table mood. 'What are our favourite things?' He dropped on Robert first, who was unhesitatingly triggered, 'A new sponge and not being directed by Peter Brook.'

Sheridan Morley, I for long assumed, had been named on a theatrical whim, for Richard Brinsley Sheridan. Not so. But the theatre came into it. He was born while his father was playing Sheridan Whiteside, at the Savoy, in *The Man Who Came to Dinner*.

I don't always come to lunch, so I miss some. Catch some too, of course. Michael Caine, temporarily repatriated from Hollywood through a tax window. He contributed, to a passing gynaecological discussion, a memorable Cockney synonym for what A.P. Herbert, in his long-anonymous verse on The Portions of a Woman, had deplored as 'Such a very short and unattractive word.'

We once persuaded A.P.H., to declaim the immortal lines at a Christmas party. Bawdy so beautiful that it comes out clean. After his death I had doubts about including it in a commemorative radio biography, but was told to go ahead. John Reith had long departed those once-prim temples.

With radio, again, I always felt I had stepped into a world that I doubted my place in. Such misgivings, in the hothouse bonhomie of the studio, must have been somehow suppressed. I would hear myself saying, on 'Any Questions?', 'Well, I agree with a lot of what Gerald's just said': Gerald being my sudden but fleeting friend, Baron Gardiner and Lord High Chancellor. Or I would stroll back from Broadcasting House with Yehudi Menuhin, discussing the problems of humorous writing and violin-playing, until we got to Claridge's, where he went in and I went on. I opened an interview with Lord Hunt, not long down from Everest, by inviting him to demolish the myth of the Abominable Snowman. 'It certainly exists,' he said. Not a good start, but I still might have cultivated our acquaintance. It was some time before I saw him again, in the milling ticket hall of Victoria tube station, where he looked bemused. It seemed no moment to renew the association.

'Don't forget, now, call me,' Vincent Price had said, giving me his Hollywood number. I was to be in Los Angeles presently, with Phil, making a rare visit to Toby and his family. 'When are you going to call Vincent Price?' they kept saying. But, somehow. . .

'Who will be *Punch*'s next editor?' asked *The Times* diary column in October 1968. Bernard, after several ineffectual operations on his knee, had given up the tiresome task of getting it to the office. 'Should the job go to an insider; or should they [Bradbury and Agnew] plump for an outsider with a big name, who would be likely to create a stir?' Bernard Levin was rumoured: Hugh Carleton Greene, about to quit the director-generalship of the BBC.

> The present staff does have at least one ambitious young man, Alan Coren, who is known to have strong ideas about the development of the magazine. Coren is around 29, and became an assistant editor at 24 – the youngest ever. He has been sharing responsibility in Mr Hollowood's absences with Mr Peter Dickinson and Mr Basil Boothroyd. Coren would clearly love the job.

I don't know if Peter was ever asked. I was, with a sidelong tentativeness. I protested my limitations. But along came Bill (in the words of the Wodehouse song lyric). Bill Davis was as much a bolt from the blue as Malcolm had been, fifteen years before, but more devastating. Malcolm had strolled in; Bill exploded.

By the end of his inaugural staff meeting I knew it was the end of me. Drinking wine, and absently passing the bottles, he talked as he drank. Tie wrenched loose, sleeves rolled up, hair out of control, he snapped through the current issue of the paper, the axe falling. This would have to go. That needed tightening up. 'We'll lose that. My brother will write a money page.' (John Davis, another swift acclimatiser, already City Editor of the *Observer*). All was to be changed in the twinkling of an eye. We wanted names, big names. A circulation of half a million. He came to my page, turned it with barely a glance. The film and theatre notices had no edge. Who was Richard Mallett? Oh, yes, and in future there would be no more word-play.

I recognised this as the final bang on my coffin nail. Word-play had always been one of my things. On the way home to Sussex in the train I thought of Phil, never demanding, but there had been talk of a rise in the housekeeping money. I thought of Toby, poised for his public school, not one of distinction, but with quite distinctive fees.

Then I went down the corridor and was sick. That could just have been the wine, but I doubt it.

As for the word-play, it soon transpired that Davis hadn't been talking about me at all, but a small verse item we were running regularly at the time called Word Play. Though marvellously assimilating his adopted language, he could be excused for finding the English pun without appeal.

I raised the housekeeping money. Toby went to school.

Bill was a hard man to talk to, with any hope of continuity. Ideas of his own were always grass-hopping in. I said to him one day towards the end of my time there, 'William' – very earnestly – 'will you do one thing for me before I go?'

'Of course. I think we ought to run some profiles.'

'It's only a small thing. Will you let me—'

'People are interested in people.'

'What would make me very happy—'

'Where's Caroline? I've lost my bloody traveller's cheques.'

' – would be if, just for once, you would let me finish a sentence.'

But he was out of the room before I finished.

The Times had been right in describing Alan as an assistant editor. We were all assistant editors. But Alan was by now Deputy Editor. There was a difference. When he eventually moved into the Editor's chair it was no jolt; for much of the Davis reign he had been in it already. Bill was continually flying. Figuratively up and down the office corridor with a wide and unpredictable range of engine noises, serenely rushing, or with an angry scream of reversed jets, intimations of emergency landings on anybody's desk. But physically, too, he was often up and away. Washington, Los Angeles, Paris, Berlin. Phone calls and telexes flowed remorselessly in, while Alan, in effect, got the paper out.

Bill was always signing traveller's cheques. When he could find them. 'I hate them. I hate these bloody things,' he broke out one day in the middle of one of my sentences, scribbling his adopted signature on a thick pack. Time wasted and nothing to show. Good grief, he was already thirty-five before getting to edit *Punch*. It had taken him that long to get there. Every minute counted.

And every post was a staging-post. *Punch* included. For me, achieving that remote, misty plateau, even as an assistant editor, was enough. I settled for it, content just not to slide off. Bill left it to become a millionaire. Seemingly without effort. A natural progression.

I met him again one day after he had accumulated what he called 'drop dead' money (once you have it you can tell anyone to drop dead). It hadn't changed him. He was still hot, tousled, shouting with laughter, his shirt half out, withdrawing attention from anything being said as some more serviceable thought took his mind.

This was in his own publishing kingdom, a spread just off Trafalgar Square. I had looked in on the way to somewhere else – not without a precautionary phone call: I'd heard him broadcasting from Los Angeles a day or two before – as well to check. He poured champagne, but had me on a proud tour of the premises before I had time to drink any, and back in his own room to interpret the photographs on the wall, his place in the Bahamas, another in the south of France; no, he'd got rid of the one in Sicily.

I borrowed his telephone for some corrections of a *Punch* proof. He left, shouting for somebody, but was back in time to hear me explaining that the printers had corrected something I had wanted as written. 'It's supposed to be a joke.' Bill's laughter drowned me out. A joke. It was itself a joke, about the joke-world over which he had once held sway. 'Jokes,' he gasped, at last recovering. 'Do you remember "word-play" that time?' I did, but was surprised that he did. I said goodbye to his backside, as he bent over somebody's desk. It had been nice to see him. 'Yes', he said, 'I've got to go to Florence tomorrow.'

Caroline, whom he had taken with him from *Punch*, and who loved him like a mother, loaded me with the current issues of his publications. The top one, I saw in the taxi, had a long piece by William Davis datelined the Caribbean. I kissed Caroline goodbye. We were old friends. 'It was so good of you to cheer him up,' she said. 'He was feeling very rejected.'

That was a year or so ago, in 1985. I haven't seen him since, except for the tail-end of an appearance on a Wogan programme. He must have suffered. The unstemmable Bill, stemmed by the unstemmable and self-promoting Terry. From what I saw it looked as if this was the way things had gone.

I don't know where he's rushing now. If he had bought out Rupert Murdoch I suppose I should have read about it, if only in the City columns of the *Observer*.

Alan Coren, his successor as Editor since 1978, is also unstemmable, but with a difference. Not just words, but wit. He ties lesser tongues. Given time, most of us can put a funny line or two on paper. But we need the time. Some of us, even with the spoken word, can shape up a laugh, yet miss, in the shaping, the chance to raise it before the conversation shoots off elsewhere. The Coren reflex is instant, spouting preposterous fancies and bizarre metaphors, classical and historical allusions, quotes from films made before he was born, or from music-hall ditties sung before I was. All at top speed. Nothing dwelt on, the gag never milked, each absurdity a springboard for another.

There are few vainer exercises than trying to bring dead wits back to life. (Capturing the living Alan is proving hard enough.) How funny was Oscar Wilde? In any event, he polished his shafts in private before loosing them in public. Perhaps Alan comes closer to Sydney Smith, whose daughter did better than most resurrectionists to revive him. She wrote of 'the multitude of unexpected images that sprang up in his mind, and succeeded each other with a rapidity that hardly allowed his hearers to follow him, but left them panting and exhausted, to beg for mercy.'

That comes as near to Alan's performance as I can get. How do people do this? And, in his case, preserve the grimly serious core essential for any editor, even of *Punch*? Perhaps particularly of *Punch*. Humorists are a tricky lot to handle.

Davis had been different – to leave it at that. It was he, all the same, if with only an editorial side-flick, whose random thrashings around led to a strange *Daily Telegraph* headline in December, 1969. 'Boothroyd is Prince's Biographer.' Other papers carried the story, tinged it seemed to me, with the surprise I felt myself. *Private Eye* was quick with 'an extract from the forthcoming work'. I felt it didn't quite catch my style, but subjective judgements can be unreliable.

Anyway, there she was, pretty as a picture if you get the drift, and I wouldn't have minded being in the running myself. Still, no hard feelings and all that sort of rot. You can't have everything as the saying goes, and I'd be pretty stuck without a saying or two. Mustn't grumble. I never fancied playing second fiddle to a monarch, and he's welcome to it as far as I'm concerned. That apart, if you can't marry the heir apparent, next best thing is to write a book about the hubby. Anyway, it's nice for an old gent like me to take a year off from *Punch* and get away from that new fellow they've got in – never thought he was much cop – Davidson? Dobson? Some name like that. . .joking apart, actually, as the saying goes, by and large, give or take a little, all things considered, what?'

They were right about the old gent. I was already looking sixty in the eye when Davidson, Dobson, some name like that, launched the threatened profiles. Failing the Queen, not accessible to such approaches, Prince Philip was the highest he could go as a starter. I said I would like to do it. Oh, no, thought Bill. As Editor, it was only proper that he should arrange the interview and write the piece. I quite saw that. I went back to whatever I was working on, those pithy pars, or ploughing through unsolicited manuscripts, or something searching of my own, about tropical fish, or piano-tuners.

A cover caricature was commissioned, suitably disrespectful of the profile's subject, a week fixed for publication, preliminary negotiations opened up. None of it anything to do with me, until Davis looked in one morning and said he had to go to Geneva – Moscow? – somewhere. 'You'll have to do the Duke.' So I did. It was an odd operation. No interview, I now learned, was to be granted. But submitted questions would be answered. I submitted the questions. Most of them were answered. From these, without at all suggesting that this was how it had been done, I wrote the profile and called it 'Working Prince'.

That was the last I thought of it until some weeks afterwards Mark Longman, Chairman of the publishers, came on my office phone and asked if I would care to discuss a matter to do with the Duke of Edinburgh. It was late on a Thursday afternoon. I was then only doing four days a week in the office. I'd done my four days, and as usual was exhausted. I was an old gent, after all. I said no, but I would call him back on Monday, and toiled off up the slope of Bouverie Street, my thoughts dominated by the ruling anxiety at that time of day: what chance of a cab to Victoria.

'Anything happen today?' This was Phil, and the time-honoured question to returning breadwinners.

'Not a thing. Oh, a publisher rang up.'

'What about?'

'I don't know. Something to do with Prince Philip.'

'What sort of something?'

'He didn't say.'

'Didn't you ask?'

'No.'

She raised it musingly once or twice over the weekend. By the Monday, refreshed and ready for another week's digging in the fun-mine, I was feeling a twinge of curiosity myself. When Longman and I eventually met he showed me a letter which the working prince had sent him from some remote spot abroad. It had enclosed the *Punch* containing the profile, and proposed that I should be asked to write the Life, an inevitable project anyway, with his fiftieth birthday coming up in eighteen months' time, and several genuine biographers already contending.

I got the feeling that Longman's heart wasn't in the idea. Rather like asking Elton John to take on Figaro. I at once said yes. Not at all in character. He took it well.

Why I said yes like that, so promptly, crisply, professionally, I didn't know. In the months that followed, waking up in the night, I saw why. I had been off my head.

Nine

ROYAL SOCIETY

'WELL, HELLO,' SAID Lt.-Commander Slater, RN, greeting me cheerfully on the squelching lawn. 'Come inside and meet the Queen.' It was one of Norfolk's wetter mornings.

Coming inside didn't mean Sandringham House, where the royal car from King's Lynn station had sped on after dropping me, but Wood Farm, a cottagey outpost on the estate. Sizeable as cottages go, but in a state of comfortable disorder: convenient that day as a base for the shooting; at other times when Prince Philip or members of his family fancied a short escape on their own without the fuss and expense of opening up the house.

In fact I met the Queen Mother first, not at once identifiable, perched on the arm of a chair in a bundled-up looking macintosh of some iridescent fabric and a hat in poor shape. She was welcoming and apologetic. 'How awful to drag you up here in this weather!' It was no worse, I said, on an ungraceful impulse, than being landed in the lap of the Royal Family. She laughed. 'I shouldn't worry about that. Jock, why hasn't he got a drink?'

The Lt.-Commander was Jock. To all, including me within a few hours. The Queen's equerry, but at everyone's bidding.

'Jock,' Princess Anne was later to call across the tea table, 'why no kipper pâté?' He nodded gravely, and ostentatiously tied a knot in his handkerchief.

I leaned on him heavily that weekend. He answered all my nervous questions. Mealtimes, tipping, who was who in the rest of the party, right up to my closing doubts about the thank-you letter. Prince Philip had invited me. The Queen was my hostess. 'Oh, do write to her,' said Jock. 'She loves getting them.' I worried about addressing the envelope. 'Just put "The Queen" and send it to me. I'll see she gets it.' It all seemed agreeably casual.

But even he could hardly help with the writing. I scrapped several drafts, including one with something about having been entertained royally.

One of the things I asked him was whether someone could be

found to drive me round the estate on the Sunday afternoon. He tied a mental knot in his handkerchief, and presently came to my room to say the Land-Rover was at the door, which it was, Prince Philip waiting at the wheel without noticeable impatience. Jock had found someone.

Inside the crowded sitting-room at Wood Farm my hostess soon approached, in jeans and an orange jumper and stepping over retrievers. 'I'm afraid,' were her first words, 'we seem to have an enormous lot of dogs in here.' What did I say? That that was perfectly all right?

Somehow and suddenly we were then discussing aircraft noises over Windsor, and I am sure I sympathised. Residents in the Castle apparently suffer not a little from the sitings of Heathrow runways.

Prince Charles struggled from behind a sofa. 'I knew I was right. I thought it was you.' This, I felt, was something he had been looking forward to.

We moved into lunch. More properly lunches, since the party was divided in two. Prince Charles and Princess Anne (headscarf, weathered jeans) took their party into some room beyond. The Queen and Prince Philip stayed with mine. He had first drawn my attention to photographs on the walls from his book *Birds from Britannia*, ending with one on the inside of the loo door. 'My favourite.' It was of some bird squatting low on its nest in an attitude of strain.

I forget what we ate. Something unremarkable. 'I think,' said Prince Philip, after helping me to decide about vegetables, 'you might try to get something into the book about my family. Not much is known about them. They were quite interesting people.' A remark later to lead me into the tangled branches of royal family trees. Monkey-puzzles. I could already see, even starting from the graspable fact that George V, Kaiser Wilhelm II, Tsar Nicholas II and Prince Andrew of Greece (Prince Philip's father), were all first cousins, and Grand Duchess Olga of Russia was his maternal grandmother, that this was going to be something more challenging than articles about Celia and the Washing-up.

He thought I might usefully talk to his sisters, Princess Sophie of Hanover and Princess Margarita of Greece. 'Usefully' was one of his words. He was always thinking of useful approaches. No insistence. Possibilities opened. The sisters lived in Bavaria.

'Would they talk to me?'

'Of course.'

Just a matter of fixing up to meet them somewhere. Munich, say.

I could get lost in Munich. To some degree I was lost already. February was imminent. The book was to be out before June 10 next year. I am a slow writer. I go to wrong airports. I hate research.

And as yet not a word on paper.

The invitation had come informally enough, by telephone from the palace. 'The boss thinks you might find a weekend at Sandringham useful. How about the one after next?'

I think the speaker was Bill Heseltine, then the Queen's press officer, now Sir William and her Private Secretary. A man of endearing openness and daunting intelligence, he was to be the smoother of all my paths. But it may have been Major Randle Cooke, the Duke's equerry at the time, and another rock of support. Whoever it was, I was given a selection of trains to King's Lynn: and asked my size in Wellingtons, which of course would be supplied. Details are looked after in those circles.

My first thought on receiving an invitation of any kind is how to get out of it. I would have paid money to get out of this one. There was no way. When I came back from the telephone and told Phil we rivalled each other for pallor.

I dwelt gratefully on the Wellingtons during the lunch at Wood Farm. The rain still fell, and was to continue during the next three hours of bogged-down walking under slaty skies. It was my first and last shoot. At least I was not to participate actively. It had not been suggested that I should bring a gun, though for all anyone present knew I could have been a lifelong twelve-bore man and the terror of every fowl that flew. While various of the royalty and nobility banged away, I mostly trudged beside Lady Rose Baring, lady-in-waiting and instantly companionable soul. I confided my haziness about Sandringham, how it was run, staffed, paid for.

'You must to talk to Charlie,' she said. 'He's coming to tea.'

'Charlie?' I said. 'It's all very well for you lot, loosing off these first names. But for a visitor from outer space. . .'

She was laughingly abject. 'It isn't fair to do that, I do see.' Charlie was Lord Tryon, holder of the Privy Purse-strings.

An area having been shot over, there were intermittent rushes for the convoy of cars, jeeps, pick-ups, beaters' vans, suddenly moving on, as if at a secret signal, to the next scene of uneven contest. I sometimes had to board briskly or get left behind, and once scrambled into the back of something already moving to share it with the Queen and a muddy dog, both invincibly cheerful.

No conversation sprang readily to mind. The weather, per-haps? Or I could have asked what entertainment was derived from these exercises by a fellow non-participant.

It was the one-on-one dialogue that always gave me most pause. Walking down the long corridor to my room on one occasion I saw that I should have to pass my hostess, cutting up dog-food at some sideboardy piece of furniture. I could have said, 'Hello,' which would be familiar. Bowed, which would have gone unseen. Pretended not to notice. Disrespectful. But I plumped for that in the end.

Things were easier at mealtimes, even at tea, without benefit of alcohol. More people, more talk.

Tea would be 'immediate', said Jock, as the party finally queued up at the House for a hand-wind bootscraper (said to have been an invention of Prince Philip's, but I never pinned him down on that).

'Come and sit by me,' said the Queen, patting a chair and pouring tea from something almost urnlike, in silver and on spindles. I understood the size of the teapot as the company drifted in. We ended up with a dozen or so, Prince Philip last and opposite, Princess Anne on my other side, Lord Tryon, the Keeper of the Privy Purse, also at our end. The rest, so to speak, nowhere.

This was a family tea, a spread of scones, toast, jam, cucumber sandwiches, chocolate biscuits wrapped or unwrapped, fruit-cake, sponge layer cake, several assorted pâtés – though no kipper. Princess Anne went on at Slater somewhat, in mock-complaint, even after his handkerchief knot. 'I mean, why not? I don't see. We did have kippers for breakfast.' They exchanged grimaces.

When the first cup left base I passed it on to her. She passed it back. 'The big ones are for the men. There's no women's lib in this place.' I suppose I looked questioning. 'Actually, the real reason is just that we haven't enough of this service to go round.'

On my left, my offer of cake was graciously declined. The Queen thought that would not be 'at all wise', and didn't eat much of anything, was partly preoccupied with a couple of hungry Corgis and a threat to stockings (having changed into a short yellow dress), partly with some argument opposite, where her husband was pressing Tryon to release funds for the refur-bishing of houses on the estate. Tryon resisting. The Queen supporting him. 'Don't you rise to it.'

Tomorrow was Sunday. The talk moved on to ecclesiastical undermanning. Five local livings, three of them in the Queen's gift, two in other people's. How could they get together and work out something? At present, only two priests for five churches.

'So you see,' said Prince Philip, drawing me in, 'there are some Sundays when some of them don't have services.'

'Yes, they do, darling.'

'No, they don't.'

'Yes, they do. It only means that if Flitcham has matins, then Sandringham can only have Communion – Oh, Jock, you will go along tomorrow to see the church is warm? Last week in the hymns our breath was going out like trumpets.' Tea over, the Queen and the Earl of Westmorland departed together, in an atmosphere faintly conspiratorial, disappearing into some kind of antechamber. Prince Charles wanted to show some old silent film comedies. 'I don't know,' said his father, rising on a sigh. 'Your films. And my in-tray's overflowing.'

We all saw them eventually, Prince Philip with enthusiasm, putting words into the wordless lips and chiding those dead comics for standing in the line of hosepipes and custard-pies which they could easily have evaded.

Prince Charles had taken station at the door of the ballroom, and ushered us in. I said, 'I thought you were taking the money.' Was this a thing to say? Too late now.

'All contributions gratefully received,' said the usher. As the rest of us broke up from the tea table, Jock had felt it among his duties to explain about the vanished Queen and Earl. 'It's all a bit comical.' Westmorland, it seemed, long a Lord in Waiting, was to become a KCVO. This, even for an earl, involved knighting.

'If we'd been at the palace, there would have been a great ceremonial to-do. Lord Chamberlain, all the Household, me in my uniform with aiguillettes and all. But as he's been asked down here to get it, and to shoot into the bargain, she just takes him next door and does it.'

The couple presently reappeared, the new knight a little pink. There were handshakes. 'What's happening?' someone asked. 'David's just keen knighted,' said somebody else. 'Yes,' said the Queen. 'I've dubbed him.' A mischievous inflexion on the 'dubbed', and her transforming laugh.

Monday's *Times* carried the formal announcement.

There's a story about A.E. Matthews, said by brother actors to have played so many lords that in the end he thought he was one. He was a great checker of props, and on one first night went down on the stage to make sure that the cigarette box had cigarettes in it and the book he was to read was the right way up.

'Very respectful stage-hands in this theatre,' he reported, back in the dressing room. 'Went down just now, three of them bowed to me.' Interested, other members of the cast followed him the next night to spy from the wings. What Matthews had missed was that his inspection coincided with the pulling up of the 'iron', or safety curtain, which meant the crew's facing inwards from the audience side and taking the strain of the ropes, bending from the waist.

The pun is commonly held to be the lowest form of humour. I rate the anecdote lower, being second-hand at best and without the spark of originality. Despite this, I quite fancy my hand at telling a story, given that I have it well ordered in my head, and that the flow of the talk admits it without too obvious a wrenching.

At dinner that night the conversation had at least touched on the theatre, Prince Philip recalling his only Shakespearian role, as Donalbain, in a Gordonstoun out-door production of *Macbeth*. I asked if he'd been any good. 'No. They just needed someone who could ride in on a horse.' Prince Charles said that when he was himself at the school his father's acting reputation had dished his own chances. This was denied. 'I always liked the bit of *Macbeth*,' said Prince Philip, 'when someone comes on in the middle of a terrific slaughter and says, "What's amiss?"'

I then told the Matthews story, and even as I came to the word 'lords' realised with a chill that it was not an ideal choice for that particular dinner table. It lacked impact, since all the guests were lords – and their ladies – except me.

But for light exchanges in royal circles topics are elusive. The commoner has nothing in common. His account of a fearful traffic jam outside Honiton, or his latest stunning rates demand, is not something he feels he can embark on. The temptation is to ask questions. At least I was there in an enquiring capacity, but the things I wanted to ask were born of a universal curiosity. 'What is it like to be Queen?' would have put it in a nutshell. I fought it down. There was really no journalist in me. Had there been, I could have kept an ear open for wonderful scoops for the popular papers – and betrayed the trust placed in my discretion, not only by the Queen and Prince Philip but all the people surrounding them, who throughout the writing of the book, in which the Sandringham weekend came quite early, before, in fact, I had written anything – held nothing back. It was hard for them. Prince Philip had directed them to open their hearts and books and records. He wanted what I wanted: a true account of him. But for them it was all against the habit of the courtier's ingrained reticence. Breaking the habit, sometimes with detectable unease, they at the same time did me the courtesy of assuming my own disregard for the trivia which keeps so many 'royal' journalists, including the zoom-lens photographers, happy and, if not glorious, at any rate prosperous.

That dinner was towards the end of a strainful day. 'I think I'm going to be sick,' I said to Lady Rose (my prop and stay during the afternoon's shooting) as we went into the dining room. 'Don't worry,' she said cheerfully. 'We'll get you out.' She would have, too, but somehow, the need didn't arise. It seemed natural that I was there. Not that I felt that. Just that everyone else made me feel that they felt it.

With the coffee I took out my cigarettes, and vainly tried to pocket them again before anyone noticed. 'Oh, do,' said the Queen. 'I don't, but I don't mind it a bit.' I thought of the times without number, at more public dinners, when I had had to contain my addiction until the blessed release of the loyal toast.

Perhaps I needed nicotine because of an unhappy exchange with a lady on my other side. Her name, like some others, had failed to register. The film, *Oh, What a Lovely War*, then newly out, had prompted me to express an admiration for it. Did she share that? 'Not really. You see, my father was Haig.' This was Lady Astor, wife of the second Baron (of Hever), who must also have been at the table somewhere. She had understandably been no relisher of John Mills's bloodthirsty caperings in the movie caricature of the noted field-marshal.

I really must be more careful.

After dinner we all trooped into the ballroom to see another film. Was its choice yet another duty of an equerry? Or were preferences expressed? It was *A Fistful of Dollars*, the first of the so-called spaghetti westerns, one of those German-Italian-Spanish co-productions where the cast, to ease multi-lingual dubbing, either kept their backs to the camera or, if in vision, uttered plotless rubbish for the sake of matching words of any kind to the lip movements. Not that we could hear much, partly because of the ear-splitting bombings and general explosions, shootings, whining ricochets and screams of stunt-men being set fire to; partly because everyone was laughing too much. Prince Philip enjoyed it even more than the earlier silent antics of Fatty Arbuckle. He and the Queen clutched each other helplessly –

having, with the Queen Mother and Princess Anne, the worst
seats in the house, nearest, that is, to the screen, though in the
comfort of armchairs.

'Can anyone tell me what this is about?' asked Martin Charteris
mildly during a rare hush. There were no volunteers. We braved
it out, and returned gasping to the big drawing room, where the
past ninety minutes' mayhem dominated the conversation.

I would give the experience less space but for the sequel. Prince
Philip left the room early, his in-tray still neglected, to goodnight
bows and curtseys. Soon afterwards the Queen, Queen Mother
and Princess Anne also withdrew, to the same respectful obser-
vances and presumably bound for bed. Presently, discussing the
spaghetti western with Lord Brabourne, himself a film-maker, I
heard cries of 'Bang, bang, you're dead', and was just missed by a
flying ping-pong ball. The three royal ladies, armed with the
young princes' pump-guns (this was 1970, remember), had
opened fire from a high scrollwork gallery at the end of the room.
Prince Charles and some friends countered with a thrown
cushion or two. I felt this would be over-boisterous in me, and
restricted my part to returning ammunition for reloading. The
engagement was soon over.

It was the kind of incident difficult to record here without
suggesting that, in such company, there was something extraordinary about perfectly ordinary high spirits.

Readers of memoirs must often doubt the reliability of the writer's recall. How can he be trusted, past time intervening, with the
where and the when, the who said what to whom?

I hope to dispel such reasonable misgivings. When all at Sandringham slept but me, I sat up late with my tape-recorder, con-
fiding the still-sharp events of the day. I set up the machine on
Edward VII's emblazoned blotting pad, amid other needs of a
guest: the rack of crested stationery, forms headed Court Telegram, pens, pencils, china ink-wells with choice of red and black,
matches, sealing-wax, a bowl with a moistened sponge, scissors,
calendar, paste-pot, an ivory paper-knife monogrammed 'AE',
with the Prince of Wales's Feathers.

It took time. The hour of one strikes on the tape, from the clock
over the desk: one of those, no doubt, always kept fast by George
V, until Edward VIII, long annoyed by the practice, ordered that
real time at Sandringham should be restored.

This clock was in fact ten minutes slow.

The room was big. Furniture heavy. Clothes-hangers roughly

poker-worked EIIR. Central heating grumbled under the window seats. Swagged curtains. A wallful of books whose titles mostly failed to stimulate. *One Hundred Years of African Commerce, 1795–1895. A Military History of the Madras Engineers*, six volumes of Gibbon. Twenty-eight, bound with much gilt, *Minutes of the Proceedings of the Royal Artillery Institution.* From a sampling, all seemed to have book-plates: The Library of George Frederick Ernest Albert, Prince of Wales. Honi Soit Qui Mal y Pense. Ich Dien.

There was a shelf of more readables, the plates inside saying more simply, 'The Queen's Book'. And a notice asking borrowers to fill in a card and leave it in the empty space.

I borrowed, filling in no card, *Hornblower in the West Indies.* But with no real need to read myself to sleep.

Sunday dawned grudgingly in mist and rain. The motorcade for morning service, splashing through potholed lanes, arrived at the church on the first stroke of eleven. Punctuality is a matter of pride as well as courtesy.

'Prince flies in on the dot,' said an Ottawa evening paper a week or two later, when he put us down there in snow on the way to Florida, Yucatan and Mexico. Periodically, on that long trip of short hops, cards would be handed back from the RAF co-pilot who took over when there was nothing to do but routine flying. These gave position, height, speed, estimated time of arrival at, say Goose Bay, and had a space for 'additional information'. Here the Goose Bay card said, '30 minutes behind schedule', and was received coolly. I kept that one because of some sketchy technical-looking drawings on the back, accompanied by a note of my own: HRH (after giving me this instrument lesson before going up front) 'Oh, well, let's see if we can find this place.'

The service at Flitcham might have been in any country church. The familiar hymns. The traditional contest for pitch and tempo between organ and congregation. Probably a better than average attendance. But something unreal for me, in joining the 'Amen' to 'A Prayer for the Queen's Majesty', personalised by the slight, pink-coated figure in the pew in front.

There was a departure from the general form when the service ended with the national anthem. I failed to notice, busy with my reedy but loyal baritone, if all the occupants of the pew in front took part. It would have meant an adjustment to the words.

'Send me victorious'? Hardly, I should think. Queen Victoria
might have done it.

That night after dinner, says my tape:

'. . .a general exodus into the, I suppose drawing room they
call it, big, with the TV going, a documentary about Pavlova, and
we all distributed ourselves, watching it, some sitting on the
floor, and I realised the Queen wasn't there, then she crept in
wearing something gold, short sleeves, a plaster on one arm
because she's in the middle of inoculations for Australia and New
Zealand, and knelt on a stool at a colossal jig-saw laid out on a
table there at the far end. . .'

I felt a pang of negligence. I was sitting beside Sir Martin
Charteris. I said, 'Does she mind just being taken no notice of?'
He assured me she was perfectly content. 'Don't feel you have to
spring up or anything.' So I didn't. But still felt I should.

'Well, good luck in Mexico,' said the Queen later, retiring for
the night. Jock had dutifully reminded her that we should not be
meeting again. I should be leaving for King's Lynn after Monday's early breakfast. Prince Philip, also about to disappear (both
to bows and curtseys), asked what time I was going. I told him.
'Oh, well,' – laughing – 'in that case, goodbye'. Prince Charles
had already roared back to Cambridge, in something fast and
sporty.

Princess Anne said, 'See you in the morning, then.' This was
so. When she appeared at breakfast I said, 'I didn't think you
meant it.' 'I knew you didn't,' she said, collecting scrambled egg.
It was good manners for one of the family to see me off.

At the station my chauffeur, with EIIR on his hat, unloaded not
only my bag but two pheasants in a cardboard box with a tie-on
label printed 'From Her Majesty the Queen', and my name filled
in. This I held prominently when I later joined the taxi-queue at
Euston. No one took any notice.

I had left a farewell note with Jock for Lady Rose. She presently
wrote back to say she was sorry we had missed each other. Some
muddle over times. I had cheered up the weekend, she said, and
I wondered how. There was a postscript: 'So glad you weren't
sick.'

Ten

THE BOSS AND THE BOOK

I HAD A green card to get me past the policeman on the gate. Still have. It should have been handed in at the end of 1971, when the palace and I had no further business together. No one asked for it. It had no photograph. I would sometimes just hold it up, from the car or taxi, and be waved through. No doubt things have been tightened up since then. Even more feloniously, I hung on to a couple of lapel badges, red and gold enamel crowns, one with a safety-pin fitting, the other designed for a buttonhole.

These were useful for outings, especially abroad, identifying a member of the royal party. It was pleasant to be approached by our hostess in Greenland, at a grand US-Danish reception, wondering if she would be out of order in asking the guest of honour to sign her visitors' book: even pleasanter to agree to put in a word for her.

Otherwise my souvenirs are few. Going through photographs for the book I found one highly characteristic of its subject, full-face, listening, intent, at some conference or other. This I stole, but must have owned up. Jumbo Thorning, Detective Chief-Superintendent, who had been one of the small Mexico contingent, served me with a summons or charge-sheet, signed 'Jefferies, J.', ordering my appearance before the Board of the Green Cloth (a body exerting judicial authority over offenders within a two-hundred-yard radius of the palace). I didn't appear, but kept and framed the picture, by then autographed. It hangs beside one of Prince Philip's paintings, also autographed, which he sent me that year with a royal Christmas card.

And I have the cufflinks. A gilded 'P' under a coronet. There had been a parting exchange of gifts. I wanted to give him something. He had fitted me uncomplainingly into his crowded life. Randle Cooke, his equerry, had seen no bar to this. 'Something small and useful.' A gold ball-point with his birth-date engraved seemed about right. 'Snap,' he said, producing from his pocket the green leather box. I wore the links for some TV occasion, round about publication time. 'Ah,' said the keen-eyed

interviewer – '*Punch* cufflinks.' For once I disclaimed that treasured association.

But all this lay ahead.

On the morning of our first meeting I was in a highly nervous
state. This seemed communicated to Prince Philip – he was
nervous, that is, for my nervousness – and the tape of the interview is full of his rasping throat-clearings, not natural with him.
Bill Heseltine, the other member of the planning party, held, I
felt, in his quiet easing of the discussion, a watching brief as
much as for me as for the boss. Well, I needed help, the boss
didn't. But he withheld none from me, either then or afterwards.
We had, of course, a unity of interest, both wanting the book to
be right – at any rate true. It was probably as hard for him to enter
my world as for me to enter his. He may or may not have had any
inkling of my doubts and insecurities – I mean over the whole
rash project as distinct from that particular morning. They were
in any case irrelevant. This was an exercise that had been decided
upon. The thing was to get on with it, directly, practically,
economically. His very quick mind, taking a point immediately,
made me feel even more bumbling. Though I had sent, through
Bill Heseltine, some preliminary ideas (which in execution, as
with any blueprint of mine, proved useless at the workbench). I
hear myself on the tape, during consideration of some point or
other, with pauses and throat-clearings, saying anything for the
sake of saying something, thus getting into shallow backwaters
where I never wanted to be. These navigational muffings were
patiently   considered.   'Well,   of   course,   you   could   do
that. . .[Hrrm]. . .It's up to you. But wouldn't you perhaps have
thought it better to. . .?'

I continually would have. My original ideas about how to do
the book seemed more and more superficial. All the marks of any
magazine penny-catcher about the Royals. He had my notes on
his knee, and made the point thoughtfully as he turned each now
dreaded page. From quite early, on the transcribed tape, I can tell
that the point had already pierced me, with a stab of inadequacy
for this whole crazy exercise. My questions got wilder and more
useless. I had asked about speech-making. Why had I asked
about speech-making? Though, by chance, I could back it with a
topical reference.

B. What happened last night, Sir? Did you have a good reception for your speech last night?

HRH. Well, it's almost impossible to tell. You know, you make
a speech and people clap. Sit down and go home. Period.

B. I was thinking, hearing. . .I heard a bit of your speech on the

news this morning. It was. . .I. . .in fact this thing about pollu-
tion and mess of car-dumps and things that you've said many
times, I was thinking of the. . .you have to find a new way, the
things you want to keep saying. . .[Founders to a halt]

HRH. [Helping] Yes, up to a point. I haven't actually said it all
that often. The folklore builds up. You say something once, and
because people remember it they think you've said it about ten
times. Because normally you have to say a thing ten times before
they notice it at all.

B. Yes.

HRH. And if they're conscious of hearing someone say something they automatically assume it's the only thing he ever said.
It's his gramophone record, you know?

B. Yes.

HRH. And then, of course, much more is read into it than was
ever there.

B. Yes.

HRH. I mean, a casual remark of absolutely total insignificance
on a television programme makes an indelible impression,
whereas something where people get up and cheer, at a dinner,
doesn't even get a line the next day.

The tape remorselessly records my further casual remarks of
absolutely total insignificance, until I somehow wrench things
round to asking if I could attend affairs he was speaking at, or
visiting, or opening, or presiding over or. . .

HRH. Oh, surely. That's the easiest thing in the world. Yes.

There was a pause. Though muffled on this side of the palace,
and the tape doesn't get it, I remember the boom and blare of the
Guards band in the forecourt. People would be pressed against
the railings, wondering what was happening inside.

B. [Plunging about in my copy of the notes] I've got myself so
organised over this that I don't know where I am.

Bill and the boss both laughed. That's always something.

Bill. When you wrote you were wondering about going to
Australia and New Zealand.

B. Yes, I. . .Oh. well, I put that in my letter to His Royal
Highness, I think rather nervously slipped in after the stuff
about. . .

HRH. You were thinking of coming to New Zealand?

B. Well, I wasn't specifically thinking about. . .but if I could see
some sort of foreign. . .

HRH. In that case I think I can think of something which might
suit you quite well.

That was how Mexico drifted in. He was going there in February after an official visit to Cape Kennedy. 'Then I go on to Vancouver and join the Queen. The point is that I shall be flying myself by Andover all the way, and as I do quite a lot of this it might be quite interesting for you. But it's five days' flying. You would have a lot of time on your hands and take your typewriter with you.' Laughter. I was feeling better. 'But the thing I couldn't do would be get you back, so I don't know how you–'

B. [Emboldened] You're not going to charge me for the outward journey though?

HRH. No, you won't even get. . .I don't know quite how we do that. [Laughs] I could make you a temporary private secretary.

Bill. Yes, why not. Extra equerry.

B. That would be nice.

Bill. What about seating them all? This isn't a very big aircraft.

HRH. The thing is I wasn't going to take the staff anyway, only a policeman.

B. And no Press?

HRH. No fear.

B. Perfect.

That tape came out in transcription at thirty-eight pages. It will be clear that I haven't quoted much. Silly questions. Tolerant answers. There were things I wanted more sensibly to ask, but had delicate misgivings. I hadn't felt I could ask about money, a curiously taboo subject at all levels of society. But he wanted me to ask about money. Indeed, suggested it. 'Leslie will tell you everything.' (Poor, reluctant Leslie Treby, HRH's accountant.)

Some of my questions opened up windows. Or the answers did. About his early life ('Talk to my sisters'). About the Navy ('Get on to Mike Parker'). About Gordonstoun ('Go and see the Margrave of Baden').

But most of the talk sought to solve my problems about how to do the book. Prince Philip, who had done books of his own, and was to do more, had ideas, but didn't push them.

B. I'm just groping for something that feels like a form.

HRH. Well, I would have suggested that you don't even contemplate the form until you've collected the information. I think that if you decide now, you'll begin to look for information to fit the form. Then if you come across something later on, you're stymied, because you won't be able to fit it in. I'm only saying this, because I found this very much with Cawston's film [*The Royal Family*] for instance, that he'd rather made up his mind how he was going to make it and the result was that it was almost impossible to go back, because if you suggested anything he said well, it doesn't fit in, I mean I can't, the pattern is like this, you know?

B. Yes.

HRH. I mean, start with a blank mind, collect the material and see where it leads you. Then if you sat down again, you see what I mean, you're in a position to say all right, let's do it like this.

B. But this has got to be done in a year.

HRH. There's no reason why you shouldn't spend about a month doing that.

B. But—

HRH. You've got to do it sooner or later.

B. I know I have.

HRH. I'm not trying to tell you how to do it. I mean it's just the way *I* would proceed.

B. Yes. Do you feel you want to see this stuff, piecemeal as I write it?

HRH. No.

B. Or at all?

HRH. It's up to you. Whatever's helpful to you. I can certainly look through it if you like. If you'd like me to. If not, I mean, obviously not. Use me as it suits you. If you say look, I'm stuck, what do I do next, or I've written this bit, do you think it's lousy? If on the other hand you want to work like an artist, with a shroud over your head, and on no account is anyone to see, that's up to you. *I'm* not making any conditions.

B. So I can come and see you when I'm in trouble?

HRH. Certainly. Oh, yes. Oh, lord, yes.

He got up. My slot in his day's engagements had run its course. 'Well,' shaking hands and laughing – 'will that start you off?'

On my first day working in the Pine Room at Buckingham Palace I found a note safety-pinned to one of the small, decorative chairs: 'Sir, I would not use this, as the colour comes off the seat. Eileen.' Another note appeared after a week or two, reporting that the seat had been re-covered and was now usable without risk.

The room overlooked Constitution Hill. Nowadays, rarely passing that way, I still look up at its long windows and remind myself, though with difficulty, that I once regarded it as my own. 'It's a pretty scruffy hole,' Prince Philip had said, leading me into it from his own room adjoining. It was large, high and L-shaped, with royal portraits, some model ships. I would have preferred something smaller, a working womb. It was hardly my place to say so. I decided to work in the small leg of the L, at least snug on two sides. A desk at once arrived there. It was probably to Bill Heseltine that I complained of the remoteness of the telephone, at the far end of the longer leg. Energies must be conserved. The next day the instrument was on the desk, its wall-point resited. I should have to get on to people, after all. Not always 'the boss', but his people. Admiral Sir Christopher Bonham-Carter, then his treasurer and private secretary. His equerry, Randle Cooke. HM Yacht *Britannia*. Windsor, certainly, when researches spilled over into the Queen's affairs. The boss's own general office, in the corridor below with many more, where doors were for some reason always open, and a babel of intercoms constantly chattered.

On the whole I found it easier to write to people. And appeals for information, or discussion meetings, would come better, I felt, on Buckingham Palace paper. My wish was somebody's command. Without question, a huge sheaf arrived, and lasted me to the end, a few spares remaining for the amusement of reliable friends. ('Dear Peter: Excuse stationery. Am using up old bits. . .')

In largely non-smoking premises, ashtrays were at first a problem. Outside, in 'my' corridor, a string of glass-topped cases stretched away, enviably displaying gemmed and golden trinkets. It was tempting to extract some suitable receptacle. But the Queen's room was at the far end. – I sometimes saw a hair-drier outside it in the distance. We never met in the palace, but I wouldn't have wanted to be caught borrowing a Fabergé snuff-box. So far I had been accepted as trustworthy, a state of things which continued.

When I wrote to Sir Martin Charteris, seeking an hour or two of his time, I asked if I could put him on tape to discuss Prince Philip as a father – Charteris was at the time the Queen's assistant private secretary, but had been with them both since the marriage – the response was characteristic, not only of him but in general. He would be delighted. 'I do not in the least mind tape-recorders when they are under the control of reliable and honourable people. Please bring yours.'

During our talk, I remember, his intercom buzzed. 'Yes, Ma'am, of course.' He apologised for having to leave for five minutes.

I ended up with a lot of tapes. When the book was done I asked Heseltine if he would like them back to be wiped or destroyed. 'Oh, no,' he said. 'Try not to leave them in taxis.' Not all were top quality recordings. One of them, the microphone on the cheeseboard at a scratch lunch for two in Prince Philip's office, was much impaired by the crunch of celery.

Eileen, the diligent and thoughtful lady responsible for tidying up the end-of-the-day mess in my workroom, solved the ashtray problem, though at first only temporarily. It was over this article, or rather its speedy disappearance, that we had our only meeting when I telephoned her for help. 'I know what happened,' she said, appearing with a replacement. 'That one came from the Privy Purse. They'll have taken it back. They can get very snotty down there.'

No one ever got snotty with me. They could have had cause. Their lives were full already. By a strong corporal of Marines, the girls in the Duke of Edinburgh's office kept sending up stacks of requested files, assiduously tagged and cross-referenced. I brought them occasional flowers, and arrived one morning at a bad time, armed with the daffodils of spring. The Guard was changing. Sightseers were thick. I had to get to work. 'Now, sir, quick!' said the constable at the gate, recognising a gap in the ranks. I scuttled across the forecourt, dropping a bloom or two. 'Give her my love,' yelled the crowd.

(At departure times I devised a private joke. The two sentries, at fixed intervals, came smartly to attention before marching from box to box. A pause on the Privy Purse steps could synchronise these honours with my emergence. Gratifying.)

I used to go down to the equerries' room for tea, where the sandwiches were circular, signifying distinction from plebeian squares or triangles. Most of the courtiers would turn up, asking how my work was going. They made me feel part of things. It was the same at the staff lunches, presided over with dignity by the Master of the Household. My only embarrassment was having to do my own carving from the joint. No carver, even at home, I must have left crude hackings for the next comer to the side table.

It occurs to me only now that someone must have paid for all those refreshments, so complacently accepted. A blushing thought, that perhaps those well-graced gentlemen were carrying me. Or was I a charge on the Privy Purse? I prefer to think so.

But also the mid-day breaks were sometimes useful for taking willing helpers out to lunch. Charteris, Heseltine, Randle Cooke, the Admiral, Jim Orr (once at Gordonstoun with 'the boss', later one of his right-hand men), Leslie Treby. Others, no doubt. Accountant Treby, perhaps more than any of them, had had profound inner struggles in overcoming the ingrained reticence. Money men are tight-lipped by nature. But he had been told to tell all, and steeled himself to do it.

The Savage Club was convenient for these entertainings, then at the bottom of St James's Street, five minutes' walk. It was one of my three fixed points. The palace, the club, the London Library. The path was well-trodden by the time the year was over.

Just before I was flown to Mexico in a slow, turbo-prop Queen's Flight Andover which I felt shouldn't really have been stretched that far, even with five overnight stops on the way, a group captain from RAF Benson rang with a request for my hat-size, glove, waist, leg and other measurements. 'It's just for your Arctic survival kit,' he said. And explained in the pause at my end that they could have made me up a jungle kit, but felt on balance that we were more likely to forceland in the Arctic. The fur-lined parka and mitts, the goggles, the snowboots, would be more practical there. The package, as I later saw laid out for my inspection at Benson, had other practical items: fire-making pellets, an ice-axe, a fishing-line, a hunting knife – and a whetstone for the knife, in case of blunting on too many bears. The wing-commander who showed me over the plane, with assurances that it would be adequately serviced before departure, said that in the event of ditching, a self-inflating dinghy would be automatically released. Perhaps I looked unassured, because he hurried on, 'It has a hood and everything. Very nice when you're in there.' No doubt it was all stowed on to the aircraft. I didn't ask. Preferred not to think about it. I could see 'the boss', in his natural resourcefulness, killing bears, making fires, angling through polar ice-holes, probably photographing one or two rare indigenous birds on the side. Myself, no.

The passenger load was small. Yet to meet HRH's 'policeman', I had a vague pre-vision of a uniform and helmet. Jumbo – Detective Chief-Superintendent Thorning – turned out to be casually suited, quiet, huge and affable. But with a towering presence in action. To the importunate at Cape Kennedy, say, bringing their private cameras too close, his murmured, 'I think I should put that away,' was enough. He wasn't going to hit them, but they didn't know that. It could have been a felling blow.

Official cameras, or at least professional, abounded throughout the trip. They all missed me, except for some newsreel footage showing me in a hard hat, about to follow Prince Philip up Apollo 13, then readied for launching. (We had instructions to abandon the hats at the top. Dropped from that height they would kill people.) I ought to have pushed into the photographs more. Something for my souvenirs. The hanging-back was perhaps hereditary. Old and rare family groups always show Father on an outer flank at the back, hardly squeezing a nose in. At Kennedy, where the British Consul had flown in from Miami, there could have been few shots of the Prince without the Consul beaming at his side. Up front in the Andover once I did persuade valet Joe Pearce to capture me beside my pilot, and he got the back of our heads nicely. Joe's inclusion in the party had for some reason surprised me. I idly said so to Christopher Bonham Carter, puzzling him for a moment. Then, 'But you don't expect him to clean his own boots?' I supposed not, on second thoughts.

I had other worries for the Admiral. 'Greenland? What on earth do I wear in Greenland?' This was dismissed. 'Remember you step straight out of the plane into a heated car.' That happened. Also in Stornoway, Iceland, Labrador. Fuelling stops, these, not overnight. But protocol demanded, while tanks were filled and engines checked, official calls on resident diplomats or top military brass. Much coffee flowed. Nothing stronger for my pilot. 'Coffee, coffee,' he groaned somewhere, after one of these obligatory rites. 'My stomach's washing around like a snipe-bog.' I was now feeling on easier, even companionable, terms, though not losing sight of precedence. I got this wrong, however, on one of the earliest strips of tarmac, where a formal group was drawn up for farewells. I waited to be last aboard the plane, mystified by Joe's and Jumbo's urgent signals from the cabin windows. The last aboard should of course have been HRH. I apologised as the door closed and he moved for'ard to the flight deck. 'It doesn't really matter,' he said. 'It's just that when I wave goodbye I could knock your glasses off.' I thereafter made sure that this would not occur.

In Florida the car was not heated but cooled. Also immense and Presidentially long. (HRH, as we walked in: 'Good heavens. Do they keep adding extra sections?')

In Mexico there was no car at all. Anyway for me. I knew this was to be the parting of the ways, but the habit of waiting motorcades had seized me in under a week. It was a shock, abandoned at the airport, seven thousand feet up, with nothing for comfort but a shimmering view of distant Popocatapetl. This was the end of the temporary courtier's life. I had been a power for hostesses in Sondestrom. I had chatted on level terms with Her Majesty's Ambassador to Iceland, whose son, a boy much titivated, had bowed embarrassingly low over my proffered hand.

In Government House, Ottawa, my breakfast order, solicited by a polished equerry the night before, had been brought in silver on a silver tray and placed on a warm, broad windowsill. I looked

Workroom, Cuckfield

Workroom, Buckingham Palace

Keeping an eye on my royal pilot.

Over Mexico in the Andover

Basil Boothroyd, Esq.,
Green Ridges,
Cuckfield,
Haywards Heath,
Sussex.

In trouble with
the law.

In trouble with
the law.

(See p.160)

Information has this day been laid before me, the undersigned,

In the Inner London Area and in the Metropolitan Police District

by Ivor Thorning, Chief Superintendent,
of Metropolitan Police
that you, xxxx between xxxx 1969 and .19 71 .
at Buckingham Palace
in the Area and District aforesaid, did without good and sufficient
cause take and carry away without the consent of
the owner an unsigned photographic portrait of
Schhhh........ (you know who!)

XXXXXXXXXXXXXXXXXXXXXXXXXXXXX

XXXX

Against the Peace, &c.

You are therefore hereby summoned to appear before the
Board of the Green Cloth XXXXXXXX Court

XX
A date to be arranged.
on XX XXXXXXXXXXXXXXXXXXXXXXXXXXXXXXX
XXXXXXXXXXX XXXXX aXXXXXXXX
answer to the said information.

Dated the 7th day of June, 19 71

Jeffries J.

Metropolitan Stipendiary Magistrate
Justice of the Peace for the Inner London Area.

M.C.A.2

———

SUMMONS

M.P.-69-62186/2M Pads

The receipt of this summons should be acknowledged to the Clerk
of the Court forthwith on the tear-off slip below. **Please sign and return
this slip. The correct postage must be paid.**

BALMORAL CASTLE

20 Sept.

Dear Mr. Boothroyd, Thank you for your letter.

BUCKINGHAM PALACE

BALMORAL CAST.
21 December.

Would you not think a slightly unbalanced

Dear Basil - (It may & its easier to spell!)

WINDSOR CAST.
29 December.

yours ever

Philip

Dear Basil,

Dear Basil!

SANDRINGHAM, NORFOLK
29 Jan.

In your note

H. M. YACHT BRITANNIA

yours sincerely

BALMORAL CASTLE
19 December -

Dear Basil,
Wonderous news

MEMORANDUM
From

H.R.H. The Duke of Edinburgh.

Believe me, Sir, Your Royal Highness's
humble and obedient servant,

Various correspondence

Press photograph captioned 'Prizes of Success'. The Daimler had passed through many hands, and was sold the following week for £50

At my patient piano

out, through panes misting with my coffee, at the swaddled but freezing soldier in deep snow, stamping his feet and guarding me. Well, us. At Patrick Air Force Base, in VIP quarters handy for the next day's rocketry, top US generals and space eggheads had been deferential, bringing me chairs. Astronaut John Young (43 orbits) answered my searching questions ('What does it feel like to be weightless?') with polite restraint. Prince Philip's questions had been rather better informed, when the time came for the 'presentations'. I had imagined these, scheduled in the itinerary programme, to be in the form of gifts. They proved to be high-powered lectures, with pointers, illuminated wall diagrams, and unassimilable space-talk by clean-cut American PR officers. Unassimilable for me. But speakers were apt to be interrupted, and indeed thrown, by keen interrogation from their principal guest. Unbroken fluency was their line. To be suddenly asked, 'When do you lock on to the S-Band?' 'Is it a passive dish?' 'But doesn't the attitude control system give you a slight Delta B?' was new and uncomfortable.

It wasn't as if he'd been mugging up on the plane, in the intervals of actually driving it. He had talked – about everything from painting and polo to the end of the world (sun finally blotted out by fumes); from systems and theories of government to Robert W. Service ('You mean you don't know Dangerous Dan McGrew'?' – and quoting.) The threat of extinction to the marine turtle. Or he read heavy works, one of them entitled *Institute of Biology Symposium No.19*, with a piece on 'The Optimum Population for Britain'. This, unexpectedly, at times made him laugh, or sparked him to a discourse on contraception, or a tangential tirade against bureaucracy and form-filling. Somehow before Florida he wrote a piece of his own, for something European, which amused him because it was to appear in sixteen languages. He later asked me to look at it and suggest improvements, which I was pleased to do. Extra equerries take on anything.

Our VIP accommodation within easy blast-off for the Space Centre was called 'Surfside Manor', a low shack on the Atlantic's edge rather like a set of superior holiday-camp chalets fused together. Prince Philip and I, on the evening of our arrival, strolled the sandy beach. We might have been anybody. Except that he, otherwise in holiday spirits, was disapproving of the American soldier, armed with everything short of a bazooka, who followed watchfully behind. My companion produced one of his forthright statements. 'If it hadn't been for all the security they would never have shot Kennedy.' I left it, and instead showed him a newspaper kindly provided by our hosts. It reported that Prince Charles had made his maiden speech in the House of Lords. 'Mm,' said his father.

There was to be another breath of England at that night's small, informal meal. We were half a dozen or so. Dr Debus, the Centre's Director and his No.1. A general. Astronaut Young, who was to be our next day's tour guide. The talk was relaxed. A good deal of laughter. The Director said that American reaction to the space programme was often in the form of letters from indignant feminists asking why no women had gone up yet. 'Still' – from Prince Philip – 'you did have a Venus Probe'. We were into something more down to earth with the coffee and what the menu described as 'Cordials', when the general, who may have been bracing himself meanwhile, suddenly stood up and proposed the Queen's health. It wasn't a speech, but an impressive performance, since it embodied most of the monarch's titles and dignities, which took some time. We sat down to a hush. Someone had to respond. For a paralysing moment I wondered if it ought to be me. But the guest of honour quickly recovered. 'Well, thanks very much.' And presently, to his neighbour, 'Go on with what you were saying about continental drift.'

The following morning, standing with Cdr. Young on the giant rocket-transporter, half the size of Lord's, and with an engine at each corner, I was still hard pushed for intelligent questions. 'How many miles to the gallon?' 'I guess around 270 gallons to the mile,' said the Commander, doing his best, and dodged further technical enquiries by calling my attention to some indeterminate lumps in a glass case. Moon rocks.

By the last leg of our journey, as we droned over inhospitable-looking brown terrain, I must have been showing a little wear and tear. Prince Philip, putting aside some papers, said 'Care for a stretch-out?' He got up and released a bunk bed from the cabin wall. I was an old gent. I stretched out. 'That's Maya country,' he mused, looking down. As so often, I missed my reference books. But it seems to have been Yucatan, because when I woke up he was putting us down into Merida, its capital city.

My copy of the day's schedule read:

0930 Depart Surfside Manor by car
0955 Arrive Patrick AFB
1000 Depart by Andover
1300 Arrive Merida for refuelling
1345 Depart by Andover
1650 Arrive Mexico City. Depart by car for the residence of Mrs

Pagliai, where His Royal Highness and party will stay while in Mexico City.

For once, not strictly accurate. It was all the party but me. Mrs Pagliai turned out, smiling on the tarmac, to be Merle Oberon, whom I hadn't seen since *Wuthering Heights*. His Royal Highness and Jumbo Thorning kissed her as an old friend. The cars sped off. Now, like an ordinary person, I had to find my own hotel in Mexico City, and somehow found a handsome high-riser with a garden on the roof; flowers, ornamental ponds, brilliant shrubs. Did it survive, I wonder, the fearful Act of God that wasted the world's biggest city in 1985? At the time I only wondered what I was doing in that place. By comparison, Buckingham Palace seemed like home. And I had to get back there. Scores of letters to write, seeking help. Hundreds of files to read, seeking facts. It was late February. Fifteen months for the review copies to be out. And, so far, not a word of the book on paper.

Some of Prince Philip's ideas to help me were too deep, too difficult. One day, when at last the book was thickening, two pages of handwritten foolscap arrived ('He never dictates, loves putting pen to paper,' Christopher Bonham-Carter had said). No preamble, no signature. The familiar upright hand with its feeling of thoughts directly on to the page. I saw from the opening paragraphs, a tight summary of the workings of a constitutional monarchy, that I should soon be out of my depth. Then:

When the throne is occupied by a Queen the evolutionary effect has always been deeply influenced by their personalities – Qs Elizabeth, Anne, Victoria. We are probably witnessing yet another shift in the powers and functions of the hereditary head of State. At the same time, the combined effect of the whole family creates a 'style'. I think you might like to discuss the changes in style and function since the last reign and what – if any – influence I have had on them. Influence can be negative as well as positive, in the sense that by *not* doing certain things these areas have become neglected or less important. For instance, we don't provide much encouragement or 'leadership' in the world of art and music. . .

One of the most obvious changes is the ease of travel, both internally in UK and overseas. Does greater personal knowledge of the Sovereign mean less mystery? Does my travelling have any point. . .?

You might like to say something about the Cmmwlth. Monarchies & Republics, 'Old-White' and 'new-ex-colonial'

Black. . .The problems of an absentee Monarchy & what might be the next stage. . .

This was hardly my field, but that of the serious writer, the constitutional historian. There was nothing for it but to write back saying so, and at some length, to take the bluntness out. I heard nothing more on that. No hard feelings. I see that my copy reply has a scribbled note in my hand. 'Dictated at palace. Their spelling mistakes.' That was the sort of thing I was better at.

Phil went to Munich with me; it was an outing; we weren't seeing much of each other. But she declined to meet the Princesses. It was always her line, and I had long given up trying to talk her out of it, that people didn't want to see her but me. The opposite, had I ever been able to persuade her, could often have been true.

Princess Sophie of Hanover had written charmingly. She and her sister would be delighted to drive in and talk about their brother. They had much admired my article about him in *Punch*. They suggested a meeting at the Hotel Vier Jahreszeiten on the Maximilianstrasse. Five stars, I saw from the AA's Continental handbook. Well, I had my credit card.

We swept in quite grandly the evening before. Buoyed by royal involvements I sent for the manager even as I signed the register, showing my card meanwhile to some underling. The manager had beautiful English, which was an advantage. For me, that is, having only three words of German. I explained that Their Royal Highnesses would be calling on me in the morning, and asked for a suitable room to be made available for private conversation. We then ate an expensive dinner and retired.

The Princesses were punctual, smiling and easy. I hadn't seen the room. But when we were escorted to an upper floor, my tape-recorder to hand, it was a surprise. It had dimension; it was hot; the polished table was symmetrically laid with sixteen fresh blotting pads. Perhaps the manager had mistaken the number of Princesses. It also overlooked the Maximilianstrasse, not only loud with traffic but in the course of being dug up down one side for the installation – perhaps merely an extension – of an under-ground railway. In two years' time Munich was to have the Olympic Games. The noise might have been governable if my guests hadn't complained of the heat, not without cause. I said I could probably have it turned down. Oh, no, they would not put me to that trouble. Just to open the windows would do. I opened them. The din drove in. Both Prince Philip's sisters were eager to talk about him, with love, animation, rushes of overlapping reminiscence. . .

'Oh, yes, that was that lovely year when we were staying with Helen of Roumania—'

'And Philip was about seven and a great show-off, standing on his head and fell off the hay wagon and broke his front tooth—'

'Yes, and of course, and Michael was about three months younger than Philip, and was King, and we went to Bucharest, and our grandmother, old Princess Henry—'

The roaring and hooting and drilling clamoured up from the street below, obliterating key words, names, whole sentences.

'. . .and. . .Hideous castle but. . .very sweet together because he had snow white hair and she was pitch black. . married Marie Bonaparte. . .mouth of the Danube. . .ponies. . .because of course Philip had never seen a horse. . .Wolfsgarten, you know, because of course the Grand Duke of Hesse. . .'

They were sweet, kind, ecstatically eager to help. There was matchless material here, but the Maximilianstrasse was too much for it. Transcribing the tape, when I felt strong enough to try, was like reassembling the shattered Portland Vase.

Periodic refreshments were brought in. Whisky-sours come to mind. But it seemed the least I could do was to offer lunch. Princess Sophie said that would be wonderful. 'Not here, I think?' She knew of somewhere else. And her husband was downstairs, Prince George of Hanover. Could she bring him too? I said that would be wonderful.

It would have been more so, the ignoble thought occurred to me in the restaurant, which was small but classy, to have eaten in the hotel and put it on the bill.

We stayed another couple of nights. We had never been to Germany and were unlikely to go again. Phil, with her persistent self-effacement, had not had much of an outing so far. The cost of two night's opera tickets, secured through the hotel desk, would be effortlessly dischargeable at the flick of a card. Unfortunately, when it came to leaving for Lake Constance, the Margrave of Baden, and Schloss Salem (where I was to learn about Gordons-toun, its parent establishment being Salem School), things went badly. The underling, now having his day off or being otherwise absent, had not understood about the card. The manager arrived, this time without being sent for. No. Nein. 'I fear we have no arrangement.'

I hadn't brought much cash. Most of it was now dispersed. It was a Sunday. A thin time lay ahead. Before setting off we lunched in the backest of streets. Bread-soup, and Beatles on the juke-box. Had I not at least had the foresight to rent a car from home, payment in sterling, things might have been worse. We thought they were going to be when we finally found the Munich rental office by long and costly cab. No, said the staff, who wore lapel slogans saying 'We try to do better.' Nein. They could find nothing about a car for Herr Boothroyd. There was no arrangement. I asked them to try to do better. After an exhaustive search of records they eventually did. But we had suffered by then. The car was not the one specified, but something small and strange. I mastered most of it by the time we made Lake Constance and our chosen non-star hotel. I am not good with cars, and Phil didn't even drive. I was tired, preoccupied with trying to place old Princess Henry in Prince Philip's family tree. It snowed. At the hotel the door of the sliding wardrobe came loose and fell on Phil. It was some weeks since Mexico, but I was missing the smoothed and carefree life.

Luckily I had little entertaining to do at Lake Constance, where the Margrave gave me a free tea. I didn't take the recorder: I had had recorders for the moment. This was just as well, as we ate on either side of a perfectly colossal circular table. If it hadn't revolved at a touch, to bring things within reach, one could have starved at it. One could also have seen a tape-recorder circling out of range as one's host fancied another slice of cake.

Not much, in any case, came out of that last pilgrimage. The Schloss was bigger than Buckingham Palace, but had a bare feeling. Its owner talked about it a lot – more than about Gordonstoun. 'We heat a few rooms and treat the corridors as streets. Throw a bucket of water down them in winter, you have the skating rink.' I didn't see the school part. I had used my three words of German to find a way into any of it. I stopped a solitary boy on his way across the acre of courtyard. Winding down my window after a search for the handle, 'Sprechen sie Englisch?' He hesitated, racking his education. 'Oui, un petit peu.'

Once more, after such adventures, it was good to be back in the palace's Pine Room, though other excursions still had to be made from there. Some with the Duke, to see him in action at drug rehabilitation centres, Awards ceremonies, Lord's Taverners evenings: others alone, to sift from files at Windsor, or lunch at RAF Benson with officers of The Queen's Flight. Such things were time-consuming, and meant absences from the typewriter. I tried to keep them near home. When, on an impulsive plunge, I proposed to accompany my subject to Helsinki, it was almost a relief to have the Admiral's memo turning me down. 'HRH says you are difficult to explain on official functions, which will be very much the case here.' It could have lost me three days. But a last few words had been added: 'Tall Ships fine, fix up with RC.'

I had asked at the same time if I could see HRH start the Tall Ships Race. Another rash request. Plymouth was a long way. But if I could get myself to Portsmouth, said Randle Cooke, fixing me up, why not go on to Plymouth in *Britannia*, which would be sailing for Portsmouth the night before? And HRH would chopper me back to Cowdray Park, his next stop. . .if I could get myself home from there.

I was the only passenger. My opulent suite had a notification on the state-room wall giving my emergency boat station as 'Royal Barge'. Before the start of the race the ship filled up somewhat. A lunch for fifty was to follow. I was strategically placed at a tip of the horseshoe-shaped table, well distanced from such fellow-guests as the Earl of Mount Edgcumbe and El Marques de Santa Cruz. When my host and pilot rose to his feet (it is a bonus for royalty that they can bring anything to an end just by standing up), I was able to make a dash for the Barge, and so to the chopper, keeping nobody waiting.

With Prince Philip at the controls of the helicopter I had hoped for some talk with him, a chance always to be seized. In the event, the machine was so huge that the pilot was on the second storey, the passenger below. We had a word or two as we came down on the Cowdray turf. 'Did you enjoy yourself?' I said I didn't think it had produced much for the book, but—

'You enjoyed yourself,' he said, laughing, and made off rapidly on foot.

My limousine, or village taxi, was waiting. 'Bring a camera,' I had told the lady driver. 'Get a shot of our arrival.' I was still thin on album material. She got the shot, which didn't come out. She was as disappointed, but less surprised, than I was. Later, the office sent me a sheaf of splendid official pictures of the occasion. All had missed me.

Despite a lurking sense of imposture, I was by now beginning to enjoy a certain reflected prestige. It brought small private amusements: as on a visit to Air Strike Command, High Wycombe, where the RAF Police, my old arm of the Service, were knife-sharp with their salutes, before jeeping me off to see Group Captain Caryl Gordon.

Gordon had long before been Prince Philip's flying instructor. Like everyone, he was eager to help, and by a wonderful stroke of luck had kept a detailed personal diary of those years. He handed it over with no signs of misgiving. He must have been of an equable temperament anyway, to judge from some of the entries.

Only a Flight-Lieutenant at the time, his briefing from the CO of the Central Flying School had ended, 'If you kill him, you realise what it will do to the Queen?' He had something of the Navy's style about him, if that can be said without offending the Air Force. Quiet, humorous, down-playing. I asked him what his job was. He supposed, he said, as if it were a thing he had given no close thought to, that it was to run the whole of the country's air defences.

Undeserved glory again shone when one of his telephones rang. 'Yes, sir, of course. . .' (I tried to think what ranks a Group Captain called Sir). . .'But I'm afraid just at the moment I have someone here from Buckingham Place.' He hung up, giving me a look. 'Nice to be able to do that,' he said, and took things up where we had left off.

But I never, with Prince Philip, quite re-established, had the chance to re-establish, the rapport, the relative intimacy, of flying and party companions, occupying spartan adjoining bunks in US Army outposts and arguing about who should be first with the bath. His calendar as usual was packed; my desk was tottering with files. He was always available, but mainly by correspondence. The book, filling my life, was only a speck on his. How was it going, people kept asking? It seemed ostentatiously self-pitying to tell the truth: that I saw no prospect of its ever being finished, and was more and more convinced, instead of less and less, that I had been an idiot to try.

Some shoulders I wept on. On none more freely – leaned on it too – than that of Michael Parker, by then back home in Australia but knowing more about my subject than anyone, in a friendship of kindred spirits begun in exultant rivalries as wartime destroyer Number Ones and nourished through Parker's five years as equerry-in-waiting to Princess Elizabeth and her husband until the Coronation (it had fallen to him, in Kenya, to break the news of George VI's death); another ten after that as Prince Philip's private secretary. Then, in 1957, though it now sounds absurd, he decided that his divorce must disqualify him from royal service, and resigned. Both Prince Philip and the Queen tried to dissuade him. It was like him to insist.

I had written to him on my first sheet of palace stationery. If I had written on a tear-off note pad the result would have been the same. I knew within reading a dozen words of his letter back that here was a friend and ally, warm, spontaneous, light-hearted, sincere. He signed it Mike. I flooded him with tapes. Questions, questions. He flooded me with answers, answers. They must have taken hours of his time and thought, delvings in records and memory, intent on being absolutely truthful and stinting nothing of aid. He added incidentals, marginal recollections, larks and laughs as well as hard stories of way back and all over the world. The time came when he was overloading me with good things. After a two-hour reminiscence of Navy days in Malta, which mentioned the practice of ships' signalling each other with Biblical references, I sent him, by cable, Matthew 14.20: 'And they did all eat, and were filled; and they took up of fragments that remained twelve baskets full.' He sent back the same day, effervescently, Acts 2.26: 'Therefore did my heart rejoice, and my tongue was glad; moreover also my flesh shall rest in hope.'

Despite even his best efforts my own hopes seem to have been sagging again not long afterwards. I signalled a dark cry, Job 19.23: 'Oh, that my words were now written, oh that they were printed in a book!' and he boosted me with Revelation 6.2: 'And I saw, and behold a white horse, and he that was sat on him had a bow; and a crown was given unto him; and he went forth conquering, and to conquer.'

When my words were somehow written, and printed in a book, Mike, a man of contacts, got hold of an early copy and telephoned from Australia. I'd got it right, he said (if rather more extravagantly than that). I felt, and still feel when old misgivings gnaw, that if he thought so, in his closeness to its central figure, it perhaps was.

He was in London once, and we met. The only time. We embraced. He was just what he had seemed from his tapes, letters and signals. Open, true, full of sparkle at the fun of being alive.

Prince Philip returned my first draft, after some days of painful suspense, in a wrapper which also bore a Biblical inscription. Navy habits endure. This said 'Proverbs 28.23'. It crystallised at once the subject's widely unsuspected modesty, and one or two murmured hints uttered from time to time about the dangers of getting carried away: 'He that rebuketh a man, afterwards shall find more favour than he that flattereth with the tongue.' Yes, I probably had been carried away a bit with him and his world: partly because I had known little of either, beyond what had been written a hundred times by other writers, most of whom had got (and still get) a lot of it wrong.

But the pages inside the wrapper, rich in comment and correction, showed that I had got plenty of it wrong as well. My opinions were never challenged, unless based on some fallacious premise, but no error of fact got past him. There were liberal interleavings. Crisper amendments crammed in the margins. I had mixed up ships. ('No. *Valiant* was already in the Med. I left *Shropshire* in Durban by troopship Jan 41, joined *Valiant* in Alexandria.') I had miscredited things. ('Steady! The variety Club got Sinatra and the matinee was their idea, I just went to it.') Somewhere I described an 'official' trip to Argentina, with some polo involvement. He deleted the 'official', but this time with a note. ('There was nothing official about it & I paid for my ticket both ways.')

Many of the interleavings were longer, sometimes running to a second leaf (of his tear-off note pad): I had said that he felt the lack of a university education. His marginal note of a single word was scored out. I could still read 'Rubbish!' under the scoring. But more kindly second thoughts expanded on a separate sheet:

I really do not feel the lack of a university education. If you count it up I've spent just as long at various courses as any student working for a degree. My concern to deflate the importance of Universities is that they are becoming a fetish and an end in themselves. We should be more realistic about their value & their purpose.

On some wrong end of the stick about his flying:

Please don't say I want to go up when the Met men are against it, for one thing it isn't true because – oddly enough – I am concerned for my own neck! For another it will annoy all fliers and Met men. Indeed there have been times when I have overruled too eager pilots & refused to fly or be flown in adverse conditions.

And so it went on. Forty or fifty. Some comments long, some short. 'The dinner was in day clothes.' 'I have never set myself a fixed numbers of pictures to paint.' 'We wouldn't have played croquet in the rain!' (My attempt to reconstruct an early meeting with Princess Elizabeth, on a wet Sunday, when he was still a cadet at Dartmouth.) Sometimes merely enquiring. 'Why are you against nannies?'

He had also found the time for a covering letter from Balmoral. Four handwritten pages.

Herewith the two volumes of your considerable labours. I have

been through them with the intention of commenting on matters of fact and I think most of the notes refer to facts rather
than opinions. Some are to do with the selection of incidents,
but these are only meant as comments as I don't want to inhibit
your freedom to say what you like. . .

Then floods of suggestions. About form, arrangement, the
cumbersomeness (not his word) of trying to combine first-hand
observation with evidence that 'has had to be dredged up from
other sources'. And much more.
The ending was less disheartening, and meant to be:

If none of this appears sufficiently enthusiastic or eulogistic
please forgive me. In fact I enjoyed large pieces of it. I like the
general tone and in several instances you have shown a very
clear perception of the situation.
   I hope all this is of some help.
                    Yours sincerely
                         Philip

Though the time was shrieking past, and the publishers not
silent, it was all of some help. It helped me to cut, correct, amend
and resubmit the whole thing. It came back quickly. I read the
new covering letter first this time, the eye skipping.

. . .strikes me as greatly improved. . .wonders with the style
. . .bits of it hilariously funny. . .let a great friend of mine read
it. . .laughed in what I hope were all the right places. . .!
   Does it mean that you are positively finished with the book
as of now, apart from galley-proofs? Anyway I hope you have a
splendid Xmas and a well deserved rest.
                    Yours sincerely
                         Philip

No, it didn't mean that. Looking with more care I saw that
there were 'still one or two points which need checking and I
have inserted slips.' Fewer than before, but plenty. Embodying
them would be a splendid way of spending Xmas – not to say the
start of the new year. And I had a last short chapter to write. I sent
this to the publishers without letting him see it. But I sent him a
copy, pleading pressure of time. I called it 'First Person Singular'.
I was the first person. It tried to sum up, with snippets of what
he had said, done, written, feelings about him that had been

unmanageable to get in elsewhere. If they were of the sort that 'flattereth with the tongue', his rebuke was gentle.

Sandringham, Norfolk

Dear Basil,
    The other reason why you only sent the carbon is that you suspected I might hash it about & you had every right to suspect that I would!
    I see I ought to have been considerably more discreet in my letters! Is nothing sacred?! After reading that last chapter all I can say is – stand by for the critics. . .!
    It must be a marvellous feeling to be 'delivered'. All that remains is to wait for reactions and sales. I hope you've got a good nerve!

Yours ever
Philip

The book in fact topped the best-selling non-fiction lists for some weeks. People say those things don't mean anything. It meant something to me. Less perhaps than what its subject wrote in my own copy.

Discharged with full remission for considerate behaviour after two years hard labour.
    With gratitude for taking on this appalling task.

Philip
1971

There was another letter that I now re-read with discomfort. Not for what it says, but for one of mine it was answering. It was not from Prince Philip, but from the Queen's Private Secretary, and with all the courtesy of that courteous man. He thanked me for my letter.

I have shown it to the Queen and she greatly appreciates your offering to dedicate your book about the Duke of Edinburgh to her. There are, however, certain rules about such matters which Her Majesty has herself approved; they are not, I should add, concerned with artistic merit. In the circumstances I am to say that Her Majesty does not feel able to accept your kind offer.'

It ended with a note in handwriting. 'So sorry to send you a negative answer, Yours sincerely, Michael Adeane.'

The dedication was eventually to Phil, and embodied a bad bit of word-play on Christian names, as if making her the second choice wasn't ungrateful enough. She had had a poor time of it since that weekend when Mark Longman hung over us both as a questionmark. It barely salves my conscience that at least when the American publishers offered a crazy six-week promotion tour, eighteen major cities and a standing speech in any city where I could still stand up, I insisted that she came too.

That was the next thing. I was still not 'positively finished' with the book.

Eleven

TELLING AMERICA

WHERE ARE YOU now, Casper Citron, Nami O'Shima, Nick Cal-anni, Lucia Perrigo, Arn Zenker, Bella Stumbo, Dick Guildenmeister, Starr Yelland, Irv Kupcinet, Sol Gramalia, Ruth Owvades, Jim Schmiedbauer, Don Azars, Lorraine Alvigi, Judy Muntz, Cheri Gay, Bill Balch, Ron Demories, Diana Fatt, Boone Erickson, Mary Lou Dekker, Lois Cress, Jerry Lange, Judy Lebedoff, Herb Nestler, Phoebe Lieder, Joe Quasarano and Earl Doud?

We were such friends once, you lovely media people. I'm talking about some years back, but if I'm still around, why shouldn't you be? Have you forgotten me? You bet. I would only remember you as shadowy figures with your reporter's note-books, cameras, microphones, in and out of TV and radio studios, hotels in Detroit, Denver, Washington, New York, Cincinnati, on benches in parks, walking backwards in steep San Francisco while I walked forwards beaming on to your video-tape, or capturing me addressing literary clubwomen in the dear old *Queen Mary*, now locked in cement to a jetty at Long Beach. But I can cheat. I have your names still, but no related faces, in my American publisher's schedule of promotional engagements. And the friendships were pretty short, after all. An hour here, half an hour there, often for breakfast TV, which meant leaving the hotel with no breakfast.

I never, to be truthful, met Earl Doud, and I hope he has forgiven me, if he remembers me, for not turning up on his great show that day, 'Earl Doud's Banana Paradise'. But I had been three days in New York by then, and on that day, which had begun at 7.15 with WABC-TV, and gone on in hourly dashes through King Features, 16th floor of something, WOR-Radio, 24th floor of something else, back to the Algonquin for *Women's Wear Daily*, out again for NBC-Radio and WNEW-TV, which were God knows where, I found myself lost and weak on Walnut Street. A banana paradise was too much. I telephoned the public relations arm of the publishers and said so. She was a strong girl called Jane Pasanen, who had fixed up all these things, but even she quailed at the appalling news. I could hear her quailing. She had about another forty things fixed up right across the continent – studios, press conferences, speeches, intricately interlocked air tickets – and here was this ninny, not out of New York yet and already crumbling fast.

She rallied. It was no good the pair of us dying. She agreed to unfix the Earl and his bananas. And clearly, in my state of health, thought it no time to remind me of the not too distant Gail Benedict Show, TV taping at 36 East 60th, and Terry Schartel, of *Family Weekly*, shortly afterwards expecting me on top sparkle in the Algonquin's famed Rose Room.

I made them. Just as I was to make, with a mounting sense of indestructibility, the Betty Groebli Show in Washington; the Colorado Authors' League in Denver; *News and Views* in Minneapolis; the Dick Spangler Show in Los Angeles (more accurately, an hour's drive down the San Fernando Valley, in a cab whose driver couldn't find it); the Virginia Graham Show on Hollywood's Sunset Strip; an interview over chopsticks in San Francisco's Chinese Quarter; the late-night radio phone-in, I forget where, but I know the refreshments were paper cups of water and it lasted three hours, people phoning in to ask questions about marquesses.

The trouble that lost me for Earl Doud was merely starvation. Eating, unless scheduled and in the company of interviewers from the *Cleveland Plain Dealer*, the *Philadelphia Bulletin*, the *Washington Evening Star* and suchlike, was hard to fit in. My advice to authors not yet sucked into the US promotional maelstrom – not that there can be many – is to place eating high in their priorities. Even above trying to get a pair of socks washed and a bag relabelled before the dash for today's airport. On Banana Paradise day, after collapsing into a bowl of French onion soup, I came out fighting, and henceforward shuttled from city to city with the restored equanimity of a man who in Lincolnshire, after all, had once moved unruffled from Horncastle to Brigg, Spilsby to Spalding, taking them all in his stride.

I was a week in New York, the first and longest stop. This was November. It was cold and mostly wet. I can't remember or imagine now what my wardrobe bag contained in the way of rainwear. It had been purpose-bought, of ideal design for short stays and hurried departures, with an all-around zip. Unzip it, hang it by its hook on the bathroom door, and your all was gathered together, clothes with time to lose some creases, a large recess for shoes, sponge-bag and a bottle of brandy – the last, which is not my drink, hospitably waiting in the small hours of my arrival. I thanked Jane Pasanen for this. She disclaimed it. Too late to thank them, I later found it was from my London agent's US affiliates. It travelled with me everywhere and was a great if well-intentioned nuisance. You may not drink brandy, but it defies nature to throw it away.

The only trouble with the wardrobe bag was that on the second night its hook pulled out, leaving it an unwieldy and sagging burden of spread-out leather, which from then on had no place but the floor. Or the bed. Moving it from the bed, after a late-night phone-in, was no way to end another day, particularly as it disgorged, at a touch, shoes, sponge-bag and the kindly bottle, and slipped my coats off its jangling hangers into crumpled heaps.

The McCall Publishing Company were doing us proud. In New York we stayed at the Algonquin. Only first-class hotels would be good enough for us. Air tickets, too. Once, from Detroit to Cleveland, a short flight, I found myself alone in the exclusive forward cabin, and was still unbuckling my seat belt when the stewardess wheeled in a virgin leg of lamb, her carving knife poised for my lonely meal. Airline economics, like American publishers', would make quite a study.

Whether it was under McCall's prodigal arrangement, or an agreement privately arrived at, Phil only spent a few days with me in New York City and then went West. She was eager to see Toby, Kaaren and Angie in Los Angeles. Between studios I somehow got her to Kennedy, by night, in blinding rain. Even with my own preoccupations, as always taking precedence over her, a thought which recurs ever more painfully since her death, I felt a tearing wrench. It was like sending her to the moon.

But at least it would be sunny there.

Staying away from the studios, in the interest of our nervous systems, she had seen more of the city than I ever did; down to the Lincoln Centre, up the Empire State building, into Central Park, round the Statue of Liberty (boats hourly from Battery Park, 90 cents). All I saw was the indistinguishable insides of WNEW-TV, WABC-TV, NBC-radio. . .callers from the *New York Post*, the Council of Better Business Bureau. . .

We had sandwich trouble on our first night; more properly about 1 a.m., Eastern Standard Time. Too exhausted to eat, but needing a little something to pacify our jet-lagged stomachs, we rang down for the sandwiches. After a long delay, even by American room-service standards (Hollywood films are not faithful in these matters) a large trolley was manoeuvred in. It needed the size to support its two gigantic steaks, showing all round their rye-bread slices. When the man had withdrawn, for five dollars, we pushed the trolley out again unbroached. I had had in mind something of the sort on offer in the royal equerries' tea room: for that, we should have specified 'regular' sandwiches.

Steaks, indeed everything on Algonquin menus, not to say those of the Terrace Hilton, Cincinnati or the Chase Park Plaza, St Louis, were bigger than I could look at, let alone eat. It would have interested me, given the time, to go round the back and look at their dustbins, since I noticed that I was not alone in relinquishing every course only half eaten. It is the custom of the country. No solicitous waiter ever asks, 'Something wrong, sir, with your Pan-Fried Maryland Clam Cakes?' He scoops away your still-heaped platter and carries it off balanced on his arm.

In the end – no, before that – I could no longer witness a meal at the Algonquin, far less sit down to one. I found a hash-joint round the corner on Sixth Avenue where I could get a coffee and a regular sandwich, not only better for my immature English stomach, but easing a grumbling conscience over the cost of all this. It seemed wrong for McCall's to be investing so heavily in pig-swill.

But the conscience must have been slow to stir. Before leaving New York for Philadelphia I left it, on my own initiative, for Basket Neck Lane, Long Island, by chauffeured limousine. As a public relations exercise, a visit to the Wodehouse residence was hardly a legitimate charge on even the most amenable of publishers. I charged it. The round trip was something like two hundred miles. It took place on a Sunday, blessedly marked 'Nothing Scheduled' in the day's itinerary sheet. I could have stayed in bed. Looking back, I take credit, if not of a financial nature, for putting the day to better use. The chance would never come again.

I had invited myself, by telephone: Ethel Wodehouse answered, in the practised role of guardian dragon. 'Oh, no, that would be quite impossible. No, no. He never comes to New York.' It took quick thinking to make my identity and intentions clearer before she hung up. All was then changed. But how wonderful. Of course I must come to lunch. Plum would be delighted. They would both be delighted. She had always, I imagine, stood between his old manual typewriter (two-finger operated, very black ribbon) and the real or outside world, and at this time with particular vigilance. His ninetieth birthday, only a week earlier, had been a fearful interruption in routine, work suspended as cameras and crews invaded all privacy – with the declared and self-defeating aim of capturing 'an ordinary day' in the life of P.G.

Wodehouse. He pondered the absurdity of this, over his single statutory martini before lunch, and was honestly perplexed by the general fuss and commotion triggered by the birthday. He must have felt somewhat the same, I thought, about that equally intense, though less agreeable, uproar over his German broadcasts thirty years before, and the witch-hunting cries of 'Traitor!' None of this, of course, came up at our meeting. He was chiefly eager for news from home. How, for instance, was *Punch*? (He was writing for it eight years before I was born.) What was William Davis like? I did my best there.

He could no doubt have lived palatially. I remember the house as small. That could be an over-dwindling against vague but different expectations. Other houses were visibly dotted about beyond the garden. 'I should have bought that piece of land,' said Ethel, looking out of the window at another house. She seemed to manage everything. This included her 'Bide-a-Wee' animal shelter, for which the Wodehouses were probably better known locally than for any wider distinction. 'Plum was very good about that,' she said. 'He gave me five thousand pounds towards it.' Plum fondly stroked his favourite birthday present, I forget from whom, a large brown leather pig beside his armchair, the Empress of Blandings to perhaps a one-third scale. 'Dollars', he corrected. Ethel said, 'Turn your toes out, Plum.' The atmosphere was very settled. They had been married for fifty-seven years. She was the elder. Great age was not a thing to be associated with either of them. He was still large and bald and beaming, as in photographs remembered from years before. He seemed, he said, to be writing more slowly just at the moment. He mused. It must be something to do with the weather. She differed little from Muggeridge's picture of their first meeting, decades ago. 'A mixture of Mistress Quickly and Florence Nightingale, with a dash of Lady Macbeth added.' At lunch there was a maid, not young and of glum aspect, to hand round the boiled potatoes. There appeared some urgency about getting the meal over, so that she could get off home.

He talked of plans to visit England. Ethel gave me a small private shake of the head. He never would. He said to me, a sudden thought breaking through misty visions of staterooms and captain's tables, 'I suppose you flew?' and received my affirmation with a nod. Accepted that the world beyond the typewriter was changing. As he had never really been in it, no comment was called for. That was how, as Wooster would have said, the ball rolled.

After our farewells, which were almost affectionately demonstrative, I felt, back in my limousine, that something had been missing. For me, if not for my American publisher, it had been a rewarding pilgrimage. But the absent element, I concluded uncertainly, had been any ability on my part to equate the man with the works. I told my chauffeur whose guest I had been. He thought he had heard the name.

Jane Pasanen not only took care of the bills. From hotel to hotel ready cash intermittently awaited me, or its readily-convertible form. Usually the gilt was slightly knocked off it by a covering memo headed 'Addition to your schedule for Minneapolis.' Or wherever. She was often only a jump ahead with things fixed. Chicago could suddenly spring an English Speaking Union reception and speech. Or I was requested to be in my Detroit bedroom at 2.30, on an afternoon scheduled as free for sleeping, to sparkle on the phone to a disembodied DJ, feeding me in live between the discs.

People are doing these things all the time. Now. As you read. I make no special case. Except that they are gifted acclimatisers with a high charge of self-sufficiency, and probably don't, like me, feel suddenly faint after handing a cab-driver $300 instead of $3. That was in Washington, a quick jaunt from the Hay-Adams hotel to the Lincoln Memorial. US dollar bills all come the same size, though friends with better eyes assure me the colours are different. It was a Saturday. It would be. My credit card company were charming on their answering machine, thanked me for calling, and would be open for business on Monday at nine.

On Monday at nine I should be airbound for Cincinnati. Though I called her home number, Jane was also charming, but backed the charm with action. Living carefully, I thought I should be able to hold out until St Louis, Tuesday, and the Chase Park Plaza. There the desk clerk handed over my refunding envelope. It also contained a covering memo. Margie Freivogel, of KDS-TV, was an addition to my schedule. Whoever she was, at least I could afford to buy her a drink.

Before setting out on this harlequinade I had written to Sid Perelman, then on one of his periodic sojourns in London, asking him to name a friend in New York who would show me a thing or two. As if I would have the time to be shown anything that stuck up less than sixty storeys, but I didn't know that then. He named and wrote to *New Yorker* writer Philip Hamburger, and I somehow found time for him to show me great kindness, the inside of the Century Club, which could have been in Pall Mall or St James's Street and caused no leather-chaired surprise, and the almost equally impressive inside of the *New Yorker* offices, from which articles of mine had from time to time rebounded. It was evening, and the place was empty, but a great soberness hung over it as we moved through the editorial rooms. 'Of course I can't take you in that one,' said Hamburger. 'That's the power-house.' I tried to envisage a visitor to the *Punch* office being matter-of-factly denied a glimpse of the editor's room. Perhaps we should take ourselves more seriously. There were two floors of filing and checking. Anyone who had ever been mentioned in the paper, or written a word for it, was in there. Perhaps the actual word. I remembered Humphry Ellis, whose articles did not rebound, having a grave query raised about one of them. It had something to do with gardening, and had quoted the average number of earthworms to a cubic foot of earth. The *New Yorker* men were worried. All efforts to check this number for accuracy had been defeated. Would Mr Ellis please give his source?

Perelman had written back to me:

Phil Hamburger is a nice fellow and one of the two or three colleagues on the magazine I regularly consorted with. Some of them tend to have a ramrod up their arse, acting as though they invented the paper. I well recall an occasion when Thurber was going on ad nauseam about his influence, and how he'd set the style for the whole enterprise. I finally got a snootful and said mildly, 'Come, come, it's just another 15-cent magazine.' Though nearly blind he leapt at me and tried to throttle me. It took two burly copy-editors to drag him off.

But writing of what lay ahead:

I have been through a species of that mill and I feel for you. You of course realize that this kind of activity is a wonderful gim-mick the publishers discovered, a substitute for spending their own money to advertise one's books. The Author as Salesman dodge was accidentally discovered when Simon & Schuster put Alexander King – whose book wasn't even reviewed in the press owing to a newspaper strike – on the Jack Parr show. King, who thought he was dying of kidney troubles, felt he had nothing to lose and virulently attacked the Catholic Church, stupefying Parr and the audience.

At the end of it, Parr said helplessly, 'I don't know who this man is, folks, but,' he went on holding up a copy of King's book, 'this is a very funny book and I advise you to run out and buy it.' Within a month it was selling 10,000 copies a week, and when King died, far from his usual pauperized state, he was worth a million and three-quarter dollars. I know all this because I brought the book to Simon & Schuster in the first place.

One or two points arise between the lines, allowing, as a matter of course, for the Perelman hyperbole: on that, Thurber's side of the attempted throttling would be interesting, and I doubt if it even got as far as striking Perelman with a rolled-up galley proof. The two burly copy-editors could just have been editor Harold Ross stirring impatiently in his chair. Sadly, none of them is now available to check.

Even Jane never managed to 'put me' on the Jack Parr Show. If she had, I doubt if it would have made me a million and three-quarter dollars. I doubt if it did for the railer against the Catholic faith, though the figure has a pleasing cadence.

I don't know what Earl Doud's Banana Paradise would have done for me if I hadn't missed it, or what all the other shows did, which I miraculously didn't. If the lot of them sold a hundred copies, I should be surprised. That would work out at a couple of copies a show. It's true that I signed two hundred and forty in Higbee's Bookshop, Cleveland, but no one had bought them yet. This was different from Harrods, where I signed a lot fewer, at spare intervals and feeling silly. The customers held their receipt in the other hand.

Yes, possibly McCall's were pursuing the wonderful gimmick of saving money on advertising. But they shelled out plenty on me. What with that, and a foolishly profuse advance, engineered by Hilary Rubinstein, my kindly and unscrupulous agent, I bet they never saw back a bean. Still, I never asked. It didn't matter to me. My concern was to come back alive.

Even the taped programmes I never saw or heard: though once, as a porter wheeled my wardrobe bag in the quieter precinct of a railway terminus – Jane sometimes had me in trains as well as planes and chauffeured limos – there was a most wondrous revelation. I heard my own voice. It was hard to locate. On the twitch of an old reflex I looked round for a hairdresser's. At London Bridge station I had once had my hair cut to the sound of my own voice on the radio. It was a longish talk, ending as the barber brushed the hairs out of my neck. 'What did you think of that?' I said, professionally interested. 'Think of what?' he said. I pointed to the loudspeaker, by then on 'The Week in Westminster'. 'Never listen,' he said.

But there was no hairdresser's this time. The porter, black and whistling, seemed to notice nothing, but would naturally be less finely tuned to the familiar vibrations. I then pinned them down to the bag. Some jolt in the handling had activated my tape-recorder with a rehearsal speech for a ladies' luncheon club, Brown Palace, Denver.

Disappointing. It often seemed to me that the programmes, particularly radio, could never have got beyond the building, never mind the city limits. I had been brought up on the ordered formality of the BBC, where radio studios were radio studios and could be nothing else. Most of these could have been anything else. Often were. The back ends of unidentifiable halls, stacked chairs under dust in the distance. Dim ante-rooms belonging to some quite different business. Even with television, where pal-pable communications equipment could hardly not be on view, it seemed to be haphazardly assembled, arousing misgivings on whether anything was actually plugged in.

None of this damped the bouncing bonhomie of the profes-sional communicators, on Christian name terms at once (rhym-ing my own with Hazel). Their programme was often already under way by the time I panted in. If television, this meant seeing, on the monitor, my soon-to-be host, highly psyched with jollity as he processed my predecessor. I once shared my waiting-time in a cupboard of a room with a man who was editing an old Gary Cooper movie, at the same time picking from the Yellow Pages a series of numbers where he hoped to run down a particu-lar shade of paint. Somewhere, I forget where, the face I had seen on the monitor hailed me with radiance and a 'Hi, Bazel,' con-fiding at once that they had a call in to Bucking-ham Palace and were waiting for the Prince to come through. However, he didn't.

That, I think, was entirely a books programme. They were better. At least the front-men knew why I was there. They some-times surprised me by being front-women, named on the day's schedule as Terry or Gerry but proving to be brisk black ladies. Or programmes listed as radio would turn out to be TV, which I had not dressed for. Choice of fellow-authors' works was often dis-composing. To see mine, on WMAQ-TV, Chicago, laid out on camera with such competition as *Sex and Sanity*, *It Needn't be in Bed* and *The Sensuous Couple*, prompted misgivings on how things would go when thrown open to general discussion.

There were occasional one-offs. Just me, that is. On one of these my radio host, stuck for tactics and not having read the book, suggested that I did so, aloud, and excused himself from the studio. To buy some paint, perhaps. I read for about forty minutes.

Mostly they were miscellaneous rag-bags, where I found myself chummy with unpredictable company. Gene Hackman (whose *French Connection* had newly brought him fame and fortune). George Hamilton IV, who suddenly sang 'It's Impossible'. Characters thought dead: Buddy Rogers, Bobby Darin. Or there was Pierre Salinger, on that big 'Sunset Strip' audience show. I congratulated him on a book written by Arthur Schlesinger, to whom Philip Hamburger had introduced me in the Century Club. Unshaken, he then played the first, or easy, movement of the Moonlight Sonata, on an eight-foot concert grand wheeled in for the purpose.

Hosts were bland and all-encompassing, whether with royal biographers, Chinese actors, inventors of artificial snow, or health pundits. Health was always to the fore. I forget America's disease of the year that year. But it was serious. Even footballers were getting it. By the time I had heard a dozen doctors on it, I felt that I was getting it. But all was brightly handled. One radio man, having squeezed me dry, and such listeners as there may have been, wound up with, 'And next week, breast cancer. We talk to a lady who has had a toomer removed.'

My own health remained good, even improving on being reunited with Phil for my impact on the viewers and listeners of California. From then on, until home, we should be together. There would be San Francisco, but after that only another city or two on the return to the East. I had already seen all the airports I wanted to. La Guardia would be the start of a beautiful tapering off. Then Kennedy, Heathrow, Sussex. Aircraft had been a flying refuge. I had fallen gratefully into scores of them. For an hour, two, three, nothing and nobody could get at me.

I had earlier phoned her from New York, not without difficulty. The American telephone, like much else, is not always what it is cracked up to be, though the operators are sweet. When I told this one that no amount of dialling would raise anything but a low, musical note she was interested. 'Gee,' she said, 'just how lucky can you get?' People still say 'Gee'. Or did then. And better. I heard a man in a Baltimore bar say 'Attaboy'.

And Phil had written back, cheerful, and with diagrams, which she liked. I remembered her first-ever letter, all those years before, telling me how to get to the Bank of England sports club. She already knew that I couldn't find anywhere. The diagrams were labelled. 'Fig. 1', 'Fig. 2', 'Fig. 3'. And a footnote: 'Hope you like figs.' We married because we made each other laugh. There are worse reasons. But my laughter became professionalised, one cause of hers becoming less frequent. Being married to a serious funny man is no joke.

It was useless writing to me after New York. I was never anywhere long enough. Her cheerful letter, in fact, with encouragement and love, and jokes, had been a brave exercise. She had arrived from a wet New York in a wet Los Angeles, or its environs. Toby and family lived in a small Hampsteady enclave some twenty miles from downtown LA, where both he and Kaaren worked, driving back and forth daily on those blood-curdling freeways.

As their house was too small to accommodate visitors Phil stayed with Kaaren's mother, Ellen, who also worked, a high-powered executive of some kind. This meant that Phil didn't see a lot of any of them, but was marooned in Ellen's house – pool and all, should the Californian weather turn Californian – with an unknown dog. Of course there were evenings, weekends. Ellen was the soul of kindness, driving her out somewhere when she could. Toby, on his way to being a lawyer, was spending much of what should have been leisure in heavy books. It all gave Phil plenty of time to wonder if I had been mugged in the subway, lost myself in Detroit, or was bobbing amid aircraft wreckage on Erie's polluted surface.

Moving with me into the Beverly Hills Hotel was better. So by now was the weather. November bees buzzed outside our window. For our last afternoon, a period of peace and respite set in for us both, but it was short-lived. Awned from the sun by palms we were sitting beside the pool eating toasted bacon sandwiches (regular). A few screen faces were dotted about, older than we remembered them. I had nothing scheduled for two hours or so: then the big audience-show taping at KTLA-TV, 5800 Sunset, my last point of sale before San Francisco.

Looking down at my sandwich for the next bite I saw something irregular. My only unnatural front tooth, top middle, had snapped off its plate and stuck in it. Speechless, or not yet venturing on speech, I displayed this disaster. Phil laughed and shrugged, thinking I was calling attention to flaws in American foodstuffs, even at Hollywood prices. When the horror got to her as well, there was nothing, for once, that even she could do for me.

Hurriedly back in the foyer I came across Dick Van Dyke and showed him the tooth. He was waiting for someone. Anyone but me. God knows why I told him the story. Hoped, perhaps, for a fellow showman's sympathy. Oh, yes, he knew the Virginia Graham Show. Been on it. He sought to cheer me with a lantern-jawed impression of what it would be like to be on it with a top front tooth gone, and praised his personal dentist, who unfortunately practised in somewhere like San Diego, down Mexico way. Anyway, not handy. I peeled off at speed for Reception.

I was disappointed with Reception, having innocently assumed that here, of all places, where teeth worth millions could be at risk, there must be some nookful of dental technicians on stand-by for emergency bridgework to get actors back on the set before production budgets ran out. Not so. Reception's young ladies were kind, sympathetic, and didn't laugh when I smiled, but they had no dentists, had no directory of dentists, knew personally no dentists, and could only prescribe the phone book's Yellow Pages. These proliferated dentists. Had it occurred to me to borrow Reception's telephone, and have the calls put on the bill, I shouldn't have had to keep going back there, from the call-box, until I had squeezed them dry of small change for the slot. By now the time was galloping. And it wasn't only quarters I was running out of, but dentists. And nothing but negative results so far.

I have no memory for addresses, but I can still give you 435 North Roxbury straight off. It was from there that an angel voice said that if I made it right away they guessed they could fix me. It was a long way by Yellow Cab. The traffic was bad. I remembered the address, but forgot the dentist's name. That didn't seem important until I got to 435 North Roxbury and it proved to be a smallish tower block entirely occupied by dentists. The search for the angel voice was prolonged. Floor by floor, enquiry by enquiry. Girls in white coats were already locking away trays of teeth. The dentist, found at last, took in his clock and my tooth with a single glance. He said I had a problem there. I agreed. At 5800 Sunset they would be lining up the cameras.

But he fixed me, and threw in two free tubes of glue.

In the end, when I tripped – in the sense of litheness – down the property staircase to greet the steep-tiered audience, my smile gave the arc-lights beam for beam. Said my hostess, her diamond ear-drops flailing, 'Well, folks, if I'd asked central casting to get me an Englishman, they couldn't have done me prouder.' She little knew how nearly she'd got one with a stiff upper lip.

So that was America. On Tuesday we should be home. I was positively finished with the book. Somehow, and for some reason, I had managed to get a couple of reports back to Buckingham Palace. Among the mounds of mail a crested envelope was waiting. It was his turn, said Prince Philip, to be 'breathlessly admiring'. Still, he had only had my side of the story. I may have played it up a bit. For once I was not dissatisfied with my performance. Not for the mikes, cameras and press. Just as a survivor. And not only from America, but the whole unnatural business since taking on the 'appalling task'.

CONFUSIONS IN CALIFORNIA.
PART OF A PAGE FROM MY AMERICAN PUBLISHER'S SCHEDULE.

Punch had suffered. That could be better put: but the year before it all started the index had shown seventy-five entries under my name (not too bad for a fifty-two-week-year). In the next two years, seven, and a phenomenal crop, all things considered. However, some of those were only short verses, and one of them a book review, the book being my own, which was Bill

Davis's idea, and showed that he was fast learning what sort of jokes we thought funny.

I was less severe than *Private Eye* had been in its look ahead to 'the least eagerly awaited book of the year, a mishmash of old newspaper cuttings, sycophancy and facetiousness'. But ended my notice along not dissimilar lines:

His Royal Highness comes out as a bit of a paragon, between you and me (sorry, keep skidding into the Boothroyd style), though he appears to have fought unsuccessfully for a frailer picture. He clearly won the author's heart, a thing which shouldn't on the whole happen to biographers, pleased though they may be with the company they're keeping.

Other critics were more lenient. Well-educated ones less clear. *The Listener* entitled Roy Fuller's very long review, 'The Divine Man's Substitute Victim'. I never knew what that meant.

Officially, *Punch* had only released me to write the book. I was then to go back into the office. But I had had eighteen years of the office. Peter had gone. So had No. 10 Bouverie Street, in its one-time capacity as our home, the small, formal manor house in the middle of Fleet Street's clatter. As I write, its windows are dusty and blank. Before that, it briefly housed some ancillary depart-ment of the National Coal Board. United Newspapers had bought us, a cog in a mightier engine, and moved us round the corner into Tudor Street.

But it would still be the top of Bouverie Street where I should have to pray for a cab to Victoria. I didn't want to come to Victoria in the first place. I had been spoiled for commuting. Now I work long-distance. The indexes have filled up again. It is better not to be in the office too much. The laughter is there, but given smaller voice, and submerged in a general hum of electronics. The other day, looking in on Alan Coren before the Table lunch, I thought catalepsy had got him. He sat in a trance at Malcolm's once editorial desk. Thank God, all was well. He was only waiting for the revisions of his weekly article to come up on the screen. By his elbow – by everybody's – the phone that remembers its own numbers. Or those of the most regularly called. As mine remains, at the time of this old-fashioned typewriting, one that he can call on Monday mornings without the prodigal time-waste of dial-ling, I am not entirely against scientific advances in office life. I just regard them, like warm bank-notes out of the wall, as dehumanising. Bertie Clover would be cramped for gaiety today, programming his processor with rude comments on the clientele of Lloyds Bank, Horncastle, and getting the screened response: DO NOT UNDERSTAND.

The morning Phil died, it was Alan who first knew. This might have been so in any case. Neither she nor I now had many friends. By our choice. More accurately by mine. Too busy. Always too busy. Too locked in my own small corner. I had been too busy and too selfish ever since 1939. This was 1980. She had occasionally had in a few acquaintances to play bridge, widowed ladies whom I would deign, at coffee time, to visit briefly before returning to my literary workshed down the garden, where I was content with the hermit's life.

When she was taken off by ambulance I called the office to explain why something I was writing would not be written. Three hours later Alan called back to ask about her. I only had the most stunning and unbelievable news. There was a moment or two's hollow pause at the other end. Then, 'Look. As soon as you can, get on a train and come up here. Come to the house. I'll be there.'

She had been in good spirits that morning, was all ready to leave for London to record a book she was enjoying for the RNIB. Taking high precedence, a letter had been on the mat from Toby, her constant expectation. It was October, so there were other Californian expectations, which the letter itself looked forward to. Phil and I were to go out there in November. It meant, for her, that she would see our grandson, arrived since our last visit nine years before. For me – always ready to dodge any venture upsetting routine – a combination of business and pleasure. Business predominating. What was there new to write about an American Presidential Election, Alan had despairingly asked. 'Well,' I said, 'I have a son standing for the California State Senate.' 'Great,' said Alan. 'Go out there and do a piece about that.' He didn't think expenses would run to a wife as well. I was glad to raid my own pocket.

In the event, that did not arise. I went alone, still quite stupefied. Everyone thought it would be best for me: including one of the bridge-playing widowed ladies, June Mortimer. I knew from Phil that she had a warm and willing heart. I had sought her help, instantly forthcoming, to clear things up. I wrote her my letter of thanks on the outward flight, somewhere over Montana, and we got married the following year.

So sensible, everyone said. Two lonely people. In fact it was nothing so coolly practical. We fell in love, surprising ourselves and each other.

Twelve

AS THINGS ARE

PRAISE OF A wife is suspect in autobiographers, often undeservedly so, I dare say. But for readers with wives of their own, whom they prefer to keep in with, public eulogy can smack of private strategy. Better slip in a few kind words about the old girl. For some reason, no matter how sincerely felt, any tribute to her grace, devotion, apt laughter and watchful monitoring of clean shirt and gin supplies, comes out specious at the writer's end and squirmy at the reader's. What to say about June is a puzzle. Shall I just compare her to a summer's day? The rest of Sonnet 18 also goes well.

However, she might have mentioned, earlier in the progress to the altar, that although she was June to a forest of friends and relations, her birth certificate had her down as Kathleen, which she had always hated and never been called by or known as. We were to change her surname. Why not the other, making an honest woman of her? Simple.

She left the idea with me one morning, and belted off at the usual high rattle in her clapped-out Clubman; to dispense meals on wheels, collect for the lifeboats, cook for the housebound, perform secretarial functions on some village committee. There, in case the picture emerges of a leathery do-gooder, she would be writing me love notes masquerading as minutes.

I too was under the accustomed pressures. Disruption must be minimised. Fitting in the wedding was going to be a day lost. I accepted that. But I was awash with TV scripts. *Punch* was still coming out every Wednesday. The habit of after-dinner speaking had not at that time been kicked, and I had long-standing obligations to bankers, cricketers, ladies' far-flung literary circles.

And the bachelor life itself brought distractions. Failing the arrival of a pie on the front step with a love note, '30 mins. med. oven', I had to keep my own body and soul together. Distant, but implacably approaching, was the prospect of transferring my piano, creative aura and a thousand books three miles off into a converted police station, humorously house-named 'Peelers'. I

knew that I should there be under-rehearsed with other names:
those of my more immediate step-family, a cloudburst of Annes,
Jameses, Olivers, Kirsties, Christophers, Carls, Peters, Janes,
Jeremys, Barrys and Sams: to know nothing, in those early days,
of numberless step-cousins, several called Betty, but running
into a confusion of Joans and Ginas and Jeans.

My hermit days were fast to recede.

We thought it best, or more probably I laid it down, that our
intentions should be kept secret until that was no longer possible.
Once revealed, I could be having interruptions from well-wish-
ers, by post, telephone, and being stopped in the street. Security
had to be tight. Particularly on June's part. All the family had
keys to the police station, convenient for leaving videotapes,
returning books, borrowing eggs, and scanning her engagement
book on the hall table, whose pages had to code me as the
window-cleaner, the Red Cross bring-and-buy, pub lunch Tony
and Peggy, or drinks with the hieroglyphics, 6.30.

We wanted it secret but quick. The calling of banns would be a
giveaway, and slow. A special licence was plainly the solution,
said the Vicar, sworn to silence but helpful. He put me in touch
with the Archbishop of Canterbury: more strictly with his representative in these matters, a harassed man stationed at No. 1, The
Sanctuary, hard by Westminster Abbey.

The institution of holy matrimony may be on the wane. There
was no sign of it there. At a desk rolling with taped-up parch-
ments he wore a beleaguered look. His phone kept going. 'Born
where?' he would say into it hoarsely. 'Is that still in the Com-
monwealth. . .?' He turned to me during a respite. Why a special
licence? The short answer – I had to get back to the typewriter –
was that it was the vicar's suggestion. This touched a sore spot.
'I'm fed up with some of these incumbents,' he said, shaking
scrolls from his sleeve. 'It's every day the same. Half of them
don't know the difference between special and ordinary. You
could make it ordinary and save yourself eleven pounds plus
VAT, do you realise that?'

But he gave me an application form, politely requiring fairly
straightforward particulars under two main headings: 'As to
Gentleman' 'As to Lady'. ('Gentleman and lady created he them':
Genesis 1.27.) Some research was naturally called for, which
yielded some surprises. For instance that the Lady had been born
in Leeds. And I had to check with her on the planned date of the
ceremony. She was taking care of the minor details, and had
personally bought the ring, instinctively sensing that the Gentleman was no shopper. He has meant ever since to ask what he

owes her and also, as a matter of curiosity, to dig out her six-year-old engagement book some time and see how she coded the wedding.

But complications set in with the accompanying sheet of instructions. Approval in writing was required, from the parties' next of kin. An assurance from the Vicar that he would permit the marriage to take place. Letters 'from a non-family person, recommending each party to His Grace the Archbishop of Canterbury'.

What had I got myself into? Other parties, living in what used to be quaintly called sin, do so in enviable simplicity.

Like all my impending step-family, the bride's next-of-kin, or son, was accessible enough, twenty minutes' drive and unlikely to stand in his mother's way. But it would mean blowing our cover. The groom's son, or next of kin, would probably give his approval too: and on stationery headed TOBY BOOTHROYD FOR STATE SENATE, likely to carry weight even in archiepiscopal circles (though like most Democrats he had been buried in the Reagan landslide). But time was now getting on, and correspondence with southern California is not swift. Besides, my glad tidings (later to be received with great joy) would need full and careful drafting. Time, time.

It was perhaps in the interest of blessed and legal unions that His Grace's representative in the end waived this supporting evidence. He could have lost us to a register office. But I had to sway him by cogent arguments. They took longer to get on paper than the articles I should have been writing instead.

So things were now moving well.

Unfortunately, the altar in sight, progress was abruptly arrested. This was my fault. I suppose a dashed-off note to Peter Dickinson, asking him in one breath to be a best man and to win over the Archbishop with a character reference, speediest, was bound to overlook the finer detail. Whereas my application had called the bride Kathleen, negotiations for the change still preoccupying our lawyers, Peter only knew her as June, and called her that.

The Sanctuary took a stern, and doubtless harassed, view. These people. How many women was I marrying?

I forget at what point the bogus June became the true one, but remember that the lawyers also showed signs of harassment. It seemed a simple matter, but their legal minds were baffled. Deed polls for a change of surnames, no problem. Christian names were less easily dislodged. The lawyers read expensively in thick books, telephoned me in the middle of difficult dialogue passages to urge consultations in depth. June (as yet Kathleen) went off to attend those. I was busy. She returned with on the whole satisfactory findings. Though such changes, it appeared, had been ruled illegal in the ancient precedent of ABC v. Parrott, it seemed that the later ruling, of XYZ v. Partridge, might well be deemed to suggest. . .

Well, good. I may have got the names of the birds wrong, it hardly matters now. Beyond a last time-consuming attendance at Westminster, to swear an oath and pay £29 plus VAT, our path was clear. The lawyers sent the bill. His Grace sent the licence. For the size and language alone this was worth the money. We keep meaning to frame it, but at eighteen inches square, and a ribboned seal hanging out of the bottom, it could be tricky.

> *Whereas* it is alleged Ye have purposed to proceed to the Solemnization of a true pure and lawful Marriage earnestly desiring the same to be Solemnized with all the speed that may be *That* such your reasonable desires may more readily take due effect *We* for certain causes Us hereunto especially moving to do so far as in *Us* lies and the Laws of this Realm allow by these Presents. . .

You should certainly feel married, with a thing like that. What we still both agree, contemplating the whole improbable adventure six years on, is that we feel nothing of the kind.

Index